Praise for *A Girl's Guide to Missiles*

"Karen Piper's A C̶̶ ̶̶G̶̶u̶̶i̶̶d̶̶e̶̶ ̶t̶o̶ ̶M̶i̶s̶s̶i̶l̶e̶s̶ reaches back into the body of American war an̶̶ ̶ ll beating but not beaten. Her mem̶̶ ̶̶ itting, holding my breath as she made ̶ ̶̶ ̶̶ ̶̶ ̶̶ girl and growing up in the military ir̶̶ ̶̶ ̶̶ ̶̶ ̶̶ Lake missile range. Gender, family, war, and ̶̶ ̶̶ ̶̶ ̶̶ nake this an unforgettable book and a radical act of truth telling."

—Lidia Yuknavitch, author of *The Book of Joan*
and *The Chronology of Water*

"Karen Piper lived the escalating levels of insanity of the cold war from the inside, playing her girlhood games in the top secret labs and working beside her parents in a hidden corner of the Mojave. The bombs of tomorrow were a family affair, and the truth was always tricky. For Piper, who writes like a dream, failed test shots mirror busted romances, and the excesses of the era eventually lead our missile girl to communal life in a bomb-proof Oregon. *A Girl's Guide to Missiles* is a family portrait, a missile-science primer, a coming-of-nuclear-age. Piper captures the soul of an era that might not be so long gone as we would hope."

—Bill Roorbach, author of *Life Among Giants*, *The Remedy for Love*, and *The Girl of the Lake*

"Brilliantly overdetermined setup, one that yields both black comedy and sickening lurches of insight."   —*Harper's*

"[A] fascinating memoir . . . [Piper] offers an incredible view of a little-known community, from WWII all the way through 9/11, and examines how her family navigated life in a town built for war."   —*Booklist*

"This is a fascinating look at growing up in Cold War America, as told by a sharp and affable narrator."   —*Publishers Weekly*

"A little-known corner of the Atomic Age comes into focus through Piper's skilled storytelling."   —*Kirkus Reviews* (starred review)

PENGUIN BOOKS

A GIRL'S GUIDE TO MISSILES

Karen Piper is the award-winning author of *The Price of Thirst*, *Left in the Dust*, and *Cartographic Fictions*. She has received the *Sierra*'s Nature Writing Award and the Next Generation Indie Book Award and fellowships from Carnegie Mellon, the Huntington, and the National Endowment for the Humanities. She is currently a professor of literature and geography at the University of Missouri.

Also by Karen Piper

The Price of Thirst: Global Water Inequality and the Coming Chaos

Left in the Dust: How Race and Politics Created a Human and Environmental Tragedy in L.A.

Cartographic Fictions: Maps, Race, and Identity

A
Girl's Guide
to
Missiles

Growing Up in America's Secret Desert

Karen Piper

PENGUIN BOOKS

PENGUIN BOOKS
An imprint of Penguin Random House LLC
penguinrandomhouse.com

First published in the United States of America by Viking,
an imprint of Penguin Random House LLC, 2018
Published in Penguin Books 2019

Photograph credits:
Insert pages 1 and 4: J. R. Eyerman/The Life Picture Collection/Getty Images;
page 2: U.S. Army Air Corps; pages 8, 11, 13, and 14: U.S. Department of the Navy.
Other photographs courtesy of the author.

ISBN 9780735220393 (paperback)

THE LIBRARY OF CONGRESS HAS CATALOGED THE HARDCOVER EDITION AS FOLLOWS:
Names: Piper, Karen Lynnea, 1965– author.
Title: A girl's guide to missiles : growing up in America's secret desert / Karen Piper.
Other titles: Growing up in America's secret desert
Description: New York, New York : Viking, an imprint of
Penguin Random House LLC, [2018] |
Description based on print version record and CIP data
provided by publisher; resource not viewed.
Identifiers: LCCN 2018025068 (print) | LCCN 2018027674 (ebook) |
ISBN 9780735220386 (ebook) | ISBN 9780399564543 (hardcover)
Subjects: LCSH: Piper, Karen Lynnea, 1965– | Naval Ordnance Test Station
(China Lake, Calif.)—Employees—Biography. | Piper, Earl Marwin, 1922–2005. |
Piper, Mary Dahlstrom. | Guided missiles—United States—History—Anecdotes. |
Electronic technicians—United States—Biography. | United States. Office of
Strategic Services—Biography. | California, Southern—Social life and
customs—20th century. | Young women—West (U.S.)—Biography. | Cold War.
Classification: LCC VF373 (ebook) | LCC VF373 .P57 2018 (print) |
DDC 358.1/7092 [B]—dc23
LC record available at https://lccn.loc.gov/2018025068

Printed in the United States of America
1   3   5   7   9   10   8   6   4   2

Set in Horley Old Style MT Std
Designed by Cassandra Garruzzo

For Mormor and Sis,
and those who survive before and after us,
especially
Earl Marwin Piper
(1922–2005)

Twelve thousand inhabitants, mostly Ph.D.s, entirely air conditioned, in the middle of the most howling of wildernesses. The whole directed exclusively to the production of bigger and better rockets. It was the most frightening exhibition of scientific and highly organized insanity I have ever seen. One vaguely thought that the human race was determined to destroy itself. After visiting the China Lake Research station, one feels quite certain of it.

—*Aldous Huxley, 1950*

Contents

A Girl's Guide to Missiles

PART ONE

Becoming China Lakers

Missile Guidebook:
Do not become enamored with missiles. A missile
does not make meaning. It destroys meaning.

Chapter One

Born into Missiles

D on't touch any ordnance," the guide said. "If you see any lying around. It could explode." Fiftyish and portly, he was wearing jeans and a T-shirt and might have passed for a truck driver if not for the B-2 bomber on his cap. Above the plane, the hat read "Northrop," where I assumed he must have worked, maybe even on the B-2. The group of twenty or so tripod-toting tourists, there to photograph the largest collection of petroglyphs in the Western Hemisphere, looked around warily. A few people laughed, others fidgeted. Only my mom and I knew that we really could explode.

"Ordnance, what's ordnance?" the woman next to me whispered with a plaintive smile as we began our walk into the canyons. One glance at her tripod made me worry. It was almost as tall as her, and she looked wobbly already.

"Missiles, bombs, that sort of thing," I said. She stopped and stepped back, her smile dropping. What did she expect? I thought.

We were at China Lake Naval Weapons Center, after all. Things were *supposed* to explode.

I had grown up here, but now only my mother remained behind to keep watch over my father's body in the warm earth. My sister and I had left long ago, and only an old black-and-white photograph of my family in front of some petroglyphs had drawn me back. In the photo, we are all together and happy: my dad, Earl; my mom, Mary; my sister, Christine; and me. I could not remember if the photo had been taken here or during one of our family road trips, hopping from one desert to another. So here I was, trying to remember something about a childhood locked behind the base gates, my memories in files that would never be declassified. I had lost my security clearance, and after my mom retired, our last access was stripped away with the sticker on her car. My family had once roamed these desert ranges freely, but now we were in exile, tourists to our own pasts. The only way we could visit the base was on a petroglyph tour.

"Don't pick up a missile, Mom," I whispered, leaning over conspiratorially. She just shrugged. She was seventy-four and impish as ever, slightly plump but ever ready to go. With her wispy gray hair, bare face, and polyester pants, she was quintessential China Lake. Not a place for fussing over hair and makeup.

"I'm not the one I'm worried about," she said, chuckling. I knew she was right. Though once prone to hide behind her skirts, I had become the kind of person whose feet would make a beeline to what I needed to know. Nothing could stop me. I would pick up ordnance just because I *had* to read the fine print. My mom followed me around as if I were a toddler, hoping to keep me alive.

Our giggling and whispering brought a swift glance from the man in the B-2 bomber cap. We both looked down, feigning invisibility, and he continued after a pause. In the wispy dead desert grass, I noticed a stinkbug startled by our shuffling feet. It raised its behind into the air, awaiting predators with a different kind of explosion, a stink that would go unnoticed by the giants towering above. I tapped my mom on the arm. "Stinkbug," I said, pointing. She nodded and smiled.

Located in Southern California's Mojave Desert, China Lake had been built so rocket scientists could design and detonate weapons in the same place. The spot was chosen for both its emptiness during World War II and its proximity to Pasadena's California Institute of Technology. The United States Navy claimed to have found the perfect "desert wasteland," a place with nothing there to kill. Caltech's rocket scientists could drive two to three hours and blow things up at a safe distance from LA's suburban sprawl.

At first, it was all about making rockets better than Hitler's. But after the war, a strange thing happened: China Lake kept growing. It was built to be temporary but had slowly developed a life of its own. Before long, it expanded from a cluster of Quonset huts to an area the size of Rhode Island, more than a million acres in all. Soon seventy-five percent of all "free world conventional weapons"—the non-nuclear, non-communist kind—would be designed at this odd inland navy base. My home.

The center of the base, where everyone lives, is at the bottom of Indian Wells Valley, though the navy also owns the small desert mountain ranges on three sides—all used as testing sites. On the fourth side, to the west, are the highest peaks in the "lower forty-eight," the Sierra Nevada mountains. Owens Peak is our peak, the tallest we can see. It determines when day and night begins at China Lake. Next to the base town is a large desert playa, the base's namesake: China Lake, named after the Chinese laborers who once mined borax from the lake bed. Outside the dry lake's edges, the valley is blanketed by creosote bushes, which over time form rings of clones to protect the "mother" at the center from the bracing wind. Test pilots say the pattern looks like a bull's-eye, but they're the only ones who get to see the base from above since even the airspace is restricted. There are aerial photographs that show the valley littered with bomb craters and targets like white-painted Xs, fake houses, and old military airplanes, tanks, and railroad cars. Almost anything can be blown up. There is even an old Vietnamese-style bridge left over from that war, half-exploded in the rolling brown hills.

I grew up in the age of missiles, which are essentially rockets with brains. They can hunt you down and will not just fly off willy-nilly to who-knows-where. If you're lucky, that is. China Lake is famous for its target-tracking missiles, dubbed "smart weapons," though it can be hard to get those missiles to hit their targets, to be as "smart" as they should be. More often than not, they are like errant children. This is why the base's first logo was a cross-eyed jackrabbit riding an out-of-control missile. Nevertheless, the right mixture of a successful missile test, perfect desert blooms, and blue skies will bring a smile to any China Laker's face.

China Lake is a strange ship in the desert, but it was also my home. Every morning at seven fifteen, my family would drive through the main gate, showing our badges to a U.S. Marine standing outside a closet-sized guardhouse. My dad went to work on the Sidewinder missile—it was his job to make sure it hit its targets—and my mom on the Tomahawk. My sister worked on base inventory, counting circuit boards and bombs. I worked as a secretary as soon as I could drive. Of course, we could not talk about anything we did on the base, even to one another. We lived in secrecy.

My mom and I walked down into Renegade Canyon as basalt walls closed in on us, blackened with the lichens and molds of age. Into this dark surface were etched images of two-headed bighorn sheep, men with helmet-sized heads, and women with giant earrings and spears.

"And remember, this is an active bombing range," the bomber man said, as if reading my mind. "*Do not* get lost." My mom glared at me. Then he added, "But don't worry—they don't bomb the canyon . . . or at least they try not to." He chuckled again. I liked him already.

As sunshine, desert wildflowers, and cacti flooded my senses, memories came rushing back. The incongruousness of the place made me want to laugh out loud, to become delirious like a Paiute on drugs. I started a skip-run like my father's into the canyon and felt that desert elation seep inside me, the living wilderness embracing me. The guide faded into the distance. The ordnance was forgotten.

I knew where I was. Home?

Chapter Two

Journey to the Lake

We made the trip from Seattle to China Lake in our sky-blue Plymouth Valiant, which had more than two hundred thousand miles on it, though we proudly made it last to four hundred thousand. Christine and I sat in the back seat, where I clutched a stack of desert postcards that my dad had sent from China Lake. He had moved there several months before us, while my mom stayed behind to sell the house. Now we were all together again, my dad having flown back to collect us after the house sold. The highway signs read "Fifty-Five Saves Lives" as we began our twenty-hour trek to our new home, my dad in the driver's seat. All I knew about where we were going was from the postcards in my hand. One was covered with paintings of desert animals—jackrabbit, antelope, tarantula, coyote, horny toad—and the other was a photo of a desert tortoise eating small yellow daisies.

Christine was nine and precocious, with stringy blondish hair and always a bit too skinny. No matter how much she ate, she would not fatten up. I was always bigger and taller, with a twisted brown mop of thick hair. "All you needed to do was shake your beautiful curls and you looked so nice," my mom once told me. "Christine looked nice too, but it took more time." It was enough time to make her hate me, it seemed. She counted the minutes it took to become beautiful, while I grew up effortlessly.

To counter those unfair minutes, Christine told me I was adopted. She said the proof was my "green" skin, which others might call "an olive complexion." To her, it was absolutely alien, leading to far-reaching ancestral explanations from Gypsy to Italian to Sami. Luckily, my thumbs were flat and wide, like my mother's. They were proof I was not adopted. Even though I had to walk around with my thumbs tucked inside my fists to avoid mockery, at least I knew I belonged. I would not be sent back to the Gypsies or Italians or Laplanders.

I always knew I was my sister's "usurper," the one who took her place. As my friend Meli, a psychologist, once explained to me, "A child can only survive without constant attention around age three. If a new sibling arrives before then, the first child can feel that her very survival is at stake." Unfortunately, no one told my mother that. Sis and I were two years apart, so I was fit for nothing but murder. "Stine hit me" were my first words, recorded forever in my baby book.

My dad kept us from fighting in the back seat of that Plymouth by leading us in endless folk ditties. You could stop Christine midpunch with, "Singing, ditty-ah, ditty-ah ding . . ." Outside, the world gradually turned drier and more brown, as if someone had taken a straw to the plants and sucked the water out. "I am going to miss watching our cherry tree bloom," my mom said, sighing, from the passenger seat. Just outside our front door in the Seattle suburb of Newport Hills, that tree had bunches of blossoms so big that they hung down like lanterns. Yet even those blooms were smaller than the giant orchids my mom would wear as corsages on special days such as Easter or Mother's Day. She would look striking with her jet-black hair, pink or yellow tailored suit, and matching pillbox hat with a tiny veil. Her dark pink lipstick would offset the pink of the flowers as she leaned down to me to brush the blossoms on my face. I would giggle at the tickling feel of petals and their rapturous scent. I always associated my mother with the mingled fragrances of cherry blossoms and Chanel No. 5.

Then, suddenly, her suits were all packed for China Lake and that world was abruptly taken from us, fading into emptiness on our long drive into the desert. Seattle was to be a beautiful cherry blossom–scented ghost. Gone were the glistening, raindrop-covered trees of my childhood and the cloudy days on the beach digging for clams. As we skirted the base of the Sierra Nevada mountains, which towered over us with their snow-covered peaks, the sun stunned with its ferocity and miles of open desert lay ahead of us like a giant pancake. We were left in a daze.

"Listen to this—" My mom began to read from a guidebook: "'The region surrounding China Lake is rich in the scenic beauty of desert valleys and majestic mountain regions.'" She sounded happy, which made me happy too. "'Death Valley is about ninety and Mount Whitney about eighty miles away, and on every hand are the historic sites of the Old West.'" The base had sent us this little booklet with a picture of Michelson Laboratory on the cover, where my dad had already begun working.

"Why do they call it Death Valley?" I asked.

"Pioneers used to die from the heat while trying to cross it in wagon trains a long time ago," she explained. "There are no roads across the Sierras from China Lake. I guess we'll be cut off from the world." My eyes got big, while my sister, who had the practical mind of a scientist, nodded in excitement.

"It describes why the navy chose this spot. . . ." Her voice rose with piqued interest. "'This nearly uninhabited desert valley, the clear skies and good flying weather, the ample water supply, the accessibility of highway and railroad, and the proximity to the Los Angeles manufacturing area all combined to provide a setting that ideally suited year-round weapon development and testing operations.'" Despite the few details in the guidebook, it felt as if we were heading into the complete unknown when we finally turned off Highway 395.

"Antelope," I said, looking down at the postcard to calm myself, reading the labels printed beneath the animals one by one. "Coyote. Tarantula."

We started down a ten-mile side road straight into a sandbox. In the middle of the box was a big dry lake, which looked like snow. My dad said cheerily, "Sure is nicer than the first time I came here," not noticing that even our black-and-white cockapoo puppy, Patches, wanted to hide, tucking her head under my leg and shaking.

After a pause, my dad retold a story we all had heard before. "I flew in on a tiny twin-engine plane from LA," he started. "It was really bumpy." We looked around for an airport, seeing only sand.

"Hey, I see it!" I pointed off to the left, where a single airstrip sat next to a white box of a building, not much bigger than my old bedroom.

"Yes, imagine flying into that and having no one there to meet you. No air-conditioning and not a soul inside. There was only the kid who had flagged in the plane and then busied himself putting brakes under the plane's wheels."

"It was really hot!" I piped in.

"A hundred and ten degrees, in fact. The first thing I noticed was that the pavement squished beneath my feet. You'll see. There was no taxi in sight, so once the pilot got in a car and drove away, I started to worry. I thought about hitchhiking the ten miles to the base—"

"Earl, don't encourage them," my mom interrupted, thinking we would start hitchhiking immediately.

"—but I hadn't done that since the war. And I was in my best suit."

"The gray one?" I asked.

"Yes, that's the one." He sounded pleased.

"So I went inside and sat next to an old rusty fan and waited. The kid—he looked like a teenager—was still unloading cargo from the plane. Finally, he came inside and stood behind the counter like no one was even there."

I could picture my father fretting about whether to approach him. I knew he did not like to bother people. At Boeing, he brought flowers to his secretary every week but was afraid to talk to his boss. "Ahem . . . Any chance I could get a ride into town?" he must have finally said.

"And this kid says," he went on, "he can give me a ride, but he'd have to shut down the airport first. I had to wait four hours!"

"Your suit must have looked a mess by then," my ever-practical mom said. "Too bad they wouldn't let me come with you. I could have ironed it before your interview."

"You wouldn't have enjoyed the barracks, Mary," he replied. "Anyway, I got the job."

"You did."

As we drove, what had once looked like dollhouses thrown across the desert floor turned into real buildings with names. We passed Three Sisters Restaurant, Grumpy Bears Groceries, and a church made of sun-damaged lumber like the kind they have in John Wayne westerns. We passed a feed store with a life-sized plastic horse on its roof. Strangely, all the stores and houses were on the right side of the road while there was only a barbed-wire fence on the left, behind which was nothing but empty desert.

"Coyote," I said, clutching the postcard harder, expecting to see a real coyote any minute. "Coyote." I petted the imaginary post-card fur.

Finally, we went through the base's main gate, where a U.S. Marine checked my dad's badge. A sign next to the gate read "Loose Lips Sink Ships" in big red letters over a picture of a sinking ship. The marine saluted briskly when he saw my dad was a captain, and my dad saluted back, crisply and more sure than anything I had ever seen him do. "Makes you feel important, that does," he said over his shoulder, "though they are so sloppy about salutes these days." At our insistence, he demonstrated how a proper salute should be done, while my mom urged him to keep both hands on the wheel.

Past the gate, the street was wide and lined with sycamore trees and automatic sprinklers that sparkled like rainbows in the sun. But then we turned off the main road, and it was all tumbleweeds and dirt again, with rows and rows of identical duplexes on identical street blocks. The buildings were washed out and faded from the sun, their paint peeling. In this hostile environment, even the paint could not cling, so the houses were a cracking, flaking gray. The government seemed to love gray. The streets were a palette of light brown sand, gray houses, and black streets. At that moment I realized we were moving not to a world of brilliant wildflowers and desert antelopes, but to bland, blocky government houses. The desert did not know that I wanted flowers *now;* it did not care that time for a child is *forever.* I would have to wait.

Rounding the corner to our new house on Rowe Street, we saw that the lawn was a dirt patch with a few clumps of dried grass. The duplex, an ash gray box with a flat roof, looked like an abandoned cell block, with a front porch tacked on that may as well have been a half-finished room: just four cement walls with window-sized holes to look out from. It was not at all like the pictures in *Life* magazine, which showed a smiling family—including a beautiful teenage daughter—standing on a nice lawn surrounded by flowers and a picket fence. Another *Life* photo depicted the living room of their huge house, where the family sat around in suits and high heels, everyone laughing. ROCKET TOWN! the magazine headline had read. I felt betrayed.

Inside, the house smelled of cigarettes and vague foodlike substances trapped in the forest green shag carpeting. My mom rushed to her familiar Ethan Allen couch, which had been moved in earlier by the navy. My dad followed, and they sat in silence, staring down, as we watched them tentatively. Then my dad looked up at us and smiled, saying, "Well, at least I don't have to stay in the bachelor's quarters anymore. This is our home, Mary!" He patted her thigh lightly, more out of nervous energy than affection, like the way he sometimes obsessively tapped the steering wheel.

"Don't do that." She caught his hand the second time. "You know I don't like it when you do that." But he never stopped, for the rest of his life.

Our house in Seattle had azaleas, alders, and our blooming cherry tree. Our duplex had one dying cottonwood. It also had no garage, no garbage disposal, and no washer-dryer hookup. Instead, we went to the base laundry; my dad insisted we avoid the one off base, which was better. "He was probably worried about me being able to get on base again," my mom explained later. She didn't have a badge. In the bedroom, a loud swamp cooler hummed, and the kitchen had a stove and refrigerator that looked as though they were from the forties: round and white with a big "General Electric" logo in silver. A sign on the refrigerator instructed us to call Public Works, number 7177, for repairs or problems with the house. My mom pulled the flyer off the refrigerator and went into the living room. She sat again on her Ethan Allen couch, covered in perfect pale blue linen, and began to rub its arm as if to invoke some magical genie that would restore her real home. Christine and I stared at the walls of cement and asbestos slapped over chicken wire to avoid looking at her.

"You know there was no way to get a better house," my dad reminded her, reading her disappointment. "Not until I'm promoted to GS-12. At least we didn't get a trailer." He seemed to think this would make my mom appreciate the duplex more. I later learned she had assumed we would be able to move if we didn't like the place the navy picked for us. My dad had broken the news to her shortly before we arrived. "The navy doesn't work that way," he had said. We were stuck.

Only as an adult did I discover the base housing regulations, tucked away in my mother's files, which explained how it all worked. If my mom and dad had been childless, I found out, they would have been assigned a motel-sized room with only an electric range. If Christine or I had died, they would have also had to go to that apartment building, since our house had a two-child minimum. If my dad had packed up and left us, my mom would have had five days to move out. It was all in the housing regulations. Mom was completely dependent on him, and us, for even this tiny space. We all had to stay alive.

As for me, my only disappointment was that I had not seen any wild animals.

"Mom, uh," I asked quietly, "where are the coyotes?"

No one replied.

Instead, Christine grabbed my postcard from me. When I tried to grab it back, she pulled my arm behind me and twisted, hard. I screamed, "Mom!"

"Say uncle, say uncle," my sister commanded. And I did. As she dropped my little arm, I sighed in relief, feeling safe again, not knowing more elaborate dangers lay ahead.

Chapter Three

The Push to Weaponize

People don't become weapons developers because they want to kill people. They build weapons because they want to do something else but cannot get a job in that something else. My dad wanted to build airplanes but was pulled into weapons when he was unemployed and worried about being able to feed his kids. Others wanted to build bridges or rocket ships. But once people end up in the world of weapons, they tend to stay. The benefits are that good. After a while, knowing that war fills your bellies, peace can feel like starvation. Even China Lake's top brass once lamented "the rigors of peacetime malnutrition." Without a war the money dries up, people start losing their jobs, and housing values tumble. We knew our town could be closed down and our homes bulldozed. It is hard to explain what a salve war can be. Even as it devastates one community, it feeds another.

My dad divided his life into three stages: poverty, orphan, war

(POW). Once he got to the last stage, he never got out. To be clear, he was not a real POW—he was just a person who ended up permanently stuck in war.

Orphaned by age twelve, my dad had been born to John and Esther Piper in a small iron-mining town in the Upper Peninsula of Michigan. John Piper worked and died in the iron mines like his dad, William, whose arm was blown off in a mining blast when he was fourteen. William survived his accident and wrote a poem that started "There may be a crack in life's wall somewhere / Where the tender roots may find their way / To a fairer clime, as some declare— / I'm unconcerned while on the way. . . ." The only religion my dad's family observed was stoicism, and they were good practitioners. Eventually, William got a wooden prosthesis.

His son John Piper was not so lucky in the Cornishman's endless battle against the mines. In England, William's dad had mined tin. In the U.S., it was iron. They kept mining like a hydra-headed monster, and John was just another fallen soldier. His death certificate said he died of "pleurisy," or inflammation of the lungs, but my dad never trusted that explanation. His obituary presented a different theory, stating he "died of a broken heart." I think that's the version my dad believed.

My dad never spoke of his parents, which led me to grow up thinking no one had grandparents. It always surprised me when others disagreed. Eventually, to fill in that blank space and keep up with the grandparent stories of my friends, I would prod my dad about what his parents were like. "They were nice people," was all I ever got. "Nice people," he said, as if they were strangers he met on a bus and liked. I suppose it was the same for me, that they were only "Esther and John," never Grandpa and Grandma. Nice people.

Esther had died the same year as John. "But from what?" I asked my dad.

"She had a headache for a year and then died," my dad said simply, as if that were normal. Eventually, he added, "Her eyes were sensitive to the light, so we had to keep the blinds drawn." Only much later did he confess to me that he thought it was his fault. When her headache was particularly bad, he said, he had insisted she get out of bed and take him to a Gene Autry movie. "I begged and begged, and the next day she died."

He never insisted on anything after that.

Esther's obituary claimed she died of heart disease, but this did not make sense to me either. Did heart disease make you want to live in the dark for a year? In the end, all I learned from my grandparents was that obituaries and death certificates lie—and that death does not like to be pigeonholed.

By the time John Piper died, my dad was already the lanky, undernourished-looking boy he would remain for the rest of his life. He had thin, light brown hair with, thankfully, a little curl to cover its sparseness, big ears, and a chin that seemed pointy only because his face was so thin. His sister, who was four years older, got married to avoid being sent to an orphanage, but my dad did not have that option. He was too young. Instead, he went to live with his aunt and uncle, the Bergs.

Unfortunately, Mrs. Berg died shortly after he moved in. My dad must have thought this whole family would be the next to go, that he might kill them too. Decades later, I found the invitation to Mrs. Berg's funeral in my dad's box of keepsakes. It read, "From the Berg Family. And Earl Piper." I pictured him living in that space between his name and the Bergs', dangling inappropriately at the end. In fact, I knew he would have remained indefinitely and elusively attached to the Berg family if not for Pearl Harbor. As it was, he stayed only four years, until he was seventeen and Pearl Harbor was attacked. As he told it, he had been working at a factory as a tool crib clerk, a kind of mechanic's librarian, on that infamous day. When he heard the announcement on the radio, he knew he had to enlist, though he had to wait two more months to turn eighteen. Then he got a new uncle, one who would never die and leave him: Uncle Sam.

Like so many boys at the time, my dad had been enamored with Charles Lindbergh and Amelia Earhart, and so he signed up to be a pilot. But his body failed him exactly three times, which left him where all washed-up pilots end up: as a navigator.

His first failure was not passing the weight test to get into the air force. He was always too little. But the recruiter, sensing my dad's disappointment, had whispered to him, "Drink a lot of water and eat as many bananas as you can. Then come back." If not for that recruiter, my dad would not have gone to war.

The second failure was during boot camp. Thrown into a pond and told to swim out during basic training, my dad sank and nearly drowned, which he attributed to having no fat. Someone had to jump in and save him, which made him afraid of water for the rest of his life. I still sometimes picture my dad's eighteen-year-old body sinking down into the darkness of that pond where others would have floated. "Why me?" he must have thought. "Why me again?"

Nevertheless, he made it to the pilot training program, where his body failed him for the final time. He got the measles during the midterm exams and was abruptly kicked out of school. There was no time for measles in a war. No one jumped in to save him that time. Though my dad always looked embarrassed when he spoke about not being a pilot, he would undoubtedly end the tale with the part about bananas. "I had to throw up afterward," he would say, chuckling at his own inadequacy. "But it worked."

Soon he was navigating for transport flights out of Cornwall, supplying the battlefields across North Africa, Western Europe, and even the Caribbean. For the first time, it must have seemed the world was more than a spare room, an iron mine, or a forest in Michigan. He spent most of the war in a glass bubble on top of the plane, "shooting" the stars with a sextant, trying to get a "celestial fix" in a world that had become lines of latitude and longitude on a map. Because the movement of the stars across the skies had been calculated to the second, my dad could figure out where he was by finding one or two stars and triangulating his position. Then he could calculate, with the help of timetables and a mathematical equation, his place in the universe. His absolute position. Who wouldn't want that?

Between flights, my dad would practice navigation by walking the ocean footpath at night from his base in St. Mawgan to Newquay, Cornwall. He claimed he got a feel for the stars that way, timing his paces to calculate his velocity. Speed plus time plus direction plus the stars. My dad taught us all the calculations of war. I think he wanted to pass something on to us, a way to always find ourselves in the world when we were lost. "The stars will help locate you," he would say.

By the age of nine, I thought war was a difficult math problem. It never occurred to me that humans, other than the men with their slide rules, were involved. I knew there was an elaborate chart of moving pieces and equations that someone was solving far away, but it did not involve us. Besides, there were really only "operations" on the base—Operation Rolling Thunder, Operation Barrel Roll, and so on. There were so many of them that I stopped trying to keep track. There were no wars as far as I knew.

Only my dad had a war.

My favorite thing about my dad's war was all the exotic cargo. My dad talked about flying bananas from Africa to England, where people had vitamin deficiencies. He talked about monkeys in Casablanca. He talked about flying blood. He carried children who had to get somewhere fast to stay alive. But he also flew illegal goods like rum and cigars from the Caribbean. He traded Chanel No. 5 from

Paris for cigarettes in England. He brought silk nylons for girlfriends. To me, war sounded like a long sequence of barters: bananas for soldiers, Chanel No. 5 for cigarettes, nylons for girlfriends. It was a fabulous, globe-trotting holiday with lots of free stuff. Who wouldn't want to go to war?

"I was just a rumrunner during the war," my dad once said, and my mom, sitting next to him, punched him in the knee.

"You could still be arrested," she warned.

My dad said all he lost in the war was a chunk of earlobe to frostbite, which could have happened anywhere. He said he never wore hats, even during Michigan winters, to the consternation of his parents. Instead, he would check for spots of frostbite in the mirror when he got home, then try to warm them up with his mittens. So he did not blame the war even for his ear. He blamed his own stubbornness.

After the war, my dad moved to Seattle and went to the University of Washington on the GI Bill. He graduated with honors in aeronautical engineering and was recruited right away to work at Boeing. If he couldn't fly planes, he said, he could make them fly. Though everything in his life was going according to plan, something must have felt wrong, because at age twenty-nine, after seeing a poster on a street pole one day, he ended up at a Billy Graham tent meeting.

Long after my dad died, my mom showed me a note he wrote to himself after that meeting, titled "Why I Became a Christian: My Testimony." The sight of my father's crisp writing style, fine-tuned from years of drawing perfect lines on graph paper for a living, shook me to the core like he must have been shaken then. "I realized I had no control over my life," he wrote. "I didn't like the way I was living but couldn't do a thing about it."

"Is he talking about drinking?" I asked my mom. She nodded. I knew my father drank during the war but never imagined it was a problem. He used to joke about "having a beer with the kids," when we were no longer kids, simply to make my mom mad. But we knew he never would. Only after I saw that note did I realize that maybe war was not exactly what my father said it was. Maybe it was not all fun and games. After World War II, which killed around sixty million people, men and women started coming home with something they called "war neurosis" or "operational fatigue." Now we call it post-traumatic stress disorder. Maybe that is why he felt he had "no control." Maybe he knew some of those sixty million.

My dad's note described Billy Graham, "He kept quoting the handwriting on the wall, and I knew if I were weighed in any balance I'd be found wanting." So under that tent filled with ten thousand people, my dad walked down the aisle like hundreds of others. He found God, who became his new Uncle. There was Uncle Berg, then Uncle Sam, and finally Uncle God, who could not leave him.

After reading the Prayer of Salvation in the back corner of that tent, my dad was told to find a church. So when he saw a flyer outside the Swedish Baptist church that read, "After Billy Graham, What?" he must have thought it was a sign. Since he met my mother at that church, perhaps it was.

For my mom, there were only two stages in my dad's life: pre-Christian dad and post-Christian dad. We were not allowed to talk about pre-Christian dad. "Your dad did some bad things before he found God," she said. "But he was forgiven." I pictured him torturing people in some dark, gangster-filled room out of *The Godfather*. Only later did I realize she meant he had sex and drank. Luckily for my mom, Christianity erased all that, at least *almost*. I think she was still bothered by what she said was gone. Since he had been washed anew by Jesus, it made sense that she would wince when he brought up the war with a wistful smile as if he wanted to go back to pre-Christian dad.

Since my dad was half Norwegian, on Esther's side, their marriage was an unlikely alliance. Swedes and Norwegians have been arch-rivals since the Swedes invaded everyone within reach ages ago. For the rest of their lives together, my mom would be the brunt of my dad's Swedish jokes, and he her Norwegian ones. "Ten thousand Swedes ran through the weeds at the battle of Copenhagen," we all learned to sing. "Ten thousand Swedes ran through the weeds a-chasin' one Norwegian." Christine and I, though mostly Swedish, usually sided with the underdog Norway, leaving my mom out in the cold.

From our house in Newport Hills, my dad took a bridge to the south in the morning to get to Boeing and another to the north at night to finish his master's degree in aerospace engineering. My mom, who had a degree in medical technology, started "drawing blood and mix-ing stool samples," as she described her job at Swedish Hospital. While my dad made the space shuttle and the 747, my mom became an expert on parasites. They were happy, the opposite of star-crossed. My dad reveled in the miracle of having non-orphaned children, and my mom quit her job after my sister was born, thinking she was safe at last with this shy man who brought her flowers. They must have thought it a marvel that they were two adults who could survive on their own. In short, we were living the American dream until, quite simply, we were not.

Our problems began with the men on the moon. I was four and my sister was six at the time of the first moon landing. We were both too little to understand how it could ruin us. The problem was that after that "one small step for man," there was really nowhere else for them to go. Mars was too far away, and the moon, unfortunately, did not have much to offer. So no more spaceships for Boeing. In beating the Soviet Union to the moon, America's main goal had been accomp-lished. After that, we had to beat them in Vietnam, which was even more expensive. We could not have it both ways. Space walks or wars, not both. So the *Apollo* program gradually shut down, which hit Boeing hard, and my dad was fired along with thirty percent of their workforce. Boeing really should have planned a few misfires first, shooting people right past the moon just to keep the money rolling in.

After twenty years at Boeing, my dad was left with no job and two little girls who had burst onto the scene with no clue about what had gone on before. After six months of unemployment, he would have taken anything when he got the job at China Lake. My mom would sometimes blame my dad for the way things turned out. "He was too shy," she would say. "He wouldn't assert himself." And this was true.

The notes from his first interview at China Lake, which he kept in a box under his bed, described him as "shy to nervous" and said he was "a good candidate, except for his age: forty-nine." I thought of my dad as reserved, but to me that meant he was wise. The notes did not say that. In fact, it seemed a bit cruel that they gave those notes to him. He could not get younger, after all.

"He was never much of a go-getter," my mom used to say. He clearly preferred to be alone with his family, listening to his kids sing "Thumbelina" in the back seat of our Plymouth Valiant. We were little songbirds, full of life, like the astronauts from *Apollo 17* who had skipped across the moon singing, "I was strolling on the moon one day, / In the merry, merry month of May . . . do do do be do." It was the last time anyone walked on the moon. Those men had looked really silly and could not harmonize like Christine and me. But they were having such fun. "Isn't this a neat way to travel?" astronaut Harrison Schmitt had said. I sometimes wondered about them. Would they have wanted to stay up there floating above the world if they had known the time for *Apollo* missions, for singing and dancing, was over back on Earth?

Or would they have wanted to come down and build weapons too?

Chapter Four

Weapons Bride

My mom, born Mary Dahlstrom, became a weapons developer because she believed a wife should follow her husband. Her mother, Hannah Dahlstrom, was from a long line of poor Baptist Swedes, which in terms of status ranks below Lutherans but above Pentecostals. Hannah had huge brown eyes and perfectly crimped dark brown hair that seemed determined to distract from her burlap-quality clothes. In 1920, she left Sweden at the age of twenty along with a million other Swedes fleeing famine. Even though the worst had been over for decades, the momentum of famine kept going, stuck in people's feet like a motor reflex. Letters kept coming from once famine-stricken relatives raving about the good soil in America. The Homestead Act was still offering free land to anyone who settled in Minnesota—except, of course, to women. Hannah went anyway. My mom said she threw up all the way across the Atlantic.

The options available to Hannah in Sweden were not too desirable. Her parents were both dead, as was her brother, who had succumbed to tuberculosis at twenty-three. She had been offered lodging in a remote goat herder's hut on a distant relative's farm, which was a spinster's job. An isolated log structure in the Dalarna hills, the cabin was about five by eight feet with a wooden plank for a bed. Instead, Hannah boarded a ship in Gothenburg bound for New York City.

At the time, post–Civil War blacks were moving north, running from the South as fast as they could, while post-famine Swedes were moving west. My mom said that when Hannah went to look for work, she kept seeing signs that read "No Blacks or Swedes" in the store windows. Ultimately, she had to settle on "piecework," or sewing at home for a pittance, while the cousin she moved in with probably wished that she would leave.

I can only imagine what meeting Victor must have meant for her. Hannah told my mom she was "swept off her feet," though my mom always added, "Duped, more like it. He was a good-looking man." I think my mom was afraid the same fate would befall me. "Why do you keep saying you want someone 'cute'?" she would ask. "He'll be old and ugly someday. Remember that."

Hannah was Victor's second wife, sandwiched between three. Her job was to take care of his five kids, ten acres, cow, and chickens while he worked at the Brown & Bigelow factory making calendars, greeting cards, and other paper goods. Before long, Hannah had two children of her own, a boy and then my mother. After that, my mom's and Hannah's hearts beat in circles around each other, but the Dahlstrom boys were the kings. "David always stole the show," my mom said of her brother.

My mom was not allowed to speak Swedish with her parents, since they thought even a hint of an accent would hold her back. So Swedish became the language of secrets that she could not enter, a language that carried all the suffering of the generations before.

When my mom was twenty and in college, Hannah had her first

stroke. She was fifty, worn out, and with no insurance or doctors or expectation of help. The first stroke only made her a little forgetful, but then they came in clusters over the course of two years with no one to sit by Hannah's side but my mom. As the daughter, my mom's assigned role was watching Hannah die. Her brother David had by then enlisted, while my mom's heart kept swimming with Hannah's heart in the sickroom upstairs. No one was there to help her, a girl in her twenties who could not stop the suffering.

Even Victor relegated them both to the attic.

The first stroke only made Hannah limp a little. The next one, a few months later, made her mouth droop on the right side. Each stroke made my mom move a little closer to Hannah. She leaned in to interpret Hannah's slurred words or stood beside her to provide a crutch as she walked. Their bodies slowly merged into one as they tried to climb the stairs, up and down.

"It's only this far to the stove," my mom would say as Victor sat in his recliner and watched TV.

"Thanks," Hannah would whisper, and try to lift her foot. Hannah had stopped going to Sunday school long ago, because she was afraid they would make her read the Bible in English. She was too embarrassed by her accent then. Now that she was losing her voice altogether, my mom must have realized that what language you spoke hardly mattered in comparison to whether you could speak at all.

Hannah was finally confined to her bed. "I can do nothing," she said in Swedish one day, and though my mom could not speak Swedish, she knew what this meant. Hannah still thought she should be working.

"She was such a patient hard worker," my mom explained to me.

Since they could not afford a doctor, my mom had to improvise. She learned how to feed her mom after her tongue stopped moving. She simply moved it out of the way and forced the food down her throat while she choked and protested. There are millions of decisions like this made every day by those who tend to the dying. "There was no way to stop my mother's pain," my mother said. "The biggest problem was that there was no one to tell me what to do." So Hannah wasted away in that attic with no way to explain what she needed while my mother absorbed her pain and decided for her.

"I never felt so helpless in my life," my mom said. As she sat in that old wooden chair beside the attic bed, she began to calculate how to get insurance, and decided that she needed a job. Every day, she and her mom decided the same thing: it should not be like this. In their hearts, together.

Somehow, during those hard years, my mom worked toward a medical technology degree at the University of Minnesota. "It was one of the only degrees open to women," she explained. "And I liked science."

My mom was twenty-eight when Hannah's body finally, quietly, separated from hers forever. The freedom of living in one body was a shock my mother could not bear. It catapulted her to what came next.

Meanwhile, Victor began to worry about finding a third wife, saying he'd need someone to cook. Swedes were dreaming the dream of the West at the time, like so many people. There were thick, rich woods out there, which translated into easy cash. So when Victor decided to pack up the farm and move to Seattle, my mom went too. They sold the farm and bought a small house on the outskirts of town.

Victor, who lived by his looks, soon had another wife.

Maybe only then did my mom feel free. She had a degree and no one to keep alive.

When my dad approached my mom in that Swedish Baptist church, I wonder what she felt. Did she feel the same relief that Hannah had when she met Victor? Or was it something else? "There was no other way for a woman to buy a house back then," my mom explained. "We did not get raises, and our job opportunities were very limited. So we had to get married." She took the best marriage proposal she had, the one that came with insurance. My dad had a good job at Boeing as an aerospace engineer, and he brought her flowers, which no one had ever done before.

"He won me over with flowers," she said. Is that love?

My mom and dad were married in the St. Paul church she had grown up attending, with lilacs and bridesmaid dresses paid for out of the $1,200 they had saved for their new life. My mom had insisted it be $600 *each*, to start fair and square. She did let my dad buy the white roses for the altar and her bouquet. His sister sewed the wedding dress. My mom was a stunning, beaming bride, with perfectly curled short black hair, red lipstick, cat's-eye glasses, and a white veil with a train. Everything was as it should be. My dad gave her pearls and the same Chanel No. 5 she would receive on every anniversary after that.

But by the time of their wedding, my dad had run out of money to fix their blue Rambler. "We had to park the car on a hill and let it roll down, hoping it would start." And so lives began together, rickety and imperfect, blessed by hope. By getting married, my mom could own a house, though she was well aware that she was contributing too. "Although he got no money from my family," she explained, "he got a wife with no school debt and a marketable degree. My dad did help with school expenses. That's worth something." I suppose this is how marriages are decided and negotiated, cast and recast through time. Of course, I knew by then that marriages have secrets, things that are never quite equal, never "fair and square." These are the things that are scarcely revealed to oneself, let alone to each other.

My own marriage taught me that.

Chapter Five

Missile Aerodynamics

Soon, pitch and roll took over my dad's life. "Pitch" is when a missile veers up or down, sometimes turning right around and hitting the pilot who fired the shot. This happened more than once at China Lake. Once, a missile veered straight up, stalled, and headed for a group of visiting dignitaries in the bleachers. Luckily, it missed them. "Roll," on the other hand, is when a missile starts to spin on its nose-to-tail axis like a top. It is not as dangerous for the pilot as pitch, but it is dangerous for civilians on the ground. The worst thing that can happen is when a missile starts to pitch and roll at the same time, which is called "dynamic instability." More often, people will say the missile "went crazy."

My dad went to China Lake to stop all that. He worked diligently at pitch and roll late into the evenings during our first summer there. He would sit and draw symmetrical circles and curves on blue graph paper, with long equations beneath and around them. Though I loved the artistic nature of the wind, how its angles and curves were so perfect, I wanted him to be drawing with crayons with me instead. I quickly became jealous of pitch and roll.

One evening, as I inched closer to my dad's feet at the dining room table, he pulled me up onto his lap. "So, Karen," he said, tickling me, "do you want to know what I'm working on?" The green-and-yellow glass interrogation light hung above the dining room table, swaying slightly with the fan, but did not bother me.

"Yes!" I said through giggles, happy that my pestering had finally worked.

"Okay," he said, picking up his pen. "Watch this." He started to draw his squiggly lines on the blue graph paper. An equation.

I watched it come into being, until I could read:

$$RM = C_1\,\bar{q}\,S\,b + \frac{\Delta RM}{Td_e}\,Td_e + FY\,Z_{MRC}$$

"That's the roll moment equation," he explained. "This equation tells you when a missile is going to roll. The first half of the equation is here," he said, pointing at the part before the first plus sign. "This is the part that makes a missile roll. Remember I told you about roll?"

I obediently nodded my head.

"Okay, and this part," he said, pointing his black pen stamped "U.S. Government" to the part after the first plus sign. "This part is what stops the roll."

His pen hovered, shaking in the light of the dining room lamp.

"So I have to keep it balanced right there," he said, pointing at the first plus sign again. His pen stayed there for quite a while. "Then the missile won't roll. Every missile wants to roll, but you have to stop it before it gets there. You have to push it back." All I cared about was that my dad's lap was warm and his leg was bouncing up and down, which meant he loved me.

But I tried to concentrate. The missile wants to roll, and you have to stop it. So my dad's job was stopping time. "If you drop a quarter from a building faceup," he went on, "what keeps that quarter from landing faceup?"

"It spins!" I said, waving my arms about my head and twisting them behind me.

"Yes, but why does it spin?" He wanted more.

"Um, I don't know."

"Because of the wind. The wind flips it around, like it does to a missile."

From this, I learned my dad's job was like dropping a quarter from a building and getting it to land faceup. He had to find a moment in time, the roll moment, which is when the quarter starts to flip. He had to eliminate that moment.

"But how do you stop the wind?" I innocently asked.

"You can't, of course. But if you drop something heavy and pointy, it won't spin like a quarter. You have to find the right shape for the missile so it doesn't spin."

I understood a little, though I was only seven.

"Or this can stop it," he said, grabbing the purple-and-silver gyroscope he'd given me. It spun in circles on the inside while standing upright and still on the outside. I wanted to throw up my hands and spin in circles then, to dance like the gyroscope to the rhythm of his voice.

"If we put this on a missile's tail, it will slow the roll down, because it generates inertia. Like if you are on the merry-go-round, you can't jump off when you are going really fast, right?"

"I don't know!" But I determined to find out when school started.

Later I would discover that all organisms—from amoebas to humans—have an innate spinning tendency. A blindfolded person will walk, drive, or fly in circles. As a neuroscientist explained, "We get lost because we are unable to orient using our senses—such as vision—and an innate mechanism for spiraling then is revealed." No one really knows why, but people will walk in circles in the woods if they get lost. People will swim in circles with no visual cues. "People tend to walk in a spiral, not a straight line, with eyes closed," the neuroscientist discovered. "When vision becomes blocked, memory of the landscape provides sufficient guidance for eight seconds; and though the Earth is a giant magnet, humans do not, unfortunately, possess a magnetic 'sixth sense' to complement it." The Earth starts spinning inside our heads after eight seconds. Maybe this is why the Sufi mystics spin in circles when they dance. Maybe we all want to spin in circles. In a blizzard or whiteout, your memory of the landscape stays with you for only eight seconds. After that, you will not know where you are. After that, you will naturally veer away from your tent. You will naturally die.

Our senses keep us alive, keep us from spinning out of control. My dad was always fighting the spinning, from the times he walked home through Michigan blizzards without wearing a hat to the times he flew through snowstorms over German-occupied Norway to the times he tried to keep missiles on course—right up to the end, when he fought the long, hard years of spinning into death.

Pitch and roll became his way of framing things, which he tried to help me understand.

Chapter Six

U.S. Government Dog

I grew up on Rowe Street, named after the USS *Rowe*, which was once stationed at Pearl Harbor. Other streets were named after fleet admirals (Nimitz, King, Halsey) or their ships (*Hornet*, *Wasp*, *Franklin*) or their combat arenas (Midway, Leyte, Coral Sea). Living on these streets gave the impression of being in a battle at sea during World War II. I would walk down Nimitz to Midway to Groves Elementary School, named after General Leslie Groves, the military man in charge of dropping the atom bomb. Ironically, Groves chose to test the bomb by dropping it on the USS *Saratoga*, once the ship of China Lake's first commander, Sherman E. Burroughs. I wonder how Burroughs felt about his ship exploding in a test at Bikini Atoll. Maybe he had offered it up, glad to be done with World War II. Maybe he was ready for the bright future of atom bombs.

As a child, I did not know what the street names meant. World War II was just my dad's war, and Nimitz was just a pretty name to me. It was only decades later that I discovered China Lake had supplied all the rockets used in World War II, sending Tiny Tim, Zuni, and Mighty Mouse rockets to the field by the millions. When I told my mom about my new discovery, she squinted her eyes as if to get a better look at the state of my mental health, then said, "China Lake *was* that war. What did you think?"

"What do you mean?" I asked.

"I mean, we did everything over there," she replied. "How could you not know that?" But growing up in a war town does not mean you know a thing about war.

Outside, I wandered the streets, getting lost in the unfamiliar sights of war. Inside, my family started acting strangely. Christine began labeling all the books in the house, saying she was using the Dewey decimal system. "You have to check them out from me from now on," she said one day. "I will mark in my file when you took it and when I need to have it back." I gave up reading and got a hamster, naming it Snowball, my ball of furry whiteness in the desert heat.

Patches, meanwhile, did not like the sonic booms and could often be found shivering under the colonial maple end table next to the couch. I could hardly blame her for being scared. With all the unexploded ordnance and wild-looking dogs roaming around outside, it was a dangerous place to be a dog. My dad even warned my mom about this before we arrived. "I sure miss the three of you," he wrote to her, "and the card from Karen kind of made me cry a little. Patches I don't miss much 'cause we have plenty of dogs around here." It made me sad to think that Patches, my best companion, was once unwanted. "They have very strict rules about dogs here, but they don't seem to enforce them," he continued. "I wonder if you shouldn't have Patches spayed before bringing her down here. She could be a real problem with all the male dogs running loose." But we did not, and it was a problem.

We had to drag Patches out from under the table to register her with the navy. They gave her a tag that read "Naval Weapons Center" with a number on one side and "DOG" on the other. "Don't they know what dogs look like here?" I asked my mom. It seemed every-thing had to be labeled or stamped now. U.S. Government pen. U.S. Government dog. U.S. Government books. Nothing was ours any-more, not even Patches.

Around the dinner table, my mother would talk about whether my sister was intentionally scraping the fork on her teeth because we could not talk about my dad's day at work. U.S. Government dad. The fork drove my mother crazy. We talked about whether my sister ate her peas. We talked about whether I had scrubbed my neck prop-erly, since it was turning brown. We talked about the problems with Public Works and how they would not unclog the sink. U.S. Govern-ment house. Anything but work and bombs and especially Vietnam. We turned off the news when it came on. We were allowed to watch *Little House on the Prairie* once a week, but that was all. Then my mom and dad would go to their room to talk about the missiles.

Since we had moved to the base, my sister had started sleeping on air mattresses underneath the dining room table. U.S. Government air mattresses. She took all the air mattresses and blankets she could find and stacked them above and below her until she was squeezed in tight and looked like a Christine sandwich. Then she was ready for nuclear war. Sometimes she took her sleeping bag and air mattresses and slept in the closet instead. My parents would laugh and take pic-tures. We all thought it was funny. She later told me she found con-fined spaces cozy, like infants who calm down when they are swaddled.

To be safe from attack, Christine and I built a fort in a bamboo grove in our backyard. It was near the chicken-wire fence separating our neighbor's duplex from ours. The center of the grove was hollow, so we planned to hide there when things got bad. We put blankets inside and then began to dig a moat so no one could get to us. We took turns chasing each other around the yard with our garden hose gun, which made filling the moat take longer but also made my mom happy since the lawn was getting watered. Once the moat was finished, we went inside and tore down the mud bridge so no one else could get inside.

When there is a secret called "war" hovering in the air, shouted out in sonic booms then pushed down into silence at the dinner table, the body will notice even if the mind refuses to. My heart tuned into those unexpected sonic booms and began to mimic them.

"Bmp, bmp," it went one night, then stopped. I was lying in my pink chiffon canopy bed. I put my hand to my heart and looked around the dark room, which was rapidly shrinking. There were stuffed animals lining the wall, looking suddenly ominous, and the room seemed so childish for someone dying. Then my heart started racing and skipping again. I held my breath and checked my wrist, which I had seen the cops do on *CHiPs* after an epic car crash scene.

Then I started the slow journey—not fast enough to die—down the hallway with one hand on my heart and one against the wall, until I finally pushed open my parents' bedroom door.

"Wha . . . What's that?" My mom sat up as though a serial killer had walked in.

"It's my heart," I said. I knew how they would respond. In my family the fear of death seemed mixed up with the desire for death, thrown together into a big grab bag where you were never sure which one was the winning answer. Either way, death was a call to action. We were suddenly at our best.

My dad jumped out of bed and ran toward me. His face glowed like a ghost's in the moonlight as he leaned down to put his ear against my chest. When he looked up, his gray eyes jumped out of his big black plastic glasses. *Turn on the light,* I wanted to say but did not. I was sure he could not hear a heartbeat.

"Well, it can't hurt to take her in," he said to my mom. That confirmed I was dying. In the dining room, the mottled green carpeting looked full of land mines that had to be avoided in the refracted moonlight pouring through the windows.

As we drove to the hospital, my arms looked greenish white, which made me feel even more sick. I was glad when the ER doctor finally put me in a bright white room with white sheets all around me, then listened to my heart while everyone watched. The way he hung there, so close and reassuring, made me relax. "Having a hard night, huh?" he said as he listened. I wanted to cry right then but did not know why. The brilliant light shining down on me, and the certainty of the doctor, and the cleanliness, made everything, all the questions about life and death, seem crystal clear and focused in that moment.

Finally, he looked back at my parents. "Her heart sounds okay," he said, then turned back to me.

"But it hurts?" he asked again.

"It hurts when I breathe," I said, "right here," pointing to my heart in case he was listening in the wrong place.

"Well, there could be a slight bronchitis," he said. "There is some wheezing. I'm going to put her on an antibiotic for five days and see if that helps." At least he'd found something, which meant I would not get in trouble for wasting everyone's time.

"Why does she get to pick the best lollipop?" my sister complained afterward.

"Because she's sick," my mom said as she patted me on the head, which felt soothing like rain.

The next time, the doctor said, "Her heart sounds fine." I was embarrassed to have nothing wrong with me. The time after that, the doctor said, "I might hear a slight heart murmur, but it's nothing to worry about."

"Ah, I have one of those too." My dad looked suddenly pleased, as if his murmur were proof of mine. We were growing desperate for an explanation. "Mine sort of comes and goes like hers does. The doctors can't always hear it."

"They can be genetic," the doctor added, nodding absentmindedly.

Back at home, my mom tried to help by giving me a medical encyclopedia to read. "This is from my days as a medical technician," she said proudly. "All the diseases I've dealt with are in there. Maybe you can find yours." I saw pictures of people with giant boils, rashes, amputations, and that sort of thing. I could not find my particular disease and kept having more and more of what I thought were heart attacks.

My dad bought his own stethoscope at the base medical supply center so we could stop bothering the doctors at the ER. After that, when I woke them up, my dad would run for his stethoscope and put it on my little chest while I lay on the living room couch, enjoying the silence of his concentration.

"Hm, I'm not sure," he would say, then concentrate and listen more.

There were so many things to be frightened of at night—the Rapture coming, jets crashing on you, bombs accidentally landing on your house. Sometimes parachuters suddenly fell from the sky or a man flew by in an ejection seat test. It seemed there was a daily invasion going on. I knew the worst one would be the Rapture, because what if I was left behind?

China Lake's newspaper, the *Rocketeer*, had a cartoon one day about a low-flying jet snagging a highway sign, followed by the pilot getting chewed out by his captain in the next cartoon window. The week after the cartoon came out, my mom said while holding the *Rocketeer*, "Listen to this. Someone complained about the cartoon, saying it brought back memories of the time he saw a jet three feet off the ground in the rearview mirror of his truck. It was headed right for him but suddenly veered up, barely missing him."

"What's he complaining about?" my dad asked.

"He says it's a serious problem," my mom replied. "We shouldn't joke about it." In China Lake, you could report such incidents the way people report bad truck drivers, but only if you were able to write down the plane's number as it flew into the speed of sound.

Luckily, though jets were loud and irritating, they never flew close enough to snag me.

In fact, the only *real* threat to me was my sister. For instance, sometimes I would start tapping my spoon on my emptied bowl of ice cream while sitting on my queen's throne of a squishy white vinyl beanbag chair. "Stop tapping that," Christine would say from her yellow throne. But I would tap again. Finally, she would rise up, the embodiment of vengeance and justice, and grab the spoon with a yank from my hand. When I began to cry, she would punch me in the arm. "I'll kill you," she would yell, pummeling my back while I curled up into a little ball and let the tension stream out.

Then I would scream, "Mo-o-om! Stine hit me! She's hi-tt-ing me now!" The pummeling on my back made it hard to get out the words, but the world would gradually right itself again.

"Karen is being a brat! She deserved it," my sister would argue before the judge, but my mom would inevitably yell at my sister, and then all was as it should be.

Sometimes, when my sister chased me around the house like a missile, I would run and hide in the bathroom, the most secure place in the house, and pray that Jesus would make the lock hold strong. But one time, Christine's foot broke right through the door when she kicked it, so I screamed at the top of my lungs, "Mo-o-om! Help! Help! Help!" After my rescue, my dad had to patch the door with cardboard that he painted white, which took a long time and made everyone think about how awful my sister was. It stood there as evidence of our trauma, so we never talked about it after that. But they knew I was better than her.

Christine would say she was going to kill me, but she never did. We were not very efficient with our kill ratios. "Don't say you're going to kill your sister," my mother complained. "Sometimes people really do kill people. It isn't nice to say that lightly." We took that to mean that we ought to take killing more seriously, like the military. We should say we were going to kill someone only when we really could.

Christine and I were slowly becoming U.S. Government kids. We began to roam a bit too far from home, out on the base ranges, which was technically illegal, but no one cared. My mom was not afraid of the soldiers with guns or the explosions; she was afraid of the desert. It had rattlesnakes, scorpions, heatstroke, and lockjaw. One man's car ran out of gas on a dirt road, and though he stayed right there on that road as he was supposed to, no one found him until he was dead. Another man fell into a mine shaft and was bitten by a dozen or so rattlesnakes. Two girls flipped over in their Jeep in a flash flood and were trapped inside and drowned. Besides, there were cougars that came into people's backyards and bobcats out at Salt Wells Propulsion Laboratory, where they once made the atom bomb. Forget about A-bombs—bobcats could jump down in your hair from the trees to scratch your eyes out.

My mom must have known that if she forced us to stay inside all day, we would spend all our time trying to kill each other. She was in a catch-22. So she let us roam. Rather than the TV, the desert was our babysitter and our teacher. We learned our lessons from it while my mom veered between worry and boredom at home. Luckily, the navy already had a plan for her, though she did not know it. It turned out they had been trying to figure out what to do with people like her— housewives—for decades before we arrived, looking for something to keep them distracted from the emptiness of the desert. They also needed the extra labor since it was hard to recruit people out there.

Ultimately, the navy settled on a solution: turn housewives into weaponeers.

Chapter Seven

Missile Mom

At first, it was hard to attract women to China Lake. Maybe it was the slot machines at the officers' club; or the taxi to the brothels at the nearby mining town of Red Mountain; or the bikini-clad "pinup" girl in every issue of the *Rocketeer*, with captions like "Eyes are upon shapely Philippine actress Sonja." The nearby defunct mining town of Red Mountain advertised itself as a "living ghost town"—complete with women dressed like Old West barmaids and rooms above the bar where you could take them for a little living history. According to the base's first commander, the men who came to work at China Lake were "war-weary veterans, with nervous disorders and physical problems," just back from the battlefields of World War II. It was not a place that attracted missile wives.

The navy claimed the Indian Wells Valley in 1943. At the time, it was home to the Desert Kawaiisu and Panamint Shoshone, though Sherman Burroughs, who discovered the land, told the navy there was "no one there." The valley was full of mining tunnels but not many miners, the Gold Rush having ended decades before. The few miners who remained had turned into what we call "desert rats." One was living in three sedans—one for a kitchen, another a parlor, and the third for his bedroom—on the lake bed. Another was known locally as the "Mad Doctor" in the struggling town of Crumville, later renamed Ridgecrest. People thought he was mad because he gave up his job as an LA physician to strike it rich in the desert, though there was little gold to be had in the Indian Wells Valley. Crumville was a frontier town full of missionaries, saloons, brothels, homesteaders, and gunplay, with about one hundred people.

In its early years, the base was half war town and half Wild West.

But base commander Sherman Burroughs had bigger plans. He wanted a permanent research facility to rival Hitler's military base on the Baltic Sea, where engineers developed the V-1 and V-2 missiles that rained down on London in the Blitz. China Lake, Burroughs declared, should be "an American Peenemünde . . . a place where nobody knew what the hell was going on." There would be, Burroughs said, "a huge laboratory wherein men and arms would be perfected for winning this war and for safe-guarding our national integrity in the future." He wanted perfect men and perfect missiles. Today, a giant white "B" still hovers on a hill overlooking the town, commemorating Burroughs as our founder.

Burroughs's only problem was women. Unlike sailors, who had no choice where they were sent, scientists would not permanently move to the desert without their wives. So China Lake was forced to clean up its image and look "safe" enough for women. First, the navy shut down the base casinos and the shuttle to Red Mountain. A short promotional film was made of the slot machines being run over by bulldozers, guaranteeing they would not miraculously reappear. Prospective employee families could watch this video, which lauded the "family friendly" environment of China Lake.

Next, they went after the brothels. In a 1952 memo sent to all base personnel, Captain Walter Vieweg, China Lake's commander at the time, wrote, "All service personnel are prohibited from patronizing, entering, or frequenting the Owl Café and Hotel, Helen's Place (also known as 'Goat Ranch'), Mamie's Place (also known as 'Hog Ranch'), and J and J rooms." All houses of prostitution. Unfortunately, the memo had the opposite of its intended effect since it provided directions to each of these secret establishments. It was even posted on their doors, serving as an inadvertent advertisement. The first thing I noticed about this memo when I found it in the National Archives was the name Captain Vieweg, the namesake of my elementary school after Groves. I weirdly thought of second grade, prostitutes, and farm animals all at once. It didn't sit well in my stomach.

China Lake became a family-friendly environment by aggressively promoting activities such as church ice cream socials, Disney movie screenings, and the base's endless "hobby clubs." There was "Pebble Pups" (I joined), "Rock Hounds" (my sister joined), "Toastmasters" (my mom joined), and "The Wildflower Club" (we all joined). There were also clubs for fencing, four-wheel driving, scuba diving, Ping-Pong, square dancing, watercolor painting, junior rifle, and many more. Christine and I chose the rock clubs because they met in the Quonset huts across the street from our duplex on Rowe Street. There, we learned to polish and grind desert rocks and slice geodes, making them perfect for our wall shelves.

But it turned out the best idea for keeping women in town was simply to hire them. The navy began to advertise a class called "Housewife to Draftsman in Only Twelve Weeks" in the local *Rocketeer* in 1951. Over time, this turned into a quota system for hiring women on the base. So when my mom suddenly said, "I need to get out of the house, Earl. I'm going crazy at home," we all knew what that meant.

My mom wasn't happy if she wasn't working; she had always meant to return to work at some point.

"Hm . . ." My dad thought aloud for a moment. "Okay, you could give it a try. You might have a shot."

"But I would hate to leave the kids alone after school," she said. "Do you really think that's okay?"

"We'll be all right," I quickly replied. "Christine can watch me."

She raised an eyebrow.

"We can get a babysitter, Mary," my dad offered instead.

So, just like that, my mom disappeared. She had outstrategized us, getting a job in a section of the base called "Area E," short for "Experimental Air Center," where my sister and I were not allowed to go. Her division was Electronics Warfare. She told us only that rattlesnakes liked to sun themselves on the long airstrip there, which had been built for the B-29 bomber to carry the atom bomb. Overnight, we were a triangle that had imploded. The weapons were her new babies, not us, and one big family probably stood over and looked down at the weapons, smiling and holding hands.

I wanted her back waiting at home to see if we lived or died in the desert.

My mom was assigned to Code 35203 as a "math aid," but all I knew was that she worked with the Gerber photoplotter, a machine that etches computer-drawn circuit board designs onto negatives. I only knew this because, when I called her at work, the secretary would often say, "She's with the Gerber now." Not me. The Gerber was in a darkroom where she could not be disturbed.

What I did not know was what she did in there. Only later did I find out that through a side door she would feed the Gerber negative paper. Then its innards would slowly digest it, spitting out drawings etched with a xenon lamp. It took around ten hours. After the negative was done, it was passed to the photo lab for processing, then glued to a sheet of copper and placed in a chemical vat that would eat away everything but the etched design. The final product was installed in the missile's nose, then taken to the desert for tests. My mom's boss designed the circuit boards. My mom programmed the Gerber with Xs and Ys.

Together, they built the brains that made the missiles run.

Sometimes her secretary would say, "She can't come to the phone. She's in the darkroom, plotting." At first, I thought she was plotting against our neighbors or the Southern Baptists, but later she told me she was making photoplots, which was all she ever said about work. I would picture my mom with stacks of giant blueprints in front of her or negatives hung on ropes with clothespins. In my imagination, she was always in a dimly lit basement. A scary basement without a phone.

It was only when I got to visit my mom for Open House Day that I realized this was not the case. Open House Day was a yearly event in which families were allowed to visit even the secret parts of the base. It took place on Armed Forces Day, which should have been called "Children's Day" since it was really for the kids. It started with a Kiwanis Club pancake breakfast in the parking lot, followed by a long drive through two extra gates to get to my mom's office.

My mom's building was next to Skytop, where they tested missile motors by holding them upside down and letting their engines roar. On the outside, her building was government gray and square, like any other, but inside it looked like a hospital where an epidemic had broken out. There were white, antiseptic-looking machines and people walking around in long white doctor coats with goggles on. Some also had headphones on. We walked by the big, humming machines while I gaped.

To my left, I briefly glimpsed a room lined with scary-looking teal blue spikes hanging from the ceiling. It looked like the kind of torture chamber where the walls are lined with nails and gradually squeeze the person inside to death, like what my dad had read to me from

Edgar Allan Poe's "The Pit and the Pendulum." But my mother herded us by as though it were all normal. "That's the photoplotter," she said, pointing out a machine tucked into its own separate room with an open door.

So that's where she hides from me, I thought. But my mom kept walking.

She led us down a white hallway to her office—a closet-sized room full of desktop computers, some dusty and half-forgotten and others brand-new. Even the wall seemed to be a large computer processor, covered in reels and slots and knobs. It looked like a cluttered control room on the starship *Enterprise.* On her desk was a microscope like the one she once used to look at giardia in stool samples, but bigger.

My mom pointed at the microscope and said cheerily, "Hey, take a look in there and see what your mother does for a living!"

All I saw was a trail of snail slime on a negative. "Yuck," I exclaimed.

"That's for the circuit board," she said, sounding suddenly defensive. To me, it was not a fancy missile mounted on a velvet wall like my dad had at the entrance to his office at Michelson Laboratory, which everyone called "Mike Lab." It was just snail doodle.

I looked again and said, "It looks like scribbling. Can we go back to that room with blue spikes?"

"Oh, here I'll show you," she said, and then ran out of the room, returning with a square brass chip. "See, look at that. From the negative, which you've been looking at through the lens, we make these chips."

I still did not see what it had to do with missiles, which were fast and sleek. She tried to explain: "See, this computer chip goes into a missile and tells it where to go."

"Oh," I said, putting the chip down.

"Well, it beats working with stool samples." She laughed and turned away.

All I wanted to know was what was in the room with the blue

spikes. So I inched out of her office, hoping she would not notice if I moved really slow. As she talked to Christine, who was taking a proper scientific interest, I made it down the hallway to take a peek at the walls lined with three-foot-long Styrofoam spikes painted blue. Everything seemed modeled after *Star Trek* here.

My mom was behind me in a moment.

"What's in this weird blue room?" I asked, half-scared.

"Oh, that's the anechoic chamber," she said, flicking her hand at it as if it were an annoyance. "There's no sound or echo in there when the door is shut."

There was a suspended walkway extending into the center, and even the backside of the door was covered in blue spikes. "Can we go inside?" I asked.

Not waiting for an answer, I darted forward, wanting to be surrounded by spikes and silence.

"Don't go in there!" my mom yelled, running after me, but I made it inside long enough to notice the sound being sucked out of me.

"It's not safe right now." My mom grabbed me and pulled me back. "There's a problem with the heat melting the glue that holds the spikes to the ceiling and they're as sharp as a knife. You could get hurt."

"But what's it for?" I asked from a safe distance within my mom's certain hands.

"That's where the scientists test the circuitry, to be sure that radio and sound signals won't interfere with the missile design."

"Is that why my ears felt funny?" I asked.

"Karen, you shouldn't have gone in there," she said, shaking her head.

"Karen likes to cause trouble," my sister said in her missy-know-it-all voice while standing next to my dad. "You shouldn't have gone inside. Anyone would know that."

I stuck my tongue out at her.

Then my mom brightened up. "The guys sometimes put people

in there for fun and shut the door." She laughed. "You need sound to balance, so people fall over when they close the door. But now it's broken."

"Well, I hope they don't fix it," I said, feeling that old claustro- phobic panic sweep over me again. "Or they might throw me in there next year."

"They might," my mom acknowledged matter-of-factly.

I was relieved to leave her world behind and head to Hangar 3, where China Lake's Search and Rescue Team was supposed to be. They were the people who rescued stranded, lost, and injured hikers in the Sierras. They rescued so many people that I once assumed that was why there needed to be a navy base out here in the desert. People would fall off cliffs in the Sierras and then get picked up and dusted off by Search and Rescue and have their pictures taken for the *Rocketeer*. We would laugh at all the stupid tourists, but only if they lived, of course. It was amazing how many different ways people could find to kill themselves in the Sierras. Cliff falls, lightning, getting lost. Those mountains just devoured people. There was an old stone hut on the top of Mount Whitney that people would run to during a storm and get hit by lightning since it was the highest point. Search and Res- cue's job was to stop all that. I adored them and thought that one day I would marry one of them.

In Hangar 3, Search and Rescue had set up a climbing wall to teach people how to climb Mt. Whitney from the hard side. They tied me onto a rope and promised to rescue me if I fell. That was their job, so I was not too scared. After that, they taught me how to bring the dead rubber lady back to life with CPR and mouth-to-mouth. Both inside the hangar and out on the airfield, there were of course all the missiles and planes displayed too. I got to climb into the cockpit of an A-4 Skyhawk to have my picture taken.

There was even a boy from Burroughs High School in a bamboo Vietcong tiger cage in Hangar 3. The sign explained that these were used to torture people in Vietnam who were too big to fit inside comfortably. They were meant for tigers. The boy from Burroughs was sitting in there as his reward for building the best tiger cage. He did not look that comfortable, so I guess it was working.

"Why is he in a bamboo cage, Mommy?"

"Because that's what happens in Vietnam."

"What is Vietnam?"

"It's a country we're at war with."

"Why are we at war?"

"Because they do bad things like put men in cages."

"But didn't *we* put him in that cage?"

"It's just an example, Karen, of what *they* do. You ask too many questions."

After the tiger cage and the anechoic chamber, I started to think something strange was going on at the base. There were torture machines everywhere.

Finally, it was time to go home. I got a bracelet inscribed with a POW's name on the way out and was told I had to wear it until he was found or released. When I lost the bracelet in the desert, I was convinced that one POW never came home because of me. But I had learned a lot about war that day and about what moms do in the military. I had climbed the climbing wall and seen a tiger cage. So I was not willing to say I wish I had never gone there, gotten that bracelet, and maybe killed that POW.

Chapter Eight

Missiles and Aliens

I hate to say it, Mary, but Jim believes in UFOs," my dad said as soon as he walked through the front door. Our ears always perked up like happy puppies when we heard his distinctive door-handle rattle. He was sure and brisk with the way he put in the key and turned the handle. The hanging lamp swung a little from the way that only he would close the door. The heat blast followed a little behind him that summer when I was eight years old.

"Wow!" Christine and I barked in glee. "Cool!" We rushed into the kitchen to hear all the details.

That was to be the beginning of the long hot days full of UFOs and Cambodians. It was a confusing time. All evening long the TV played news about President Richard Nixon, who had been caught wiretapping reporters' phones and burglarizing buildings to get information on the people who had leaked the Pentagon Papers, and there was a front-page *New York Times* story about him secretly bombing Cambodia. He had kept this bombing so secret that even the U.S. Air Force pilots who had dropped the bombs had to maintain a "dual reporting" system, writing down Vietnamese targets to give to the press and secret Cambodian ones for Nixon. But when burglars were captured breaking into Democratic National Campaign headquarters, ordered by Nixon to get dirt on his opponents, Congress finally had had enough. This led to the Watergate hearings, which ultimately ended Nixon's presidency. But it went on for years.

"No, they must have dropped those bombs in Cambodia by accident," my dad said to the TV when the scandal first broke. "People don't understand. That's how war is. The pilots probably went off course." People get lost, my dad said. He had been lost during World War II, so he knew.

I did not know what Cambodia was, but I knew when my dad was upset because he would start pacing in the living room, throwing his change purse up and down, one of those black, oval plastic purses that opens when you squeeze it on the ends. It took a long time for him to get to that point. First, there would be the sound of jangling coins in his pocket, starting slowly but then increasing in rhythmic intensity. Then he would start walking. It was as though he wanted to say something but would walk instead, furrowing his brow until his purse came out with a life of its own and started flying. As my dad tensed up, so did we. We waited for what came next.

Christine and I would try to look around him when he walked in front of the TV. She had her yellow beanbag chair, and I had my white one, and we sat there in our thrones while our heads bobbed like pendulums. We had given up asking him not to walk in front of the TV. The darker path in the carpet showed that he could not stop. My dad, Richard Nixon, and Henry Kissinger were all upset that summer—the latter two because they had been caught and my dad because Nixon was being impeached. My dad trusted Nixon.

On July 31, 1973, Congressman Robert Drinan introduced the first impeachment resolution against President Nixon on the grounds that he had secretly ordered the bombing of Cambodia for fourteen months in 1969–1970. These bombing raids, which killed tens of thousands of Cambodian villagers, also left thousands of bomb craters in Cambodia. In turn, these craters had been discovered by a *New York Times* correspondent who broke the story. I am not sure how Nixon thought he could get away with it since there was no way to hide all those bomb craters. Unlike China Lake, Cambodia could not be fenced in. Someone was eventually bound to visit.

Robert Drinan testified, "I learned on that day that President Nixon had misled me and misled the entire nation." It was the third attempt to impeach Nixon in that summer after the Watergate hearings—but only by Democrats. Meanwhile, Nixon was secretly fuming, as he complained to his national security adviser, "Never forget, the press is the enemy, the press is the enemy. The establishment is the enemy, the professors are the enemy, the professors are the enemy. Write that on a blackboard one hundred times."

Luckily, my dad's office mate, Jim Jarkovich, had a bigger problem for us to worry about: UFOs. I had met Mr. Jarkovich at my dad's office once and thought of him as someone who did not notice kids. Technically, I was not supposed to go there since I did not have a badge, but security was lax and children were allowed to wander in and out as long as the guards knew them. My mom would sometimes take me to my dad's office and let me run in to get him after work.

In the lobby of Mike Lab was a welcoming room full of missiles. Since it was for visitors to the lab, the furniture was better than everywhere else. It had plush blue carpeting, big mahogany chairs with padded seats, and different kinds of missiles lining the wall. They were mounted like fine jewels on velvet backdrops, each with its own special light so it glowed. That was where we brought visitors who wanted to buy them. Next to each missile, there was a small screen and a red button that would start a video, showing it in flight.

Past the lobby was a guard behind a nice mahogany desk at the entrance to the hallways. He knew me and let me run right by. Mike Lab lost its velvety showcase charm past the guard. It was a large gray concrete building with seemingly endless additions tacked on over the years. Wandering the maze inside, I passed "Hazardous Materials" signs where chemicals were planted like minefields for kids.

The office that my dad shared with Mr. Jarkovich was drab and small, with matching gray and white linoleum on both the desktop and the floor, a tall gray metal bookcase that separated Jarkovich from my dad, and a giant school clock hanging over them both, ticking loudly. The documents on their desks were kept in colored folders that were blue ("Classified"), yellow ("Secret"), or red ("Top Secret"). If I interrupted my dad, he would stuff some papers into a red or yellow folder. Everything, including the pens, was stamped "U.S. Government Property." The branch and division heads got better offices, "executive" versions with wooden desks and padding for their chairs, but my dad and Mr. Jarkovich were doomed to standard gray metal forever. They were not "go-getters."

Mr. Jarkovich was like a piece of furniture, never turning around when I came to visit. To me, he was a slouched back in a wrinkled plaid shirt. At the top of his back he had a full mop of bushy brown hair, unlike my father, who was going bald. And while my dad was always perfectly clean and clad in a white cotton short-sleeved shirt with the collar starched, Mr. Jarkovich did not even iron his shirt. Maybe he did not have a wife, but even my dad could iron his own shirts. Mr. Jarkovich wore blue jeans rather than dress slacks. His hair never looked recently washed. He was by base standards disheveled.

But suddenly, because of the aliens, he became a superstar to me.

"Did he see an alien?" I excitedly blurted out to my dad that day. "Where are they?" I forgot that my dad did not believe in aliens so I was not supposed to either. All the drapes were drawn in the house in a desperate attempt to keep the sun out, but light was filtering in through the cracks in the drapes, lighting up the dust like little spaceships.

"No, I should have said Lemurians," my dad said to my mom, not us. "He won't stop talking about Lemurians. I don't think they are aliens. I'm not sure."

"Oh . . ." Christine and I deflated a bit. I knew all about aliens from *The Twilight Zone* and NBC but had never heard of Lemurians. They sounded like monkeys. Everyone believed in monkeys.

"He thinks they live around here somewhere." He looked concerned.

For a while, the Lemurians consumed my dad because they consumed Mr. Jarkovich. I thought they were at least more interesting than Nixon and seemed to make my dad happier. One day, my dad brought home a book about them called *Lemuria: The Lost Continent of the Pacific*, which Mr. Jarkovich had lent him. We found out they were creatures with a third eye for a brain from an island called Mu, in the middle of the Pacific Ocean. When their island sank, millions of years ago, they had to move to Mount Shasta in California, where they lived in the lava tunnels.

"So they're not aliens," my dad explained. "It sounds like they're residents from Earth but from a long time ago. They are an ancient people." They still sounded supercool. After reading a bit more, he went on to explain that after moving to the lava tubes inside Mount Shasta, the Lemurians met some *actual* aliens from Venus who were already living in Mount Shasta.

"So there *are* aliens," I insisted.

"I suppose so," my dad said. "The aliens were from Venus. The Lemurians learned to live with them, and then they all started building tunnels across the whole United States. *Cherrrhem. . .*" My dad paused. "Jim Jarkovich told me their tunnels extend out to Area Fifty-One and run right beneath China Lake."

It seemed like a lot of aliens were being spotted that summer, especially on the Gulf coast. *CBS News* had reported, "Gulfport police have received so many calls that they've posted a nighttime watch." For aliens. Even Ohio's governor claimed to have seen one. My dad said UFOs were just top secret military planes that we were not allowed to talk about. But Mr. Jarkovich worked on the base too, so why did he believe in aliens? It was confusing.

"What are they doing in the tunnels?" I asked, fascinated. I had always tried to dig to China through the ant holes, which were entrances. Now I had a new reason to dig.

"You know, this is something that only Jim Jarkovich believes," my dad said, trying to dampen my enthusiasm. "None of this is true. It's make-believe."

"But why does Mr. Jarkovich believe it, then?"

My dad did not really have an answer. Adults never had answers.

"I don't know, Karen," my dad said impatiently. "Jim seems to think it is really important, so I'm trying to figure out why it's so important to him. I want to help him."

"Well, what does he think they're doing at China Lake?" I asked again.

"Building atom bombs," he solemnly replied, patting my head to protect me from the bomb. Mr. Jarkovich believed that the Lemurians knew how to get to the old atom bomb fuses and radioactive materials that had been left behind at China Lake. He believed the Lemurians were making atom bombs underground to be better prepared for the next world war. The Lemurians had even invited some U.S. government officials to join them underground, where they were creating a whole new society. There, aliens and congressmen would meet in secret five-star hotels and discuss the future of the planet. Since the Lemurians were supposed to be wise and eternally kind, I did not really understand why they needed the bomb, but I thought their ideas sounded a lot like the Mansons'. They were waiting for Helter Skelter and preparing just in case.

Maybe the atom bomb made everyone want to tunnel, or maybe it was the desert. It was cooler underground. In the desert, all the animals lived down there. Once, a man named "Burro" Schmidt who lived nearby became obsessed with tunneling. It was during the California gold rush, though his tunnel had nothing to do with gold. Legend goes that Schmidt dug through a mountain so his burro would not have to climb over it. He was nicknamed "Burro" Schmidt because he loved his burro that much. Of course, at first he did hope to find gold on the way, but he kept digging even when it was clear the mountain contained none. He kept digging even after a road was built around the hill that made his tunnel unnecessary. After thirty-eight years of digging, he finally made it to the other side and then sold his mine and burro and moved away. Now he is famous for his tunnel.

My dad and I would wander the desert, looking for desert holes, wondering who lived inside those tunnels. He would lean down far, bent at the waist, trying to see, his brain clicking.

"Hello, down there!" I would wave and loudly greet the snake or kangaroo rat while he compared this hole size with other sizes he had stored in his memory, figuring out probabilities and possibilities for who lived there.

On the *CBS Evening News*, a cabdriver named John Lane said he dropped a passenger at Keesler Air Force Base in Biloxi, Mississippi, when a blue light landed on the freeway in front of him. Soon a being with a crablike hand walked right up and knocked on his cab window. John Lane did not say if he opened the door to say hello or if he took out his gun. Maybe it was a Lemurian. They were friendly and wise, so John Lane should have tried talking to them.

"I don't know what to do," my dad said quietly to my mom one night at the dining room table. I imagined we were all trapped in the beam of our hanging light, like when the aliens abduct you and you are paralyzed. "He talks about Lemuria all the time, says there are tunnels beneath China Lake. He thinks the navy is only dropping bombs to create new entrances to Lemuria. I'm afraid he's going to go look for them on the ranges at night. That would be dangerous."

"Did you tell your boss?" my mom asked.

"No, do you think I should? I don't want to get him in trouble."

"But they sound nice, the Lemurians," I interrupted, trying to make my dad see the positive side of the situation. After all, their ultimate goal, according to the book, was bringing wisdom and peace to Earth.

"It sounds like some kind of cult to me," my dad countered. "A lot of people seem to believe this nonsense." To us, a "cult" meant anything that was non-Christian. Lemurians were not Christians.

"Maybe if you talked to him about God," my mom suggested. "Bring him a Bible. Maybe that will help."

I knew where this was going. My mom and dad had done the same thing with the Mormons who came to our house, turning the tables and trying to save them instead. My parents even read the Book of Mormon so they could explain to the Mormons, logically, what was wrong with their religion. The Mormons kept coming for some juice and deprogramming, so maybe they liked it. An old Mormon trail ran across our valley, after all, so they had been doing this sort of thing for a century. I am sure my mom and dad posed little threat. During those long Mormon evenings, I learned a lot about talking salamanders and golden plates, and my parents seemed happy to have these new friends.

Then, one day, the Mormons stopped showing up, perhaps realizing the battle was futile. My mom and dad seemed a little sad after that, looking out the window in expectation and turning away like abandoned children when no one showed up.

"Haven't seen them on our street lately," my dad would say. "I hope they are okay."

"There are a lot of doors out there, Earl," my mom would reply.

Now it was Mr. Jarkovich's turn for some deprogramming. I wondered if he would start coming to our house with his book while my parents held theirs. Then they could fight and laugh, then hug, over coffee. I still kind of missed the Mormons.

Instead, my dad only got more worried about both Mr. Jarkovich and Cambodia. Mr. Jarkovich was getting worse, he said. Some days he did not show up for work, and other days he did not work when he showed up. My dad was afraid he would get fired.

Cambodia would not go away for Mr. Nixon either, and he only made it worse by breaking into that journalist's office and the offices of the Democratic National Convention. Still, no one had any idea how bad it could get, how the investigation might never end. It was only when Nixon was forced to release his White House recordings that people saw who he really was. Even my parents turned against him then. "The mouth on that man," my mom said. "Do people really talk that way?"

Back in Mississippi on the Pascagoula River, Charles Hickson and Calvin Parker were assaulted by claw-handed aliens that looked like little gray men. On October 11, 1973, they claimed, they were fishing off a dock when a spaceship suddenly appeared and sucked them up inside. There, they were studied by a creature with a giant eye for twenty minutes before being released. I thought this sounded like a Lemurian since he was just curious, not mean. Afterward, Charles and Calvin went straight to the police. Later, they told the press they believed in God, but this did not keep them from believing in aliens too. Maybe you could have both, contrary to what my dad said. The sheriff said there had been so many sightings that he could not sleep at night and "would seek presidential intervention if somebody didn't do something."

When I asked my dad why we were bombing Cambodia, he looked at me as though I were a student from Kent State. "You kids just don't get it!" His temper flared. "Those pilots were bombing near the border. It was a confusing situation. Nixon said he was bombing near the border. He wouldn't . . ." But his voice trailed off.

"So it was just a mistake, you think?" I wondered aloud.

"You don't understand what communism is like, Karen."

I was not sure how he did either.

Nixon blamed the journalist who had leaked the Cambodia story, saying this man had ruined the operation and violated national security, but it was a losing argument. When he left the White House for the last time, he flew away in a helicopter, off to who-knows-where like the Mormons.

After that, Mr. Jarkovich disappeared too. He simply stopped coming to work.

"What happened to Mr. Jarkovich?" I asked one night.

"Maybe he made it to Lemuria," was all my dad said. But there was no twinkle in his eye when he said this. I never knew what happened to Jim Jarkovich, aside from a letter I found from him in my dad's box after he died. Mr. Jarkovich wrote with a desperate slant, "Thanks for being a friend and attempting to understand my suffering. Tell the others from both branches I care about them regardless of how they feel about me. God Bless You!" He believed in aliens and God too. I learned a lot about what you could or could not believe from TV that year. Another brick in my walled world fell out.

Maybe Mr. Jarkovich simply had had enough of the military and suddenly quit. Maybe he was committed to a mental hospital. Maybe he went home and shot himself. I do not know if anyone else at work cared about him besides my dad, or if they were just glad for the empty chair. It could be that the whole lab went into a panic and somehow tracked him down but what they had found out was classified. National security.

Maybe, just maybe, he finally made it to Lemuria.

Today, there are still people who think we are hiding aliens at China Lake.

Others claim to have been kidnapped and held in electrified "baby cages" with thousands of other babies at Hangar 3. They call it Operation Monarch and say its purpose was to turn babies into little Manchurian candidates, or devil-worshipping sex slaves, or something like that. They had to be hypnotized to remember even that much.

My dad would call this "a cult" if he were alive. I don't know what I should call it. Disinformation, maybe. Paranoia. I can only confirm that I was in that hangar at the very time these hypnotized people claim to have been locked up in baby cages inside. There were no cages. No babies. Nada. The hangar was big and wide and open and there would have been nowhere to hide those babies from me.

As for Nixon, he was forced to resign on August 9, 1974. In the final articles of impeachment, Cambodia was not included, to the ire of Congressman Robert Drinan, who said, "Can we impeach a president for unlawful wiretapping but not impeach a president for unlawful war-making? Can we impeach a president for concealing a burglary but not for concealing a massive bombing?" It turned out we could. Nixon disappeared like Jarkovich after that, and no one spoke of him again. The next president, Gerald Ford, seemed to come and go with no one noticing. We were all too tired from Nixon.

Over the years, I came to realize my dad felt that Nixon had lied to *him* personally. He was mad that Nixon pretended to be a good Christian on TV but swore like a sailor in private. Mostly, he was mad that those bombs had landed on Cambodia without any warning. You see, in the weapons industry, you like to know where your bombs are going. You feel a little responsible. My dad felt responsible for Cambodia.

I didn't realize how much until it was too late.

Chapter Nine

Atom Bomb School

As I entered Groves Elementary School each day, I passed a portrait of General Leslie Groves, a black-and-white photograph of a large man with a square jaw, curly gray hair, and a bushy mustache. To me, he looked like a bully guarding my hallway, wishing he could punch someone in the nose. I avoided looking at him. The navy had separated me from my sister, who went to Vieweg, a block in the other direction. Oddly, the following year we switched schools; I attended Vieweg and she went to Groves. I have no idea why. There were two elementary schools and one junior high on the base; for high school, there was only the "public" school, off base, a frightening alternative to the security of navy schools.

I only recently discovered that my school was built for the Manhattan Project. It seems I grew up in the part of the base devoted to building the nuclear bomb, where the people from "Project Camel" lived. Project Camel was China Lake's contribution to the development of the nuclear bomb, though apparently no one remembers how it got that name. Some claim the name came from an old Arabian tale, which warned not to let a camel stick its nose in a tent because the whole body would follow. It meant something like "getting your foot in the door." If that was the case, I guess we thought the bomb would get our foot in the door of Japan. Others said it meant that when a camel puts its head in a tent, its breath is a foul explosion. Either way, it seems to have something to do with camels and tents. Maybe some Washington person just thought we had camels and lived in tents at China Lake.

China Lake designed the "implosion" trigger for the Fat Man bomb, while Los Alamos built the "gun" trigger for the Thin Man bomb, later renamed Little Boy. I sometimes wondered if China Lakers felt slighted that the Los Alamos folks got all the credit, though I suspect they were just proud to have kept their secrets better than the nuclear braggarts at Los Alamos. At China Lake, about one hundred people developed fuses, tested "dud" bombs, designed triggers, and worked on a non-nuclear version of the bomb that was packed with TNT. It was called "pumpkin" because it was big and round and painted orange to distinguish it from the nuclear kind. My mom's nickname for me was also Pumpkin, which she would say before patting my head and sending me off to school. "Goodbye, Pumpkin," as they said to the bomb when it left the plane at Hiroshima. Except that pumpkin did not come back.

Only a handful of people on the base knew what they were building, that it was going to be atomic. For most, it was just a big, clumsy bomb. "Is this atomic?" maybe someone asked one day.

"Do you have a need-to-know?" would have been the reply. That's the question we always asked on the base before responding to a question. If you did not need to know to do your job, you did not get to know. Everything outside of your assigned duty was secret. Only

Groves and his top scientists got to see the big picture, the atom bomb. The others were merely designing a trigger, mixing explosives, or painting a large orb orange. They did not know they were blowing up Hiroshima.

On July 18, 1945, Captain William Parsons stopped by China Lake to thank the members of Project Camel for their work on his way to drop the atom bomb on Hiroshima. (Did they feel tricked when they found out? I heard a rumor that some had cried.)

After finally watching the A-bomb explode at its target, Parsons described his feelings: "Once in many centuries, you can't shake off the Midas touch. That's what happened to us." Everything in Hiroshima became gold. But the "father" of the atom bomb, Robert Oppenheimer, did not feel like Midas. He felt like Shiva, the god of destruction, and said in tears on TV, "In some sort of crude sense which no vulgarity, no humor, no overstatement can quite extinguish, the physicists have known sin; and this is a knowledge which they cannot lose." Then he quoted Hindu scripture, saying, "Now I am become Death, the destroyer of worlds."

I suppose one man's Evil is another man's Gold.

After the bomb was dropped, Project Camel was shut down, and the bomb buildings—my school and neighborhood and the Salt Wells complex—stood as ghostly reminders of the passion of Leslie Groves. Groves had built my whole neighborhood, close to four hundred identical duplexes, and assigned a scientist family to one side and a military family to the other. He wanted them to work well together. Ironically, he never got along with intellectuals or scientists, complaining they were "willing to have other people killed and wounded to protect their own interests but . . . unwilling to participate in the dangerous occupation of a soldier." In fact, Groves had wanted Kyoto bombed rather than Hiroshima because it was a city of artists and intellectuals. His target committee argued: "From the psychological point of view there is the advantage that Kyoto is an intellectual center for Japan and the people there are more apt to appreciate the significance of such a weapon as the gadget." As if its significance were difficult to grasp. Luckily for Kyoto, the secretary of war had spent his honeymoon there and did not want to see it destroyed. Groves tried to keep it on the list but lost the battle. Of course, this was not so lucky for Hiroshima.

Because of Leslie Groves, I ended up with a military "boyfriend" in the fourth grade. If not for Groves, we would not have lived in the same neighborhood. Of course, I did not know that. To me, all that mattered was that Rich had long curly blond hair and wore bell-bottoms and puka shells and his face was freckled and beautiful. He also had a fancy dirt bike, while I had a banana-seat bicycle with flowers on the basket and multicolored tassels on the handlebars. We were perfectly complementary. But to my parents, he was military, one of the "bad guys."

My family did not socialize with people in the military because we did not think they were religious, perhaps because my dad was "bad" when he was in the military. So we stayed away from them and assumed they visited prostitutes at the "ranch," a wild tavern where fights broke out, up the hill. Military men and women also socialized at the O-Club or at the many bars in town. We socialized only at church on Wednesdays and Sundays. So Rich and I were like Romeo and Juliet.

My parents had picked the Southern Baptist church, Immanuel Baptist, after trying out the First and Second Baptists. The black Baptist church had made me cry, so that one would not do. The pastor had said, "I can tell that someone is suffering in this room. Let it out now." I thought he was talking about us, since we were the only white people in the room. We sat stiff and upright and polite in our chairs while everyone else looked so relaxed. We clearly needed to cry. After that, we tried the Nazarenes, which our church friends fled to when there were schisms at Immanuel, but the Nazarenes could not guarantee our salvation forever—and nobody wants to become unsaved once they are saved. That would be a nightmare. Then we tried the Lutherans, which attracted other Swedes and Norwegians, but we found them too "hoity-toity." My mom's family was Baptist all the way back to the time Baptists were murdered by Lutherans, so she seemed suspicious when we first walked in the door. We even tried Four Square Gospel a few times, which petrified me when people spoke in tongues. I asked my mom why those people were possessed by Satan. So that would not do. The Mormon temple was the biggest one in town, but we were not allowed inside. So we ended up Southern Baptist, even though we all missed the Swedish kind, which had nice old Swedish ladies who made pancakes and cake for coffee klatches. Coffee and sweets is a real religion to a Swede, but no one shared our religion at China Lake. At Christmas, Christine and I would wear St. Lucia candles on our heads to honor the virgin martyr whose eyes were gouged out for refusing to marry a pagan. Every night, we would take turns praying in Swedish: "Goody Good. Valsing-ya matin. . . ."

We missed those Swedes.

Since doctrine mattered more than culture, we really had no choice but to be Baptist. We believed in getting saved, getting dunked, taking communion, and going to Heaven. Most important, in that order. Heaven could be reached through death or through the Rapture, but not both. We also believed in the Three in One (Father, Son, and Holy Ghost) and that the Bible was the literal word of God. We followed the Nicene Creed, which states that Jesus is "the only Son of God" who "for our sake was crucified." Catholics believed the same thing, but they thought the creed's "one, holy, catholic, and apostolic Church" only meant them, not us. Catholics also worshipped the pope, who we thought might actually be the Antichrist. If the pope *was* the Antichrist, we would have to fight the Catholics during Armageddon, so we could not get too close to them. But we accepted them for now as Christians.

Unfortunately, Rich was not Catholic, or Baptist, or even anything, which made him especially dangerous. Only General Leslie Groves would have approved. He must have smiled down from Heaven when he saw military and civilians finally getting along at China Lake. For me, having a boyfriend in fourth grade was mainly a status move. It meant holding hands in public, which signified you were a "cool" kid, an adult kid. Like the real adults.

Rich sat in front of me in class and had nice long hair, so I put a valentine in his box when the teacher said we should for Valentine's Day. With it, I attached a note that read "Do you like me? Check one: yes or no." He put his answer back in my box. After that, we started walking home together. It was "yes."

Rich lived about three duplexes down from me, closer to the school, but he always walked all the way to my house to pick me up. Sometimes we walked down the side of the paved road, on the dirt edge, and sometimes we walked down the dirt alley behind our houses. One day, he stopped in front of his house and asked me to come in, which is how I discovered that military and civilian houses are very different inside, though they look the same on the outside. His house was full of sheepskin rugs and beads and smoke, and the windows were blacked out so it was dark and cool. Their house seemed designed for survival in the desert and was much more practical than ours. His brother even had a water bed, which I figured was in case he needed extra water—like if a war broke out—or had sunstroke. Maybe a cool water bed helped.

Rich pulled me through a doorway full of hanging glow-in-the-dark beads, where there was a bong in the corner with his brother's dog tags hanging near it. "This is my big brother's room," he said, leading me to the water bed next to a lava lamp. "He's in 'Nam. . . ."

On TV, the helicopters were pulling people out of there. People were standing on rooftops with their arms outstretched, trying to jump onboard precariously overloaded choppers. The babies went first.

"Come inside and lay down." He pulled my hand and leaned back on the bed, which squished underneath him. "We'll listen to the Beatles and space out." As we sang along with the songs on *Abbey Road*, the world seemed strange and wonderful and new. "We all live in a yellow submarine," Rich sang quietly as we rocked on the water bed. I wanted to be inside that Beatles' song, which was like nothing I had heard at home. We had only gospel music or Gene Kelly and Fred Astaire. So I drifted off into the music and the lava lamp and the slow waves of the bed. Suddenly, I noticed Rich's head touching mine. I opened my eyes and Rich's giant lips were heading straight for me. My eyes bulged in a giant "No!" and I smartly turned my head before he hit my lips . . . but just barely. He may have touched the corner. I could not be sure. This was terrible.

Running out the door toward home, I kept trying to wipe his kiss off my cheek. But it would not come off. That was when I remembered what my mother had said at our family Bible hour. We had been reading 2 Samuel 13–14, about a man who "forced" this woman Tamar and "lay with her." When I asked my mother what that meant, she took me in her bedroom and told me what I knew only from school as fingers going in and out of finger holes. "A man puts his penis inside the vagina," she said, "when they are laying down in bed. A penis is what your dad has and uses to go to the bathroom. A vagina is where you go to the bathroom. A hole down there." I also knew from church that sex was holy in marriage and a sin when it was premarital. I still did not quite understand the penis and vagina part, but I knew I had "lain" with Rich in bed and he had "forced" me. I could never tell my mother. Jesus was supposed to protect us from evildoers like the hippies, Charlie Manson, and the other Charlie, who was a gook.

But I had been lured in by the lava lights. I had sinned.

After that, I started to avoid Rich at school, riding my bike home alone. Still, I could not get that Beatles song out of my head. At church, the pastor had talked about the Beatles and whether they were satanic. Apparently, the Beatles said they were better than Jesus. Charles Manson thought they were the four angels of Revelation because of the Bible verse that read, "Their faces were as the faces of men, yet they had hair of women." That made sense to me, since they did have girl hair, but the pastor said it was blasphemous to think such a thing. It was all very confusing.

At the time, the Mansons had recently been arrested just outside China Lake for the murder of Sharon Tate, and the police were still scouring the desert looking for more bodies. The Mansons had been staying at an old miner's house called Barker Ranch, which they bought with a gold album from the Beach Boys. Since not all of the followers had been arrested, my mother was understandably scared, especially since they had been sneaking onto the base to steal scrap metal for their desert fortress. It was easy to get on the base, which was surrounded by a chicken-wire fence that you could lift up in places. The Mansons even shopped at *our* 7-Eleven in Ridgecrest, where Christine and I bought our candy. Some people said Manson sold drugs to base kids. In 1972, the *Rocketeer* reported that China Lake Search and Rescue had found another "hippie commune" at a deserted mining camp nearby. We all assumed it was more Mansons.

I vaguely knew that Manson was satanic, like Rosemary's baby or the demons inside the girl in *The Exorcist*. But when our pastor said he came to the desert to find the "Bottomless Pit," I was confused.

We already knew where the Bottomless Pit was. It was Hell, where you went when you died. It certainly wasn't in the desert. But then I found out from TV that Charlie's Bottomless Pit was completely different than ours. Ours was full of worms and fire eating you eternally, while his had golden walls and rivers full of milk and honey. Charlie said his was underground out here, somewhere, and that he was going to wait there for Helter Skelter, which was his version of our Armageddon. The battle at the End of the World.

"Mom, why is Manson's Bottomless Pit so different than ours?" I asked.

"You don't understand, Karen. Manson's crazy. That's not real."

"Okay." I nodded. I knew ours *was* real.

"Besides, he kills people," she said.

I still did not see how that was different from what we did.

"Don't we kill people?" I said.

Secretly, I decided my mom was wrong and that Charlie's Bottomless Pit was the real one. I decided that if I did not make it into Heaven, which seemed like a distinct possibility, I would go to his pit instead of ours. In fact, there were lots of things the pastor said that I was starting to not trust. For instance, the pastor said people who died before hearing the Gospel were innocent and would go straight to Heaven. But if that was the case, why did we spend all this money on missionaries? It seemed terribly wasteful when you could just as easily let them die without hearing the Gospel and know they would be fine. Besides, the pastor said, "God is Love." The Bible said it too. So what was up with this Hell thing, anyway? If God was Love, he would not make Hell. So I decided to dispense with the idea of Hell altogether. I was only nine, but this was the rational thing to do.

This was the beginning of my heretical life, which I knew I could not tell anyone about since they might try to take my blasphemous ideas away from me. I would not stand for that. Instead, I became good at hiding things, just like the navy, while still somehow worrying that the Beatles had infected my brain. If you played "Revolution 9" backward, after all, you could hear the words "Turn me on, dead man." The pastor told us that. He said it was because the Beatles wanted us to have sex with corpses. Who was I to say? So when the pastor announced that we should bring in our rock records, tarot cards, or anything else devil worshipping to church the following Sunday, I decided it was a sign.

The traveling record breaker was coming to town. Just for me.

The traveling record breaker looked so hot in his three-piece suit, but he always wore it when he came to visit from somewhere in the South. First, the record breaker would preach to us about the evils of rock 'n' roll, then demonstrate how Satan was backmasked into songs. When he shouted, full of condemnation, you could see all the way around his eyeballs, which was kind of scary, and he was as tall as Ichabod Crane. So he always looked down on you.

I waited patiently through all the yelling and formalities and backmasking, waiting for the time to confess. Finally, we began to sing the same hymn over and over again as the pastor tried to get people to come forward to be saved or renew their faith. I was shy at first and could not take that step. But a woman stepped out into the aisle with a crystal ball that was so pretty. It was the best thing I had ever seen taken to the altar, and she looked so confident in her flowy skirt, holding it close. It ended up being too hard for the preacher to smash with his special smashing rock, so he prayed over it to cleanse it of evil instead. She still did not get it back after it was cleansed, though it should have been fine then.

Then the pastor held out his hands again to us. "And tonight, I want all of you who know something of the devil, something secret that you have been hiding, to come forward and let me destroy it!" He raised his hands in triumph as we began to sing: "Just as I am, without one plea . . ." I was already about to cry, so I finally started walking down the aisle, where you were allowed to do that. The preacher eyed me as though he knew a problem was coming. The carpet was brand-new gold plush and my feet made silvery streaks as the carpet fibers turned down. Behind the altar was a simple wooden cross with the baptistery beneath it where I had been dunked last year. The congregation sang with a rising reverence: "Just as I am, without one plea, / But that Thy blood was shed for me. / And that Thou bid'st me come to Thee / O Lamb of God, I come! I come!" *Abbey Road* was my dark blot and my soul was carrying it inside me. The downcast eyes along the pews all seemed to sneak a look at me as I passed.

Crouching at the altar was the preacher, his eyes protruding with the passion of God.

I knelt down and hid my face in the gold carpet of the altar steps as I told him about *Abbey Road* and the sex and my love of Charles Manson and lava lamps and how I did not want to waste money on missionaries and did not believe in Hell. He put his hand on my back and said, "Hallelujah!" I had never felt so loved. I began to sob and sob and thought I could not stop. No one but that preacher seemed to understand what I had been through, all the levels of sin and suffering, like the black pastor had before him. I had only wanted to tell someone, anyone.

"What were you doing?" my mother whispered when I got back. She looked more embarrassed at my outburst than angry at my sin. So that was good.

I finally said quietly, "I kissed Rich."

Surprisingly, she said nothing to me. Instead, she turned to my father and whispered, "Maybe we should think about the church school. Let's see what they think." Of course, I immediately agreed.

So that was how we ended up following the great exodus of civilians leaving the base in the seventies, on to life outside the gates. It was only a mile away, but it was a safer world, a more religious world where we could live two blocks from our church. Groves's dream of military and civilians, of heathens and God-fearers, living in perfect harmony was starting to crumble, beginning with me and Rich.

We always knew those enlisted men were trouble.

Chapter Ten

Spare the Rod, Lose the War

As my sister remembers it, I was the one who chose to go to the school run by our church, Immanuel Baptist. I believe her since she never lies. Besides, I always considered myself the de facto head of the family. My dad was indecisive to a fault and my mom believed in obeying her husband, so they sort of canceled each other out. Not having anyone around to tell them how to raise children, my parents relied on Dr. Spock, who told them to "follow your child's lead." So they did. They followed *my* lead. Truth be told, Christine beat me because I had the power. I was the head of the family, the *baby* in charge.

"I want to go to the Christian school," I declared, and no one could disagree.

Our school was called Immanuel Christian School, or ICS, and its curriculum was developed by a Baptist pastor in Texas. The program of study was known as an "Accelerated Christian Education," or ACE, which was what we would be taught at Ridgecrest's ICS. Soon that same curriculum would be taught all across America, and today the world. But our school was one of the first.

Christine later told me she agreed to go to ICS only to protect me. This made my heart grow three sizes, even though when she told me, she was still mad about having to go. She thought it had ruined her career in music, since the base schools had better music programs. How could I explain to her that I had to worry about my own salvation? If I did not go to that school, I thought I might not see her forever in Heaven. Even though the Baptists believe that salvation is forever, I was never quite sure it took with me. As an adult, it made no sense to say this to her.

All I could say was, "Sorry."

Of course, I had been saved as soon as it was allowed, but there were so many things that no one explained clearly. For instance, you were supposed to wait until the "Age of Innocence" was over to be saved, the years when you were too little to understand what Jesus meant. If you died during that time period, you would still go to Heaven. But no one told you when that age ended or if the prayer still worked if you said it too early. These were the things that drove me crazy as a child.

Eventually, I decided it was seven years old.

"Lord Jesus, I am a sinner," I said while sitting on the toilet as soon as I turned seven. "I accept you into my heart." Suddenly, I realized that maybe the toilet part canceled it out, though the bathroom was the only place in the house to be alone. Even though I was not *going* when I said it, I still did not get the feeling of bliss that you were supposed to have afterward. That was how you knew it worked. I might have blasphemed Jesus with the toilet.

All I could do was say the prayer over and over in hopes that it would take in time before the Rapture. So I wandered around the house, repeating the prayer in my head, a glazed look in my eyes. My mom would pat me on the head or hand me a stuffed animal, but no one knew what I was doing. "Karen likes to be alone," my mom said. Still, I never got the feeling. It was aggravating.

Finally, it occurred to me that maybe it was something other than the toilet. There was this secret thing I did, which I called "exercising," when I hid in the closet. In fact, I did it far too much. "Exercising" was also what my mom said the planes did when they were dropping bombs, but this was a different kind of euphemism. "Oh, they're exercising today," she would say cheerily, looking at the sky. But mine was like the Sin of Onan, except for girls. Was there such a thing?

It was clearly time for the Christian school to figure all this out.

To be closer to our new school, my family picked up and moved to town. Ridgecrest had only a few small shops for things that people could not get on the base, such as Lindsay's Furniture and Corney's Shoes. We all knew the Lindsay family, who we said "ran the town." At the time, people were moving off the base as fast as houses could be built, leaving mostly military people on the base. Slowly, old base housing was torn down as it was abandoned; there were warnings not to let kids play in abandoned housing tracks, which were full of snakes and spiders.

One of the reasons people moved was religion. Technically, God was not allowed on the base, due to a constitutional clause known as "the separation of church and state." As Thomas Jefferson wrote, "I contemplate with sovereign reverence that act of the whole American people which declared that their 'legislature' should 'make no law respecting an establishment of religion, or prohibiting the free exercise thereof,' thus building a wall of separation between Church & State." Since the state owned the base, it would have had to make rules allowing Christian churches to set up there, which would both be discriminatory and mix up religion with the state. At least, that was how we saw it then. Instead of churches, we had one "chapel" on the base, and it was ecumenical, with a revolving altar for Catholics, Jews, and Protestants.

Perhaps this is why there was a strange duality between town and base life. If China Lake had the most PhDs per capita in the United States, Ridgecrest had the most churches per capita in California. One China Laker described his surprise upon realizing how religious the community was: "I concluded that six days a week the folks follow the reality of mathematics, physics, and chemistry, but on the seventh day they toss reason aside." He continued, "Before one test flight the group I was working in had a prayer breakfast. They were essentially praying that the mathematical equations were correct! I will never forget that." It was common to pray before missile tests for decades at China Lake; that was allowed, just not churches.

Of course, Ridgecrest was attractive for other reasons too. You did not have to be religious to want to leave a government gray duplex. Our new house, about a mile outside the gates, was a bright blue ranch style with a green lawn and even a flower bed with roses. Inside, there was a plastic chandelier and our very own intercom system for spying on one another. In fact, Christine and I had picked that house over another for the intercom alone. The only problem with our new house was that we were suddenly outside the base fence and cut off from the desert. Our dog, Patches, who once wandered the desert freely with my sister and me, started running frantically in circles around the backyard. On the base, our duplex had only a two-sided fence, but now there were three, with a dangerous street out front if we let Patches roam. In Ridgecrest, we stayed inside, where my mom had her Swedish Dala horses, red enameled wooden toy horses from her ancestral home of Dalarna. She had her Gaither Trio albums, her gilded Bibles, and a pretty chandelier to go with her

Wedgewood china with real gold trim. Christine and I only had each
other and an intercom to follow each other wherever we went. We
also, finally, got to walk to school together every morning.

On the first day of school, we all had on our matching uniforms:
blue polyester jumpers with pleated skirts for the girls and blue pants
with red or white shirts for the boys. Our mothers had to make them
because you could not buy them in stores or online as you can now,
since that Baptist pastor later diversified and started selling uniforms
along with his packets of God's knowledge. Underneath the jumper,
we wore either a red or a white shirt. Pinned to the jumper, we wore a
"kerchief" covered in American flags. Those we bought from our
church, who bought them from a supplier in Texas.

Our classroom, for fifth to eighth graders, was behind the church
and constructed out of cinder-block bricks made from a nearby extinct volcano. I was in the fifth grade, the youngest out of twenty, in a
classroom with a linoleum floor, white walls, and gray metal folding
chairs. It looked like the government. Long wooden desks ran along
the length of the wall with particleboard white "dividers" to separate
the students from one another. Each of us was assigned a "cubicle"
with our name on a "star chart" posted on a corkboard wall inside.
On it, we marked our progress in finishing PACEs—Packets of Accelerated Christian Education. Each day, we sat and faced the corkboard and the wall. On top of each divider was a hole in which we
could insert either a miniature Christian flag—white with a blue
square in the corner and a red cross inside of that, to remind us of
Jesus's blood—to ask a personal question or an American flag for an
academic question, which really meant asking permission to go to the
score table. Christian was for permission to go to the bathroom.
Maybe there were other "personal" questions, but I never had one in
my eight years there.

The teachers were called "monitors" because they did not teach.
Instead, they monitored us. As our founder explained, "Although

ACE recommends all teachers hold at least a BS degree, the most important degree is a BA (Born Again) in Salvation." We learned from booklets at this school rather than teachers. Only later did my dad realize that *he* would have to teach us algebra every night since the monitors could not help us. Besides having a BA, the monitors had to be "modest in dress and appearance, meek of spirit and personality, active in church and community life, clean in conversation and personal life, and a student of the Scriptures." If they met all those qualifications, all they had to do all day was go around the room answering flags—or "monitoring."

On the first day, our monitor Mr. Crackling explained what would become my daily regime for the next nine years. He looked like Santa Claus but with a red mustache instead of a white beard and an American flag outfit instead of a soft red suit. He was Scottish and had a real Scottish terrier and liked to play the bagpipes for boys' study groups that met at his house.

He also liked to yell.

"Every morning," Mr. Crackling said gruffly, "you will stand by your desk, facing me, until you are told to be seated. First, we will inspect your uniforms. Girls, get on your knees." We did as he said.

Then Miss Carter went around the room, measuring the distance between our uniform hem and the floor to ensure there was not more than one inch. At the same time, Mr. Crackling inspected the boys' uniforms and made sure their hair was at least half an inch above their ears. Girls' blouses could be opened no more than three fingers below the clavicle. Boys' pants could be neither too short nor too long, both of which signified something subversive. Miss Carter, who went to our church, was a frail-looking woman who seemed far too skinny and always had dark circles under her eyes. To inspect our uniforms, she had to crawl on her knees from student to student with a ruler. I might have felt sorry for her, but I was too worried about my uniform. If it wasn't right, then I would get sent home in front of everyone.

Mr. Crackling continued when we were done. "Next, you will pledge allegiance to the American flag, the Christian flag, and the Bible. First the Christian flag. . . ."

We all started, "I pledge allegiance to the Christian flag and to the Savior for whose Kingdom it stands. One Savior, crucified, risen, and coming again with life and liberty to all who believe." It quickly became clear to me that this school would be much like the military, with drill sergeants, standing at attention, and following orders. I was actually very good at following orders.

"Now, did I see hands on everyone's hearts?" Mr. Crackling seemed to enjoy our mistakes. "Do you not pledge with your heart? Hands on hearts!"

"I pledge allegiance to the Bible, God's Holy Word . . . ," we read.

We then learned about swats, demerits, and detention and how that all worked. When Mr. Crackling laughed, his big belly shook in a jolly way that was also kind of scary. He picked up a big wooden paddle full of holes to lessen the wind resistance and make it go faster. He swung it through the air like a baseball bat, demonstrating swats, which made me think of the Special Weapons Attack Teams that were busy in south-central LA.

After we sat down, Mr. Crackling walked around the room, giving us our PACEs in social studies, math, science, and English. As he did this, he told us we were not allowed to stand up or turn around or communicate with other students. This would lead to demerits, detentions, or swats, depending on the severity of the offense. Communicating with other students, we were told, "undermined the authority of God and the supervisors." We would get a twenty-minute break for lunch, which we could eat under the two cottonwood trees outside or in our cubicles. A lot of us opted for the cubicles, including me.

Though the atmosphere was closely guarded and quiet, and nothing moved, there were lots of rules. It seemed like you were safest if you did *nothing*. It was also best not to move too fast in case you did something wrong. I learned to freeze like an animal. Over time, I was sure I had become invisible. Literally. I even created an invisible friend, who lived under the score table, to keep me company.

My social studies PACE had a cartoon picture of a family on the cover, with the bubble over the father's head saying, "My family will serve the Lord," and the bubble over the mother's head saying, "It is God's plan for the father to be head of his family. I talk to your father about things, but he is the one who decides what we must do." The whole packet was full of bubbles over cartoon heads. On one page, the mother said, "Men are better at science and math because of how their minds work. Women are happier working in the house, while men are happier outside of the home." On another page, I learned that true peace was impossible in this world and could be found only in the next world with God. We learned that the only government that would work was "the government which will be instituted under direct and personal Millennial rule of the Lord Jesus Christ." On the base, we all knew the government did not work very well. So that made sense.

In science, I learned scientific proof for Noah's flood and that dinosaurs and humans once lived together, proven by the fact that their footprints were found together near the Paluxy River in Texas. This confused me because our preacher said that dinosaur bones had been planted by Satan to trick people into believing in evolution. He said dinosaurs never even existed. According to my PACE, proof that the world was only six thousand years old had been supplied by the first men who landed on the moon. Apparently, everyone was afraid there would be so much dust on the moon, owing to millions of years of accumulation and evolution, that the astronauts would just sink in and die. Instead, there was only six inches of dust, which took six thousand years to make. The moon proved that the Bible was literally true. We were instructed to fill in this information in sentences that read, "The moon is _____ years old. How do scientists know this? _____." The man in charge of the moon mission, Wernher von Braun, was also a creationist, as we learned in a PACE. He had said, "For me the idea of a creation is inconceivable without God. One cannot be exposed to the law and order of the universe without concluding that there must be a divine intent behind it all."

It was only the missionary books, which we called "English literature," that started to cause me problems. There was *God's Smuggler*, about a man who carried Bibles across the border to the Soviet Union, over and over again. Literally nothing else happened. Then there was *Jungle Pilot*, about a missionary who was speared by natives while trying to deliver Bibles. It seemed like the same story, again and again. If the natives did not kill the missionaries right away, they were always eventually grateful to be saved.

This was when I learned to cheat, which was also a sin.

One day, I filled in all the wrong answers in my PACE and raised my American flag. I admit I was a bit scared. Miss Carter made her way around the room and eventually got to me. "Yes, Karen?" she said. She looked so tired.

"I need to go to the score table," I said, afraid she would notice my answers were fakes. Then I would have to go and get swats. It was a huge risk, unlike anything I had done before. The missionaries made me do it.

"Okay, go ahead." She nodded pleasantly. I took a huge gulp of air and brushed her as I got up. I discovered that cheating was not that difficult. In fact, it turned out this was how most of us survived. At the score table, I pulled out the grading key and memorized as many right answers as I could. Then I went back to my desk and erased all the old answers to put in the right ones. I got to have excellent short-term memory. I even won the citywide spelling bee.

But every sin comes with its punishment, and mine was boredom. There was nothing else in my cubicle besides PACEs and the Bible. I began to dream of the "garage sale" books my mom had bought because they were only a nickel. My sister still controlled them with her Dewey decimal system, but I decided to swipe one when she was not looking. To me, stealing did not seem as bad as cheating in the scheme of things. On the base everyone stole government supplies: calculators, pens, whatever. We were all family, after all, and believed *we* were government property. The stuff was not going anywhere. It could go back to the base when we died.

So my education proceeded from the Bible to books about women who dangled from a dark cliff or got trapped in a castle tower. It seemed Gothic romance novels could be had everywhere for only a nickel. One noblewoman who lived on the coast of Cornwall realized that someone wanted to kill her for her money. In the end, she got pushed off a cliff, but a mysterious man rode up on his horse to rescue her just in time. The problem was that she did not know if he was the killer, so she had to decide whether to take his hand or risk falling from the cliff. She made the right decision and chose the man, who pulled her up on his horse and kissed her hard, which meant he was not the killer. It reminded me of the Gene Kelly movies at home, where Gene danced as though he wanted to kiss someone and made me want to kiss him too. At home, I would hide in the closet and think of him, hoping my mother would not find me.

I would always have Gene and my invisible friend, Harvey. Yes, the rabbit, beneath the score table. He kept me company.

At school, I had to be sure to keep the book in my lap or under my PACE so no one could see me. Mr. Crackling would sometimes stop by my cubicle unannounced, squeezing his fat belly against my back, which grossed me out even though there was no getting away from him. He never caught me, though.

It was only when the girl in the next cubicle threw a note over my divider that our problems began. I knew her name was Lorinda, but that was all. She was blond and a whole foot taller than me, though only a year older. She also wore lip gloss and curled her hair, which made her kind of scary.

"What are you reading?" her note said. Busted.

"Romance novel," I wrote back, hoping she was not a stooge.

Another note came whizzing over. "Can I read it?"

I wrote back, "Okay. When I'm done."

That was how Lorinda and I got to be friends during our fifteen-minute recesses—one in the morning and one in the afternoon. Sometimes we even talked to each other at lunch. Slowly, we became experts at covert ops and passed books between borders as in *God's Smuggler*. Then we became more emboldened, even locking the monitor outside during recess once by putting a chair under the door handle inside. After that, we did our best to rearrange everything in the classroom. We put chairs on the score table and hung them from hooks on the walls. We scattered everyone's PACEs all over the floors. It was a disinformation campaign. "Let's turn everything upside down!" we had agreed.

In the end, we snuck out the back door so no one would know it was us. It was a triumph. We may actually have won the war, but Lorinda was not as good at hiding things as I was. I was the "good girl," but her status was not as clear. So she fell under suspicion, vulnerable to attack.

The next morning, Mr. Crackling stopped by Lorinda's cubicle and said, "Come with me to my office," grabbing my book from her lap. I froze, waiting for him to grab me next. It seemed like hours before she came back, her face red but stiff with a glowing defiance. She nodded briefly in my direction as if to signify that she had not ratted me out, and Mr. Crackling never bothered me.

I had to wait until recess to find out what had happened.

"He made me pull down my underwear, lift my skirt, and lean over the desk," she explained. "He said it would hurt more that way."

She was eleven years old.

"My butt is all red and swollen, but he said he won't tell my parents, so at least that's good. They would kill me if they knew."

After that, I stopped stealing books, which meant I had only the Bible. I knew they could not take that away from me. I started reading it from beginning to end, which is how I discovered Michal, David's first wife. The pastor never talked about her. As far as I could tell, Michal stopped sleeping with David after he came prancing into town half-naked with the Ark of the Covenant, whatever that was. It read "Michal the daughter of Saul looked out at the window, and saw king David leaping and dancing before the LORD; and she despised him in her heart."

When she came out to meet him, she told him why: "How did the king of Israel get honor today, by uncovering himself in the eyes of the handmaids of his servants, as one of the vain fellows shamelessly uncovereth himself!" Naked dancing with handmaids? No one talked about that in church. I got the feeling she was jealous. This was where, in a good Gothic novel, he would apologize and say he would dance only for her from now on. That he had lost his mind.

Instead, his reply really bugged me: "Before the LORD, who chose me above thy father, and above all his house . . . will I make merry. And I will be yet more vile than thus, and will be base in mine own sight; and with the handmaids whom thou hast spoken of, with them will I get me honor."

To me, it sounded as if he were saying, "Screw you. Women like me. I'm better than you." David was no hero for me after that. I was done with David, even if he killed Goliath.

But as I read on, I began to see that Michal's brother Jonathan factored into things a lot. When David had to leave Jonathan to go to war, they "kissed and wept" for a long time. Then it said David loved him "more than any woman." It occurred to me that maybe that was the real reason Michal stopped sleeping with David or, as the Bible put it, "had no child unto the day of her death."

Maybe Bathsheba was just another cover. He could not say what he really wanted. I forgave David a little after that. He could not have the person he loved.

At the same time, he still bugged me a little. He sure got all the attention, not his wife, who had to just disappear and not have children for the rest of her life. So I decided to stop reading the Bible and write a novel about Michal instead—for the next eight years. I wanted people to know who she was. In my novel, Michal never wanted to marry David. She knew what was going on with her brother Jonathan, which made her resent the way David carried on with women even more. She only wanted honesty, and to be free; but there was no way out for Michal, so then she goes crazy and dies.

Luckily, because I was Baptist, I was allowed to have my own interpretation of the Bible. That was why Luther had banged his "95 Theses" onto the door, after all. He thought we should read the Bible for ourselves and stop listening to the pope, who thought he was better than everyone.

Still, I wished my novel had a happier ending.

In my cubicle, it at first felt claustrophobic to stare at the wall all day long, but after a while it seemed natural. Parents were not allowed to visit ICS and we were not allowed to visit them. I began to think of my cubicle as a spaceship floating among the stars, which was comforting. Before long, I did not want to leave my cubicle at all. I was glad they let me eat my lunch at my cubicle, staring at my star chart. And though my sister was right across the room, even she started to fade in my mind. She was in her spaceship and I was in mine, floating in our separate directions into the universe.

Outside, a war was ending and a presidency crumbling into failure. ACE had been founded, in its own weird way, to keep all that from happening. According to the Texas pastor who started the schools, parents who refused to spank their children were "part of the same socialist, communist-inspired operation trying to break down the discipline and the order in America." He was quoting his mentor, preacher Jack Hyles. Those parents were the North Vietnamese, those nonspankers. That was why we had to be there. For the war. As Jack Hyles preached, "Don't spank the child. Don't have capital punishment. And the same thing leads eventually to its inevitable end, and that is, 'We're against war.'"

At ICS, we were winning the war, one SWAT at a time.

Chapter Eleven

Snake Genocide

On weekends, we would load into the Plymouth Duster, red with a white stripe because Christine and I wanted it that way, and flee town. So did half of Ridgecrest. We ran away from the world of weapons and Richard Nixon. We were two to three hours, depending on traffic, from the amusement parks and shopping malls of Los Angeles, but only minutes from endless desert adventures. Our choices ranged from stargazing and arrowhead hunting to collecting wildflowers and exploring canyons.

On weekdays, I had only the back gate for comfort, my little door to Narnia. Outside it was a miniature desert, really nothing more than a street block that had remained undeveloped, but still with tumbleweeds and lizards and creosote bushes. That pink-peeling wooden gate sat behind a wall of tumbleweeds, blown there by the wind, for several months after we moved in. It looked as though it had not been opened in decades. Then my dad finally cleared them away and forced the gate open.

"Patches!" I yelled to our neurotic dog. We inched forward at first, sunstruck, afraid that somehow we were not allowed outside. Patches sniffed and sniffed for danger, then suddenly darted past me like a rocket, pulling me along behind the leash. It was spring, so the desert had spurted out all its stars, daisies, and buttercups, whose seeds can lie dormant for seven years or more until the rain and sun are exactly right. I sang, "Daisies, daisies, daisies! Big ones, small ones, white and yellow," while patting their soft heads. I had missed them.

Patches was frantically sniffing the ground, lifting her head to snort at the wind, while I squatted to look beneath the bushes. First, I found my friends the black ants, with their nice symmetrical holes, unlike the sloppy ones the red ants built. Once, my mom had to put me in a bath with baking soda, then gently squeeze all the red ant stingers out since they would swarm your leg and sting you. But you could dig and dig forever in a black ant hole and not get stung, or get to the bottom, though there were little egghead silverfish living down there that looked like blind white teardrops.

Besides the ants, there were all the ancient beetles: the green shiny dinosaur-looking ones, the black ones with red trim, and the yellow-striped ones. Bugs seemed more resilient than the navy to me. They could suck water from cactus or sleep underground for decades until the next rain came. I read about all of them, begging my mom and dad to buy me books. If I was lucky, I could sometimes find a tarantula and then would lay my hand on the ground in front of it and wait for it to walk on me. Tarantula feet feel like heaven, soft dancing furry heaven. Light as a misty rain. Gopher snakes are fine to pick up, too, and their skin feels slick and cool. Lizards hid beneath the creosotes, jackrabbits ate the twigs, and kangaroo rats dug holes at the base. Most people do not realize that a creosote bush is a whole animal town. If you pull one out and shake it hard like a rug, you won't be able to count all the things that fall out.

But weekends provided even vaster experiences. Sometimes the base had "star parties," when China Lakers would drive out into the desert with big base telescopes, while my dad brought his little telescope from home. There, we would all share telescopes while trying to find new planets, comets, or stars. The kids would lie on blankets, looking at the stars, while the parents told desert stories and looked for a piece of the sky to name. For a navigator like my dad, it was like being in the war again. He felt useful. As for me, I could fall forever into the stars with aliens and be happy.

Usually, Christine and I would want to look for rocks on weekends for Pebble Pups and Rock Hounds, the base rock clubs. In Pebble Pups, I learned where to find crystals, turquoise, mica, and geodes. A good geode, which you sliced in half in the lab at the Quonset hut, could win you the annual gem and mineral show, where the top prize was your own GemMaster. I was determined to win so I could slice and grind my rocks at home. I would scour the *Rocketeer* for hotels that advertised "arrowheads nearby" or "good rocks" and then declare, "Found one!" And off we went on weekend races for rocks. We had to hurry because everyone else wanted that GemMaster too.

Once, after leaving town at the crack of dawn, we started to notice that we were driving over a lot of snakes. It was not uncommon to see a few dead rattlers on the road, but this time there were too many. My sister and I started to count. "Twenty!" I yelled out. "Forty, fifty, sixty . . ." They were going by almost faster than we could count.

"How many now?" my dad asked.

"One hundred!"

We kept going, up to two hundred, before my mom noticed something. "Earl, slow down," she shouted, "I think they're still alive!"

Indeed, I noticed a few were flapping around on the ground.

"Earl, stop!" my mom screamed then. "I think we're killing them!"

My dad slowed down, surveying the scene, but did not stop. "But we can't stop," he said. "What if the kids jump out? Those are rattlesnakes!"

So we kept going on our own little snake genocide. As the sun rose over the horizon, the snakes became livelier and gradually all skittled off the pavement. I remembered what Mr. Roberts had taught us at school, that snakes are cold-blooded and like to lie on the pavement at night since it is warmer than the sand. If the pavement gets too cold, they cannot move until it warms up again. Mr. Roberts kept giant aquariums full of rattlesnakes that we got to see up close in his summer class at the public school. He taught us how to build a rattlesnake catcher out of a stick and a string. He even dissected a snake in front of us. It was frozen, so he had to thaw it out first. By making a string loop at the end of the stick, you can catch a rattlesnake by the head without it ever getting close enough to bite.

My parents started laughing, relieved, when the roads were clear of snakes. But then we all grew quiet, shocked by what we had seen, what we had done.

Finally, we saw the hotel sign: "Rockhounder Rendezvous."

"Yay! We made it!" I shouted as the car slowed down.

As soon as we stopped, I bolted from the car and off into the desert, and my mom yelled after me, "Stay close to the car!" But my sister was already chasing behind me, giggling, with Patches behind her.

Crossing a hilltop, I started to see obsidian right away. I picked up the pieces, examining them and putting the ones in my bag that were arrowheads. Little did I know that I was carting off the hard-earned tools of the Kawaiisu—from one of the largest aboriginal stone workshops in California. I was transferring these gems from their workshop to mine: Pebble Pups. My sister yelled from far behind, "Save something for me!" But I was not about to let the good things go. A good arrowhead was worth points. The more arrowheads, the better.

"Karen, come back," my mom shouted again. I decided I would have to wait, but I knew it would be good to go farther, with my parents following behind and Patches leaping and wagging her bright, white, joyful tail.

Chapter Twelve

The Soul of the Photoplotter

Back at home, my mom went back to her Gerber photoplotter, named after its designer, Joseph Gerber, who has nothing to do with baby food. Nevertheless, it was my mom's new baby. My mom said the Gerber had to be kept in the dark and cleaned often. It also emitted a moaning howl that was loud enough to require headphones and could blind my mom with its xenon lamp unless she wore her dark safety goggles. It turned out that the Gerber's sensitivities made people sensitive too.

Her boss, Mr. Bukowski, designed missile circuitry and was a world-renowned expert on "spirals," which I imagined was a Slinky so hard to design that it required a PhD. Their office, which was miles from anywhere, was a magnet for desert creatures seeking shade or water. Once, she said, a rattlesnake was found under a desk at work. Even so, it seemed to me, she was far more worried about the Gerber than that snake.

Her problems all started when she tried to change the filter in the

Gerber. Technically, she was supposed to call the Gerber people for that, but she was a Depression-era kid and believed in fixing things herself. She tried to explain the problem with the Gerber people in a memo to Mr. Bukowski: "Their willingness to declare our lamps unusable may be motivated by their desire to sell a modification to the Gerber." She thought a new filter would fix everything instead, that it would be a simple change.

But a co-worker of hers, Harris in Operations, disagreed. He was a middle-aged man with a loud voice and saggy face who thought those Equal Rights Amendment "Freedom Train" feminists were going too far. He supported Phyllis Schlafly, who said women should stay at home. So when he happened to catch my mom changing the filter, disobeying protocol, he knew he had found an easy target. He stormed in, towering over her, and shouted, "That's an Operations job. Our filter changer handles that."

My mom was taken aback by his bulk and apparent confusion. There was no "filter changer," as far as she knew. She had assumed he would tell her to call Gerber. Nevertheless, she was driven back by his size and the way he leaned in over her. "Get out of here!" he yelled.

"Is there a filter changer?" she wrote to Mr. Bukowski from the safety of her office. He had not heard of one either. They decided to wait and see what would happen next.

After a few days with work at a standstill and no filter changer in sight, my mom wrote to her division head—above even Mr. Bukowski—to explain that she was not allowed to change the filter and thus was unable to work. A simple filter change, she explained, would force the machine to recalibrate and fix the problem. Until then, any plots she printed would be bad. The spirals would not have their perfect arc. The missiles would not fly.

For Harris, that memo to Mr. Bukowski's boss may as well have been an official declaration of war. When he got wind of it, he began his own memo-writing campaign. First, he sent one to my mom, even though her office was only down the hallway from his, stating that all further requests for plotting had to go through him. He accused my mom of secretly "tampering" with the Gerber and attached a "request form" for her to mail to him when she wanted to use the plotter again.

"More copies are available in my office," he wrote.

The number of memos written, encoded, and passed between people who were working in the same hall might seem surprising to those who are not in Defense. There, everything has to be documented, double-entry-style, and preferably in acronyms. Otherwise, it does not exist.

Meanwhile at home, my mom started lying on the couch and not wanting to get up, while my dad kept having to travel for wind tunnel tests. Though he never said where he went, he always came back with gifts. There was the black Eskimo doll, made from Alaskan sealskin, that you could wear like a purse. There was a porcupine made of rabbit fur. There was a handmade Native American doll and a pretty blue dream catcher that read "New Mexico Dreams." He left me little bread crumbs, clues about where he was, which I cherished like pieces of him. My dad often complained, "I don't understand why China Lake can't build a proper wind tunnel," which at least helped me know he was not leaving because of me.

"What's a wind tunnel?" I asked.

"It's where we make the wind blow really hard so we can watch something fly inside."

"Like a kite?" My dad liked to build kites, then take us out into the desert to fly them, which was his way of teaching us aerodynamics.

"No, but someone once put a duck in at Mike lab to watch it fly," he said. I wondered then if that duck liked being put in a wind tunnel or if the men who put him there were just being mean. I did not think

I would like to be put in there. That duck would have to just fly and fly and fly while all the men laughed at him.

"Why do you have to travel," I asked, "if you have a tunnel big enough for a duck at home?"

"It's not big enough," he said. If he had a big one, he could stay.

Today, I picture my mom's days unfolding at work like a twisted ballet, with the Gerber in the middle of the stage. Dancers come and go, sometimes blocking access to the machine, sometimes hiding behind it. Mom and Harris are locked in a ballet battle until one of them dies in the end, falling in a curtain of red ballet blood. Had the Gerber been a shrine and whoever approached it a prophet, the problem would have been that Harris did not believe in female prophets. He thought my mom was a false prophet. He thought his machine was good the way it was and did not need anything but him.

In contrast, for my mom the Gerber was a finicky child who had to be coaxed and preened so it would perform well. She knew that if the needs of the Gerber were ignored, it would create bad plots, little temper tantrums that would lead to bad missiles. Bad missiles made my dad leave town to fix them. And if a missile left a navy carrier chute with a bad circuit, there would be just one big plunk and then a long journey to the bottom of the ocean with all that money trailing behind. My mom believed the troops depended upon her and did not want a plunk. She did not want to waste that money. To her, sabotaging the Gerber meant sabotaging U.S. Defense. My mom must have thought she was facing an eternal enemy of the United States: treason. And all because Harris was withholding access to the plotter.

Finally, according to my mom's notes, which told me the story of this drama, a new photoplotter operator appeared, Martha, who was petite with feathered red hair, diamond stud earrings, and bright red nails. She was a "downtime" person, which meant her "JO" (Job Order) had run out, leaving her without an assignment or funding from a particular missile program. In China Lake, to be on down-time was humiliating. It meant you were wasting "overhead," or tax-payer money. You would be shunned as if you were contagious. Downtime people had nothing to do because they were not popular or smart enough to be picked for work on a particular missile. For instance, my dad put "AIM-9L" on his work stubs for years because he was being paid with money allotted for the Sidewinder. He was a Sidewinder person, whereas a downtime person is nothing. It meant you did not stay in one place for long but were more like a "temp" worker, sent to fill in holes everywhere, and the hole at my mom's office was suddenly, mysteriously, for a "filter changer."

So Martha was sent to Harris, who put her in charge of the Gerber. One had to wonder how she got to be in charge, to the point that in the end she could stop production on the Sidearm. Apparently, she had only a high school degree. Was Harris having an affair with her and treating the Gerber like a present for her? Was she just that pretty? Whatever the reason, my mom's access to the Gerber did not improve after Martha arrived. Once, after getting two hours with the plotter, my mom had to beg Harris for two more.

Then he yelled at her, "Can't you do anything right?"

She started to cry.

And the filter was never changed, not for four long months. If my mom believed in "working as good as any man," Martha clearly had a different strategy. She believed in the power of rumors. First, Martha wrote a memo claiming my mom had been imagining problems with the Gerber and was compulsively tampering with it. Next, she started printing plots and showing them to everyone to prove the Gerber worked fine. In response, my mom printed her own plots, pointing out the problem to Martha. My mom wrote to Harris, "Only a non-trivial design, such as a modulated spiral, would likely repeat the problem."

In response, Harris accused her of calling him "trivial."

Who knows how long this "print off" might have lasted if Mr. Bukowski had not finally intervened. "The plots are bad," he wrote to Harris. "I should not have to tell you this."

Next, Martha tried a different strategy. She claimed my mom's software instructions were the problem, not the Gerber. She refused to communicate any further with my mom, who she said was being irrational. Because of this, Mr. Bukowski had to be constantly on the phone, even while on vacation, as a mediator between Martha and my mom. He even wrote to his boss to complain.

Finally, Martha hit on a winning rumor. "Why do you think Mr. Bukowski treats her better than everyone else?" she whispered, lifting an eye in insinuation. My mom overheard this and knew there was no evidence to prove Martha wrong this time. There was nothing to print, nothing mathematical to prove, which was her specialty. And rumors will always find allies. Soon my mom heard people whispering in the hallways that she was Mr. Bukowski's "pet." They questioned her credentials, wondering how she got the job without a degree in computer science, only medical technology.

One day, she heard something rattling in her desk drawer and opened it to find bullets. "They were about this size—" She held her fingers an inch apart when she told me.

"What did you do?" I asked, my eyes twice as big.

"I told some people about it, but they just shrugged. Then the janitor said he could use them, so I gave them to him. He said they were for a rifle."

"What were they doing out there?" I said.

My mom shrugged. "I assumed they were for rattlesnakes," she said. "But maybe they were for spies." Then she laughed.

At the time, she was not laughing. Instead, she retreated to the couch and called in sick. That was when Mr. Bukowski finally stepped in. To me, Mr. Bukowski sounded like the kind of guy who could take a lot but had his breaking point. His parents had escaped from the Soviet Union, after all, so he must have known plenty about cat-and-mouse games, government bullies, and espionage. He decided he could play.

"I want you to keep an eye on the Gerber room and report to me who is using it every day," he first wrote to the micro-miniature lab. They were in the room next to the Gerber lab.

Soon the spy was writing on U.S. Navy letterhead every day, "No one today." Next, Mr. Bukowski passed this information up to his boss: "No one today." Evidence against Harris began to mount. Cases were being prepared. The plan was to prove that Harris was deliberately withholding the Gerber from my mother, claiming it was in use when it was not. They needed the double-entry ledger for that.

One day, Mr. Bukowski urgently needed plots for a trip to Dallas, but when my mom went to the Gerber room, she found it locked. The secretary then told her that both Martha and Harris had gone out of town for a few days and had taken the key. In a panic, my mom burst into Mr. Bukowski's high-level meeting to explain. A sea of desert-grizzled engineering faces looked up at her.

"They've . . . they've gone," my mom sputtered, humiliated. "They took the Gerber key!"

Mr. Bukowski had to cancel his trip to Dallas, the contractors had to postpone the missile production schedule, and ultimately the missiles may not have made it to the field in time. This was when Mr. Bukowski, a mild-mannered Polish man whose parents had told him to be grateful every day for what he had, finally lost it and was no longer grateful. He wrote to his boss, "The generating of high quality Gerber artwork has always been a challenge and undoubtedly will continue to be so; but the events of the last four weeks were almost enough to make me look for some other kind of work."

And because Mr. Bukowski never lost it, a decision from above finally came down. A memo arrived from Code 35, above them all, copied to everyone involved. It read simply, "Any problems with the Gerber will be solved by Mary." The verdict was in.

My mom lost many battles but finally won the war. But war leaves scars, and living next to the enemy, even after a détente, is never easy. After that, my mom suffered from a lack of confidence. Since my parents were from different branches and could talk only on a "need to know" basis, she could not tell my dad what was going on. He started to draw the blinds when she was on the couch, afraid she would die as his mother had done. He worried about having to travel so much with all of us left in his wake, bouncing and about to upturn like a boat. My sister would stare at him with her serious glasses face, perched and waiting for him to fall over too.

The Gerber never fully recovered either. After being fussed and fought over so much, it decided it had had enough even after my mother got full custody. The fight had been too long, the adjustments too few. Its lamp exploded, destroying the mirror and the lens. After that, my mom explained, "It never got back into perfect adjustment."

I would not be surprised if Harris blew it up.

If I asked my mom what she did at work, she would always say, "Oh, I was at the bottom of the totem pole—nothing important," followed by, "People always said I was too slow." Of course, partly this was my mom's personality. Like my dad, she could be shy, humble, and stoical. She once said, "I've always been a nobody all my life. Your dad was always more popular at church." I found this hard to believe, since my dad was the quietest person I have ever known. Nevertheless, after a lifetime of hearing my mother say such things, I truly came to believe them. At least, I assumed my father had the more important job at China Lake. Imagine my surprise when I discovered her work file, which held the Gerber memos.

They also held so much more.

My mom started as a GS-3 math aid, which involved using a miniature calculator and "keypunching data and programs" into the mainframe computer, a machine that took up the whole basement and had to be fed wallet-sized cards full of punch holes. But within a decade, she wrote of her credentials, "I have a system level knowledge of Tomahawk's navigation," including its "Inertial Navigation System (INS), Global Positioning System (GPS), barometric and radar altimeters, pre-stored terrain altitude profiles (TERCOM maps), and terrain imagery." She could change a torpedo heading or launch point with the stroke of a DOS (disk operating system) programming line and, out of sheer boredom, once designed a laser bar-coding program years before anyone had heard of such a thing. She wanted to keep track of government property because she thought too much of it was disappearing. While my dad evaluated pitch and roll, my mom prepared the simulation programs and test plans for him to follow. She plotted his results. She analyzed his data. In one yearly review, her division boss wrote, "She is a perfectionist who holds the team together and could easily do any of our jobs. She needs a substantial raise." Imagine that. She not only wrote computer programs, but also converted them to other languages as computers were evolving. She could even build a computer.

After some research, I discovered that my mom's job was not that unusual for women at the time. Called "computresses," women were once hired to operate forty-pound calculators that did nothing more than add, subtract, and divide. They did the math for the engineers. Back then, this was considered "clerical," or women's work, like typing. But slowly, computers evolved from these motor-driven calculators, and women were the only ones who knew how to use them.

By the time my mom arrived on the scene, calculators were already "miniature," but computers were enormous. She was at the forefront of the shift to computers that was a room-sized IBM mainframe set up in the basement. She told stories about "punch cards" and how the IBM had to constantly be fed with them. That was "programming" then. Ironically, as computers became central to the process of building a missile, and then guiding missiles, women became central too. The men did not know how to use them. My mom once said to me, "I was shocked that these guys did not know how to do basic things like plotting. I had to do everything for them. Except for Mr. Bukowski, of course. He knew it was important to learn." Nevertheless, the men still got the big salaries.

Imagine that.

When I told my mom only a few years ago that I had found and read her work notes, she was not angry, as I had feared. She simply looked over the contraband, then said, "So now you know what I did at work, though it was a lot more than just working on the Gerber."

"I know!" I said. "You never told me, Mom."

"Well, we're not supposed to," she replied, stern and worklike.

Then she brightened up and said, "I once drove a missile to Newport Beach." She laughed.

"What do you mean?" I asked, shocked.

"I mean, I put it in the trunk of the Toyota Camry and headed off to LA. It was supposed to have some tests done there."

"But what if you crashed?" I asked. In Los Angeles, there were gridlocks, drive-by shootings, and Lamborghinis speeding by at 120 mph.

My mom said she drove slowly, as she always does, and tried to focus on the destination: Lockheed Martin. "That must have been weird," I commented.

"I noticed my hands had turned white by the time I got there. I was gripping the steering wheel so hard. So I decided to get off the freeway and go to the mall," she said, laughing. "The missile sat in the parking lot while I shopped."

"Which mall?"

"You know, the one in Brea. I shopped for a few hours, and after that, I was fine to drive. But now, when I think about leaving that missile in a crowded parking lot, I wonder what I was thinking. Anyone could have broken in."

"Was it armed?" I asked, picturing something far worse than a robbery.

"Oh no, it wouldn't fit in my trunk that way. It was just the nose. But what if the police had stopped me and wanted to look in the trunk? No one told me what to do in that case."

I think my parents have different stories from those of other parents.

Then she looked at the notes again and said, "It's a good thing I didn't write down what the real problems were at work. This was nothing in comparison."

"And I bet you won't tell me now," I said.

"Of course not. You would put it in your book."

Chapter Thirteen

President Kennedy's Lincoln

When my family first drove down the main avenue of China Lake, we passed "Kennedy's Forest," which was really nothing more than a few rows of sycamore trees. Ironically, those trees had not been planted in Kennedy's honor, but had once been blown up for him at a weapons show. They were dubbed "Kennedy's Forest" only when they miraculously started growing back. They had survived, while he had not.

Shortly before our fateful long family drive into the desert, my dad wrote to my mom of his doubts about moving. "My worst fears were confirmed," he wrote from China Lake before he came to get us. "I am going to be the aerodynamicist on the AIM-9L. I will be furnishing all the aerodynamic data, trying to solve any aerodynamic problems that come up, writing weekly progress reports, and estimating percent work remaining. . . . Pray for me."

Only now do I know that my dad had been assigned an impossible task: he was supposed to make the AIM-9L Sidewinder fly straight when it could not. I found this out thirty years after the fact, long after he was dead and the base's files were finally declassified. Before that, they were not even accessible to people on the base. After their declassification, the files were moved to the National Archives at the University of California–Riverside, which was where I read them. By then it was too late to tell my dad that it was not his fault if those missiles did not hit their targets. He could not have stopped it.

As with my mom's files, barely saved from the shredder, my dad's files—the Sidewinder files—had been all but forgotten by the time I found them in 2011. Only I kept lurking, wanting to know what my parents did, searching for answers. So I drove to a small brick building outside of Riverside, where they were stored, and I began to dig. There were stacks of boxes on the Sidewinder to go through until I finally happened upon a report by Sidewinder designer Howie Wilcox. In it, he strongly argued that the Sidewinder not be sent to the field. "Idealized missiles," he called them, claiming they were unfit for the harsh reality of Vietnam. He wrote that engineers were working in an "idealized environment," a math equation in which the missile could not miss. He meant my dad and his blue graph paper.

In Vietnam, he wrote, the Sidewinder would not work in the rain. It would not work in the clouds, in the haze, or in the smog. It would not work on sunny days above the ocean. It was a *Green Eggs and Ham* list of flaws: "Not in the dark. Not on a train. Not in a car. Not in a tree." Not anywhere, Sam-I-am, you see. Howie concluded, "Only fair-weather attacks are possible with an infra-red homing missile." The Sidewinder had been tested only in the desert. Vietnam was not a desert.

Designed to track the red glowing heat of a plane's tailpipe, the Sidewinder could not distinguish tailpipes from light refracting in the clouds. It "went crazy" over reflections of the sun on the ocean. Finally, Howie warned, the enemy could outsmart a Sidewinder by throwing a flare out the window. The Sidewinder would forget the tailpipe and jump on the flare as if it were the best thing in the whole world. That report contradicted everything I had heard about the Sidewinder growing up. It was supposed to be our premier weapon, our pride and glory, the star missile of China Lake. But here it sounded more like a perpetually distracted kitten, chasing shiny things.

Why did no one listen to Wilcox? I thought. Vietnam was hazy.

The Sidewinder had a success rate of only sixteen percent in Vietnam.

If the navy had listened to Howie, they would at least have kept the guns on the planes as a backup plan. Instead, they replaced the guns with Sidewinders, so when those missiles missed, the American pilots became sitting ducks. If the navy had listened to Howie, they would at least have taught the pilots to dogfight rather than declaring it an obsolete skill. The Topgun U.S. Navy strike fighter tactics school, about which the Tom Cruise movie was made, was only opened after one thousand planes were lost in Vietnam.

How was I to know that when my dad stopped bouncing lightly on his feet twice, as he did when he was ready to go somewhere fun, it was because the Sidewinder was not working? Granted, Howie's report was written a decade before my family arrived at China Lake. But sixteen percent is nothing to brag about. We were there for the important years, when the missiles were flying, when Roger Stone was working for Nixon's CREEP (the Committee to Re-Elect the President), when Cambodia was being bombed, and when bodies were coming home from the war by the thousands. Stone was known as Nixon's "dirty trickster" at the time, responsible for planting moles in the DNC and otherwise trolling Nixon's opposition for re-election. Though his day job was "scheduling," Roger Stone said, "By night, I'm trafficking in the black arts. Nixon's people were obsessed with intelligence." We were there for the years of dirty tricks.

By the time we arrived at China Lake, Kennedy's trees were halfway back to their original size. Soldiers were coming home with something called "post-Vietnam syndrome." To me, Kennedy represents a different path we could have taken, a path that would not have ended in defeat. People loved him in China Lake when I lived there. He was the only president ever to have visited the base.

In the armaments museum, you can still watch a video about his visit or skim through photographs and news stories about that day—June 7, 1963. This was eight years before we moved to the base, but his memory still lingered. There, you can watch him land on Air Force One at the Area E airstrip. As his plane pulls to a stop, white-jumpsuited men with white hoods, looking like a biohazard team, push a stairway up to him. They look as if they'd just run over from the chemical lab to help Kennedy out of his plane.

Then, in dazzling contrast to the white of the plane, the staircase, and the jumpsuited men, Kennedy steps out in a black suit and black tie with a white handkerchief in his pocket, looking as brilliant as his smile.

Bleachers await him, full of women in pearls and pith helmets next to men in suits, all facing an empty desert that will soon be full of exploding weapons. At a podium in front, a man says into a microphone, "The events to follow illustrate weapons in various stages of development and tests. Like parents bracing themselves for the possible embarrassment of a child's first recital, we continue."

Then the weapons begin to fly in all their Technicolor glory. Those fifteen-year-old chopped-down sycamore trees had earlier been propped back up as a mock Vietnamese forest, and when a Helicopter Trap Weapon is dropped on them, they lie down like rays around a sun. A helicopter lands in the middle. People cheer. Then Mk 81 bombs create little mushroom clouds that race across the desert floor. Cluster bombs spew shrapnel, breaking red balloons tied to the earth that are meant to represent soldiers. Napalm, also designed at China Lake, lights up the desert in a fireball. It is a symphony of fire timed beautifully to music. How could he not be impressed? Even William Porter, our friend and church deacon, got to shake Kennedy's hand. He had designed the Shrike missile, named for a bird that impales its victims and hangs their bodies on barbed-wire fences.

Finally, a Walleye missile, which is TV camera guided, is aimed straight for the president. It is the grand finale. The camera in the nose scans the terrain, looking for a target match, in this case President Kennedy. On a TV screen mounted by his chair, the President is supposed to see himself on TV. See himself as a target. Then the missile is supposed to veer away from him, right on schedule.

It might sound shocking to aim a missile at the president's head, but China Lakers were like the Merry Pranksters of weapons. They liked those kinds of jokes and tricks. For instance, a favorite gag was to hand a visiting dignitary or defense contractor a cigarette before taking him into a room to see the Sidewinder. The Sidewinder nose would be propped on a stand with the rotating glass tracker at the tip pointed into the center of the room. Since the missile is drawn to heat like a snake, it would start tracking the visitor when he walked in. Sometimes engineers would paint the missile nose like an eyeball, which would follow the visitor around the room. The visitor may have nearly had a heart attack, but everyone else had a good laugh. So it made sense they would point a missile at President Kennedy too.

But Kennedy did not jump, or laugh, as he was supposed to. When he was directed to look at the TV screen by his chair to see the Walleye missile photographing him, locking in on him, he merely looked confused. Reportedly, he simply said, "I can't say I recognized myself. I don't quite understand the joke."

Soon after the show ended, rumors began to fly that Kennedy looked worn out and had a headache. One person said he "looked like he was tired, wished he didn't have to do this, and wanted a good beer or a shot of whiskey." He asked if he could lie down for a while, so the navy rounded up all the neighborhood dogs to keep them from barking while he slept.

Finally, Kennedy got up and ended his visit with a one-minute speech in which he said it was nice to see all the healthy-looking children in California. He always liked the children. Then he said, "I cannot think of a prouder occupation when asked what our occupation may be than to say, 'I serve the United States of America.'" This is the part that everyone quotes, but it is not the most important part.

Kennedy was driven away down Blandy Avenue, named after the man in charge of the Bikini Atoll atomic bomb tests. Admiral Blandy once defended his actions amid antinuclear protests by saying, "I am not an atomic playboy, exploding these bombs to satisfy my personal whim." Kennedy *was* a playboy, though he denied it too. Women could tell, even in China Lake. They threw themselves at his car as he drove away, trying to stop him from leaving.

Here is where I always pause the tape, because Kennedy's Lincoln Continental starts to look so familiar—especially if I run it in slow motion. It looks so vulnerable, so open to attack. It is the car that I cannot look away from. It is the *same* car he rode in five months later in Dallas. It has five Secret Service agents jogging by its side, as they would do when it drove by the Texas School Book Depository. These men do not try to stop the women jumping from the crowd. One lands right on the hood of his car. Kennedy raises his hand to his neck instinctively, trying to block her. She says she only wants a handshake.

I wonder how they got that car to China Lake. I wonder how they got it back to Dallas.

Then he is gone, out the main gate, never to return.

Three days after his visit, Kennedy gave a speech at the American University. "World peace," he began. "What kind of peace do I mean? What kind of peace do we seek? Not a Pax Americana enforced on the world by American weapons of war. Not the peace of the grave or the security of the slave." Instead, he explained, "I am talking about genuine peace, the kind of peace that makes life on earth worth living, the kind that enables men and nations to grow and to hope and to build a better life for their children—not merely peace for Americans but peace for all men and women—not merely peace in our time but peace for all time."

In nearly every speech until his death, Kennedy spoke of peace with a newfound passion and sureness. Then, one day in October, he devised a plan to remove all seventeen thousand U.S. combat troops from Vietnam within two years. Secretary of Defense Robert McNamara, who heartily agreed, made the announcement the same day.

One month later, Kennedy was dead. My mom said she kept thinking about little Jack at the time, who was slightly older than my sister. "It would have been so terrible to be left with a child that age," my mom said.

President Lyndon Johnson, who immediately succeeded Kennedy, had other things on his mind. He called Robert McNamara and said, "I always thought it was foolish for you to make any statements about withdrawing. I thought it was bad psychologically. But you and the president thought otherwise, and I just sat silent." His voice sounds defensive as if he wants to show who is in charge. "We have a commitment to Vietnamese freedom," he said. "We could pull out of there, the dominoes would fall, and that part of the world would go to Communists." We would stay in Vietnam.

There was nothing that Robert McNamara could say in response. He had a new boss.

Over sixteen thousand American soldiers would die in one year: 1968.

When is the moment you could have stopped the roll from happening, set out on the right path, corrected course? When is that moment you could have kept it all from going crazy? Was it then?

Robert McNamara's new boss deployed the Sidewinder to Vietnam. I arrived in China Lake just in time for post-Vietnam syndrome, now known as post-traumatic stress disorder, when people began to notice that returning veterans startled too easily. They dreamed of being back in the jungle, gasped for breath, drank, reached for a gun, killed themselves. The world was filling up with the falling-apart. Meanwhile, the United States was developing its own syndrome, called "Vietnam syndrome," not to be confused with "post-Vietnam syndrome." It meant we secretly thought we were losers and were vaguely depressed. We felt lost, with no sense of purpose or pride.

While doctors said the only cure for post-Vietnam syndrome was talking about the war, the only cure for "Vietnam syndrome" was Ronald Reagan. I was ready for the Reagan cure. Ten years after our first fateful drive down Blandy Avenue, when I was about to turn sixteen, I was praying for Reagan to win. I needed that Gipper to save me, to save us all from ourselves. To Make America Great Again. I did not realize then that my fate would become entwined with his in ways no one could have predicted. I only knew that my whole life was ahead of me. Reagan was my future. We would be winners together.

PART TWO

A Teenage Weaponeer

Missile Guidebook:
Refuse to be its victim. It will want you to think
you are subject to its will. You are not. You are
more powerful than a missile, which can only erase
life and stories. You can create life and tell stories,
stories that are true.

Chapter Fourteen

The Chosin Few

Unless it falls on a Sunday, my birthday is always Inauguration Day. Eras change with me. Presidents come and go. I often feel lost in the shuffle between then and now, on a day when people cheer or cry, but never about me. My birthday is a lesson in my own insignificance.

Only one birthday was different: January 20, 1981. It was Ronald Reagan's Inauguration Day and also my sixteenth birthday. All the powers of the universe seemed to confer and agree that the best presents would be saved for me. The day was a spectacle I would never forget. A brass band played, the U.S. Capitol was draped with giant American flags, and Nancy Reagan changed clothes sixteen times. My dad and I stood in the living room, too excited to sit down, watching the TV. Our heavy blue drapes blocked the sun as in a movie theater, but the movie on this screen was Freedom. Reagan said that Americans would do "whatever needs to be done to preserve this last and greatest bastion of freedom." Us.

Then he said the unimaginable. He thanked our veterans who had served "halfway around the world," on "the Chosin Reservoir, and in a hundred rice paddies and jungles of a place called Vietnam." Just like that, he had broken the curse of the Vietnam vets. Our Vietnam veterans were heroes now, not forgotten, not spat upon, not sad anymore. My dad teared up, as he always did during a sappy movie.

After Reagan was sworn in and walked away to trumpets blaring, NBC said the unimaginable too. "The hostages are free," Tom Brokaw announced minutes later. "The hostages are free," he repeated, perhaps not believing it himself. For the last 444 days, a number that everyone knew by heart, the United States had watched on pins and needles for news of fifty-two American embassy workers who had been held hostage by Islamists in Iran. The days dragged on like a ticking time bomb as the new number was posted every night on ABC, CBS, and NBC. Four hundred forty-four.

Suddenly, the clock had stopped. I looked at my dad in surprise. The wells in his eyes began to flow over. Spontaneously, we hugged each other.

"There's your birthday present, Karen," he said.

I replied, "This is the best day of my life." We usually hugged only before or after extended absences and even then with an agreed-upon formality, like presidents shaking hands.

Now a new era had begun. I was sixteen, had a public school boyfriend, and could finally drive. I could also start working on the base that summer, as did most teenagers in Ridgecrest. At my high school, where you worked at your own pace, you could graduate whenever you finished the twelfth grade PACEs. I later met a woman named BethAnn who finished all her PACES in the fourth grade. She had to go to public school after that since she could not go to college at age ten. I would finish only a year early, but it still felt like an accomplishment. Little did I know then the trouble my public school boyfriend would cause, how he would make my dad turn on me. That moment of freedom and celebration, with my dad's hand lingering on my shoulder, even after the hug, would soon turn into a cold hard yank of shame.

My boyfriend, Phil, was James Bond dreamy, with thick, black, feathered hair and a secret agent coolness. I think he actually wanted to be James Bond, since he made me watch all the movies and had memorized all of his lines. I thought the movies were silly, especially the girls, but still liked having a Bond boyfriend. He was even learning to speak Russian so he could join the CIA.

Since I met him at church, my parents did not seem to mind that he was from Burroughs High School. His sister was even friends with my sister. One day, Christine handed me a checklist in church from him. It read, "What is your favorite color?" and had a blank line for me to fill in. "What is your favorite movie? What is your favorite animal?" I must have answered everything correctly, because the following Sunday he came over to my family pew to ask me to go to John's Pizza with him.

By then my sister was going out with a boy who sat four cubicles down from her at ICS. They had gone to a PACE Bowl together, a *Jeopardy!*-type game in which you compete against ACE kids from across the country. They came back practically engaged. The bowl was in North Carolina, and she got to wear her own clothes while testing her memory of the PACEs on the show. Though she did not win, she came back in love with cool, tall Mitch. Practical, good, marriage-material Mitch. She was starting her senior year in the fall and would be working in base Inventory for the summer, which meant she would have a laser scanner for counting everything, a special base driver's license, and the freedom to roam all over the base. By then, she was also a cheerleader, and even though their outfits had to reach their knees and they were not allowed to jump too high, it meant she hung out with the "cool kids," all five of them. She no longer seemed afraid of even swats. She was that popular. I was not, but I at least had Lorinda.

I went to work on my first day that summer hoping I would get a good manila envelope, one with a "Secret" badge and a work assignment in a remote location. Summer employees had to line up in the gymnasium on their first day, as if registering for college or a conference, to get their manila envelope. When I opened my envelope and pulled out all the paperwork, I sadly found I would be stuck in Building KB-2122, catty-corner to Mike Lab. Payroll. It was a two-story square cinder-block affair with only one entrance, like a payroll fort but with no money. Only pay stubs. It did not even have windows. On top of that, my badge was blue for "Classified" while my sister's was "Secret."

Later that night, I complained about my job assignment to my boyfriend Phil while we were in the desert. There, with the excuse of driving into the desert to watch the stars, we had been slowly inching closer and closer to horizontal in the back of his Toyota Corolla station wagon. He said suddenly, "Think of the base as the Force." He stroked my arm gently. "So even if you're not a Jedi warrior, you're still fighting against Evil." It helped put everything back in perspective. "You have the Force with you." We lived in *Stars Wars* then.

"Fighting against the Evil Empire," I added. In that moment, I felt so proud to have a Han Solo boyfriend, even though he insisted he was Luke Skywalker, that I kissed him a little longer than I should have. In fact, I kept kissing him even as we pulled up to my house, not wanting to go inside.

That was when I felt the yank. In an instant, the passenger door had opened and a hand reached in and grabbed me. I barely had time to see who it was before I realized I was being dragged into my house. I tried to remember how horizontal I had been before that door had opened.

Inside, my dad dropped my arm and left me standing in the living room, shutting his bedroom door more loudly than usual. I stood there, frozen, then wavered on my feet a bit. Nothing like this had ever happened before. I started to cry.

Soon I found myself at the end of my parents' bed, peering into the blackness where they were supposed to be. "We . . . we . . . were . . . just . . . making . . . out," I said between sobs. I did not want to turn on the light to reveal my shame. Nothing moved except my lungs, gasping for air.

Silence. I cried myself into exhaustion and went to bed.

Only years later did my mom tell me the reason for their silence, the source of our miscommunication. They thought "making out" meant the same thing as "making love." They lay there in shock, worried I might be pregnant, not knowing what to say. Not knowing who I was. At my church and school, if girls got pregnant, they simply disappeared and were never spoken of again. I think they went to live with a distant relative to avoid shaming their parents, or something. No one ever explained. Even the pastor's daughter got sent away like that. Maybe my parents were afraid I would be sent away too.

In the morning, we pretended the previous night had not happened. It was better that way. My dad went to the blond wooden cereal cupboard, grabbed a bowl, and sat down on the couch to eat. Each of us mimicked his actions in turn, perching in front of the TV for the morning news, bowls in hand.

But that evening, my dad called Phil and scheduled a "talk."

In the meantime, I had one window in my office in Payroll. It looked out over an inner courtyard, consisting of only a cement slab with a picnic table where no one ever sat. I was filling in for the division head secretary, who had taken ill, though no one told me with what. "Just answer the phone," my new boss said. "You can let the paperwork pile up." Then he shut the door to his adjoining office, as my dad had done with his bedroom door, and was gone. I hardly ever saw him that summer. I can't even remember what he looked like.

All summer long, I answered the phone, "Division Five, Payroll, this is Karen." Then I pushed a button and transferred the call to my boss's line, telling him who was on the phone. Sometimes he asked me to take a message on the special base message pads, with carbon copies for evidence.

Between calls, I studied the payroll forms, which looked pretty simple. Since everyone at the same "GS" level made the same amount of money, it was easy to figure out everyone's salary on the base. People were all labeled GS-1 to GS-15 depending on the number of years they had worked and their yearly evaluations. No one made much money compared with the defense contractors, but I was certainly at the bottom: GS-1. A little better than minimum wage. My dad was a GS-13. I wondered if there were some top secret Gs that we never heard about. Probably. Did they have pay stubs filled out in invisible ink?

Other than that, all there was to do was watch the hallways, which were more like prison walkways over the empty inner courtyard. People's office doors would open and close and a Payroll parade would go by each day while we watched through our courtyard-facing windows. It felt like being back in the cubicle. There were painted tan metal doors opening, step-step-step, then closing behind another mouse hole in this building. Gradually, I noticed that one man's door, across the courtyard, never seemed to open.

I got so used to my solitude that when Larry first walked through my door, it felt like an invasion. He had a spiffy U.S. Marine Corps uniform on. I had only seen marines guarding things like the main gate or base theater, so I could not understand why they needed him in Payroll. He was about fifty years old, with cocoa-brown skin and a close-shaven head, and he even walked like a marine. Perfect.

"You the new girl?" he asked, then introduced himself. "Larry, at your service, ma'am."

No one had ever called me ma'am.

It took a while to get used to Larry's visits, but then I started to enjoy them. He would walk up and plop himself in the room's only other chair, acting as if it were his own living room, even when he had nothing to say. My nervousness never seemed to make him nervous, like it did with other people. He just stayed.

Eventually, I asked him about the closed door across the hallway. "What's up with that guy?" I pointed at his door. "I've never seen him."

"Oh, he's seventy-four years old," he said, as if that explained everything.

"Is he sick?" I asked.

"No, but he puts his head on his desk and sleeps." He laughed. "All day. That's one tired old man." No one said anything for a moment. I was thinking we were lucky to have base jobs because no one would fire that old man, no matter how long he slept. They would find him dead in there first, which was one of the benefits of working in Defense.

Back at home, the "man-to-man talk" with Phil was soon approaching. I had no idea what "man-to-man" meant but was determined to find out, no matter how risky it might be. I hid a cassette player under the china cabinet in the piano room and pushed "record" before Phil was due to arrive. I knew they would talk in there, beyond the white sliding door in the room with only the stereo and upright piano. It held the Bill Gaither, *Mary Poppins*, and *My Fair Lady* records and was the room for listening. The big red button like a piano key went down with a loud *click* before I darted out.

Phil looked nervous but charming as ever when he arrived, as though he might start speaking Russian just to impress my dad. I hoped he wouldn't. Whatever they said, behind that closed door, may well have been Russian to me. I needed to know what the country of men said.

When the sliding door with the indented brass button handle finally opened, I studied their faces. Phil had the same expression he'd had when he'd walked in, smiling and nervous. He shook my father's hand and left without saying a word to me.

"I'm glad that's settled," he said to my dad before he left.

After that, the only problem was retrieving the tape recorder. It was almost dinnertime, when everyone hung around the kitchen, waiting for their TV dinners to come out of the oven, covered in aluminum foil. There was no way I could get in there without being noticed.

When we sat down under the hanging lamp, in a dining room offset from the kitchen, we began our ritual silent dinner. You could hear the silverware scraping on my sister's teeth, and my mother said, "Stop scraping your teeth!" She had braces by then so maybe couldn't help it. I was listening to the clock tick, hoping dinner would soon be over, preparing for the worst.

Click went the tape recorder in the other room as it reached the end of the tape. It was a *click* so loud that we all just looked at each other for a while, before my dad bolted out of his chair like a rocket.

He came back from the piano room with the cassette and, as before, headed to his bedroom and shut the door. "What did you do, Karen?" my mom asked.

"Nothing," I said.

When he did not return, we all knew he was erasing, which you could do only by holding down the red (record) button and black (play) button at the same time. It took over an hour. Meanwhile, the three of us kept eating in straitjacket silence until my mom got up to clean off the table.

My sister sniggered.

At work, I was glad to find out that Larry's stories were much worse than mine. His eyes would always drift back in time like my dad's, but his went to Korea. "Korea?" I said when he first mentioned the place. "I didn't know there was a war there."

"Yeah, most people don't," he replied. "People can only remember one war back, not two. Korea was before Vietnam."

"What did you do there?" I asked.

"I was one of the Chosin Few," he said. I assumed he meant the Chosen Few from the Bible: Jews. Or was it Christians? I could never remember exactly which was which. But it was the People of God.

"Many are called, but few are chosen." I nodded sympathetically, as Christians do when they recognize each other.

"Wha'?" He burst out laughing, slapping his thighs as he bent over and laughed from the belly.

"No, we held the Chosin Reservoir. In Korea!" he sputtered between laughs. "I'm talking about war, girl, not God and Heaven."

"Oh." I blushed, looking down.

"It was more like Hell, I think," he continued. "But a frozen kind. Everything was frozen there—the lake, our food, even our fingers and toes started turning black over time. We were surrounded for over a month. Lost two of them." He picked up his boot and pointed at his toes, as if I could see through his boots.

"I didn't know Korea was cold," I interrupted. I thought it was jungle.

"Boy, that's the coldest I've ever been," he went on in his pleasant, happy lilt that showed he was not from California, where we talked fast and flat. "American planes would fly over to drop napalm on the Chinese, and I'd be jealous!" he joked. "They looked so warm. You'd see them jumping up on fire and running away. And their horses on fire too. Only the ones on fire would move, see. Then we could shoot them."

I tried to picture burning horses, but nothing came.

"A bunch of our men went AWOL, even though there was

nowhere to go except out onto the frozen reservoir. It was either freeze or get shot or burned up."

"So how'd you get out alive?" I asked.

"They called it 'Home by Christmas.'" He chuckled. "Funny name. Don't it make you think of a Bing Crosby song? Operation Home by Christmas. But it worked. We got home, but we lost thirteen hundred on the way."

"That's a lot," I exclaimed.

"Sure was. We had to walk and walk with guys dropping all around. Shot. Stupid pilots even napalmed our two lead companies by mistake. Burned those guys right up. We attached the frozen bodies to ropes, and dragged them out like a sled. Everyone had a body to pull. But that's the motto of the marines, did you know that?"

"No man left behind!" I burst out proudly. This was the first time I had associated war with bodies: burning, frozen, toeless bodies. Bodies like mine, but without toes. Bodies on fire.

That summer, without knowing it, my mother taught me something about war too. We were watching *NBC Nightly News* when "Breaking News" flashed on the screen, and then Tom Brokaw said, "Two U.S. Navy jets, following what is being called an unprovoked attack, knocked down two Libyan fighter planes." Colonel Muammar al-Qaddafi had shot at our F-14 Tomcats while they were in his Gulf of Sidra.

Both Libyan pilots had ejected, and NBC showed an artist's rendition of the attack, since it was not filmed. In the last drawing, a Libyan pilot raised his hand from the ocean, clearly trying not to drown. "There is no sign of the other pilot," Tom Brokaw said seriously. "Only one parachute was deployed."

That was when my mom began to cry.

"What's wrong?" I asked, surprised.

"Those are our missiles," she said. "I don't like to see people die." I stared at her silently, afraid to draw attention to her few tears, worried that this might cause more tears, worried they might never stop.

At work, people started wearing buttons that read "U.S. 2, Libya 0." I heard they sold out at the armaments museum in one day. The mood was overwhelmingly celebratory, but I was left wondering why everyone was happy while my mom was sad. My mom's tears had confused me, each one bringing with it a moment of doubt that made me who I am today. They were tears of sorrow for a real human being, not an enemy. That was the summer I learned from Larry and my mom that war had people in it.

Did Ronald Reagan know that?

Before that, wars were memos or math equations to me. I studied memos in the "to do" file for the unnamed sick woman while waiting for the phone to ring. Nothing on those memos meant much to me, written in cryptic acronyms such as FA-18, Mk 46, and ASROC. Only the format was familiar.

At the top of the letterhead was the navy seal, an American eagle clutching a sword with an anchor instead of a tip, and then the heading to the right: "Department of the Navy, Naval Weapons Center, China Lake." The memos were always cluttered with dashes, slashes, and dots separating acronyms. In the upper right, a line read "IN REPLY REFER TO." Then the abbreviations started. There was "38501/STM:msa" and, beneath that, "Reg 385-872-81." This part I knew: 38501 was the code number; STM was the author, Sam T. Morton; :msa was the typist, Mary Stuart Allen. Then the code number again, the letter number, and the year.

Was there more to war than the way the wind looked on blue graph paper, and the acronyms, and the walks on a Cornish beach following the stars? I was growing up.

———————

"Want to get milk?" my dad said to me one night, after all the drama and erasures. This meant he wanted to walk to Albertsons, two blocks away, in the cool desert evening. With me.

"Sure," I said, hoping for a détente. As we walked, I noticed how similar our gait was, like toy soldiers in our rigidity. I tried to mimic his paces. All those late night walks in Cornwall, navigating through the stars, were being passed from him to me right then.

Then he did his *"Cherrrhem, cherrrhem . . . ,"* clearing his throat. I waited for what came next.

"They're faking the missile tests," he said.

"What tests?" I asked. This was not what I had expected at all. The air was hot and dark, but with enough of a wind to make you feel alive. The Albertsons sign was a lighthouse at the end of a desert walk.

"The missile tests," he replied. "They're editing the tapes so it looks like they hit their targets."

"How can they do that?"

"All you have to do is cut the part where it starts to spin," he replied. "They dumb it down."

"But why would they do that?" But he did not answer.

Then he said quietly, "If they send those missiles to the field, they will hit the wrong targets." It was not within me to understand any of this. All I knew was that my dad was agitated by it, but the weight between us lifted a little when we spoke. I knew not to push him, reveling in the fact that he had confided that much. So he did care. I purred like a cat inside. As we finally entered the store—a beam of bright light blaring out the door into the dark desert—he even turned to me and smiled, if only just a little.

———————

At the bottom of the memos at work was the "Copy to:" line on the left, followed by code numbers lined up flush, one on top of the other. The smallest and most important number was at the top. For instance, 38 (Department) would be on top, then 385 (Division) beneath that, then 38501 (Branch). Next to each number was a line for initials from the code head. As the numbers got smaller, they went all the way up to the top of the navy, but not to the president, who did not have a code. Or if he did, it was a secret one, written in invisible ink. Some memos must have gone to Reagan, who was commander in chief after all. But he was not in the "Copy to:" line.

That summer, the codes were, starting at the bottom: my boss, his boss, the technical director Burrell Hays, then Assistant Secretary of the Navy Melvyn Paisley, and finally Secretary of the Navy John Lehman. Then they stopped. If I had been able to type that summer, I would still only be ":klp" at the bottom. You could not expect anyone to think about me.

I sometimes wished I knew what the memos meant, but I was too low level for anyone to explain. "Need to know." Payroll dealt with all the JOs, meaning we got a glimpse into all the projects happening on the base and how the money was allocated. But I got to read only the unclassified memos, the ones that were lying around any-which-where though signed in the same way as the top secret ones. There were stamps for the people at the top so their hands would not get too tired from having to sign everything. Their secretaries also signed for them.

That summer, there was no way I could have known that second-to-the-top Melvyn Paisley was in a heated battle with third-to-the-top Burrell Hays. To me, Burrell Hays was a picture on the cover of the weekly *Rocketeer*, where he looked squeezably soft, with balding reddish-brown hair, large square wire-rimmed glasses, and the standard base attire of short-sleeved button-down shirt and polyester pants.

His signature was a stamp.

Only later would I discover that Melvyn Paisley, a bar-brawling, red-headed short Irishman who slept with or married all of his secretaries, was taking kickbacks from defense contractors such as Northrop and Lockheed—his own chosen few—in exchange for handing them weapons contracts. Those contractors did not want to waste time on writing bids. They wanted their money *now*. Paisley wanted his money too. He went on lavish ski trips in Europe and commandeered trains for football teams so he could party with them.

Only Hays got in the way. When Hays refused to go along with this corrupt scheme, Paisley tried to drop him from the projects. Eventually, he tried to shut down all of China Lake, thinking government-paid scientists were getting in the way of his plans. Little did I know those feet darting down hallways and code lines wrangling and twisting with each other might be in crisis that summer. It was all top secret. I certainly did not need to know.

Only Reagan needed to know, and he denied he knew anything at all. *People* magazine finally broke the story, writing, "Paisley, four times married, sometimes boasted of his sexual conquests like an ace counting kills. But now the devil-may-care pilot is running into flak. The recently disclosed federal investigation into Pentagon corruption, Operation Ill Wind, threatens to blow Paisley no good. The two-year probe has focused on alleged bribery, bid rigging and conspiracy among Pentagon procurement officials, weapons contractors and the consultants who bring them together." In the end, nineteen corporations were charged with crimes. Paisley went to jail.

But that summer, all those memo wars were just getting started. They would go on for years, while all that mattered to me was getting back in my dad's good graces. It was a short walk to his office, so I went to eat lunch with him one day. When he saw me, he stood up and said, "Ah, time for lunch?" We took our brown lunch sacks, each packed on our own but both with an apple and peanut-butter-and-jelly sandwich, to the cafeteria while Mr. Jarkovich ate at his desk in the days before he disappeared.

Some days, my sister would suddenly burst into my office, smiling with vitality from the desert, a sudden contrast to my gray life. She would talk about counting weapons, computers, and extra chairs, then dart off as fast as she had appeared. After she left, I would go back to my memos or to waiting for the seventy-four-year-old man to come out of his office across the courtyard. (He never did.)

At least I had Larry. It was the summer of Larry and pay chits and making out in the desert and meteor showers and *Star Wars*. Sometimes I thought about going to college but was not quite sure why I would. I did not want to be an engineer and did not know what else there was to do.

Then one day Larry disappeared without even saying goodbye. Marines can do that. I only hoped he was not sent someplace cold or someplace that required all his toes. Sadly, he was not there for my last day at Payroll, when the branch gave me a fancy leather briefcase as a going-away present. It was the executive version, stamped "U.S. Government." "It's for college," my boss said, even though I still had one year left at ICS. I had never had anything so beautiful, so adult, as that briefcase. "Don't tell anyone we gave you this," he continued. "We're not really supposed to give away government supplies."

That briefcase helped me decide to go to college. I became determined to head off into the horizon, ready or not, like all those faulty weapons. Of course, my parents had always expected this; they had worked long and hard *just* so I could do this. But I could have gone to the community college on the hill, as my sister had done. They would have been happy with that, even preferred it. Suddenly I did not want to. I wanted to get out of town one day and experience something new: a *real* city.

Before my dad grabbed me from that car, I had felt perfectly innocent because I *knew* I was not having sex. But then that hand reached in from someplace far away, maybe from pre-Christian dad. I wanted never to feel its touch again. After that evening, even though I was still "with" Phil and he said everything went fine, we grew more distant. Maybe I did not want a Bond man, a China Lake man, after all. But it was more than that. China Lake, which I had thought was the safest place in the world, was starting to feel less safe to me. It was upsetting my mom and dad. Cracks were opening up, which I did not understand, cracks to another world, like my great-grandpa had said. The roots were taking hold. I wanted to see what was through those cracks. Maybe there was something more authentically safe out there, not bombs-and-missiles safe. I had a need to know.

Today, I still sometimes think of Larry, who made me feel safe despite his tales of danger. He made me feel at home with war. He taught me how it felt. Maybe he had come to China Lake to test the ASROC missile, or work with test pilots, or maybe he was sent to Payroll just to rescue me. Only later did it occur to me that while I had been feeling sorry for Larry about Korea, he may have actually been feeling sorry for me. He was one of the Chosin Few, leaving No Man Behind. Even me.

Chapter Fifteen

How to Get a Baptist Wife

As valedictorian of my class of seven, I received a full scholarship to California Baptist College in the fall of 1982. It was only two hours away, in Riverside. So I loaded up the blue Honda Civic that I had saved up for with my Defense earnings. It did not have air-conditioning, so I drove to college late at night, when the road was full of peace and stars and coyote yaps on lonely 395. There was something about that night drive full of animals coming out to breathe that made me feel free, as though my lungs had expanded two sizes. Not Reagan free. A different kind. Better.

I took the road that Caltech scientists once drove out on with rockets on top of mattresses in the backs of their trucks, when they were looking for a better place to blow them up than Pasadena. It was the road that paralleled the aqueduct that carried water more than two hundred miles from Owens Lake north of Ridgecrest to LA. It was the road that burros had once walked down, twenty-mule teams pulling loads of borax. Now it was the road taking me away. I was its new history.

The road had swells and dips that made your stomach fly up in your throat. "Roller-coaster road!" Christine and I would shout from the back seat as we traveled back and forth to Los Angeles. The whole family would laugh growing up along that road. I would watch ravens watching me, perched from the telephone wires that looked like they had no reason being there. There was no one to talk to out there. I knew the ravens knew something that I did not. Under their gaze, I felt a euphoria that did not come from Jesus or passionate kisses. It came from a warm desert night wind that would wake up your mind like it woke up the animals. It was cool enough to breathe. It was alive. It was my road.

I passed Edwards Air Force Base, a boneyard for old planes that looked like skeletons in the dark. That was where the first space shuttle had landed, where Christine and I had waved our little American flags to welcome the astronauts home from outer space like aliens. After that was Mojave railroad junction, the only place to stop for gas, and California City, a failed mini-town I could faintly see off in the distance. Someone had once built it in hopes that it would become the next Los Angeles, but instead it became a giant dust storm—a suburb of nothing. After that was the turn-off to Boron, with its competing Twenty Mule Team and Saxon Aerospace museums, and finally the long climb over scrub-covered Cajon Pass, the threshold between desert peace and LA chaos. Instinctively, I held my breath, though I could not see the wall of smog ahead in the dark. These were the days before catalytic converters, when Los Angeles' air looked like Bangkok's or Shanghai's today. A brown opaque oven.

It was the first time I had seen California Baptist College in the dark, and it was lit up like a movie set with Spanish mission-style red tile roofs, lighted courtyards, palm trees, fountains, and long rolling lawns. So romantic. But when I got to my dorm, the scene was not what I expected. Women in sweats were dancing in the hallway to the blaring Modern English song "I Melt with You." I stood there, suitcases in hand, as the band sang, "The future's open wide." Glancing to my left, I saw a woman on her dorm bed on her back with her legs spread wide open. She jumped up and started laughing. In my room, I saw Cheri, outgoing, vibrant Cheri, with dyed-red spiky hair and a polka-dot miniskirt. She looked like Cyndi Lauper. So this was my new roommate. I put down my suitcases.

"Have you been to Chippendales?" she asked me within the week. I was still in shock that we were allowed to play the radio, especially rock 'n' roll.

"No," I said.

"Like, wow," she replied. "Then we've got to go!"

These Baptists seemed much different from the ones back home. In terms of doctrine, they were the same, but *no one* would drink at my church, let alone go to Chippendales. Dancing was a mortal sin, since Baptists believed it led to lust and premarital sex. Surprisingly, I was allowed to go to my boyfriend's high school prom, where I danced for the first time—other than with Gene Kelly in the living room. ICS did not have a prom with dancing. Instead, we dressed up and drank punch in the gym, chaperoned by our parents. So it would take a while to adjust to college, where so many things were *allowed*.

Then there was the disorienting speed of things, the noncubicle chaos of the campus hallways and classrooms. Here, professors stood in the front of the class talking while the students seemed to copy down what he or she said. I had never seen a "lecture" in my life, only sermons, and we did not take notes at those. I could barely concentrate with everything going on at once—talking, note taking, reading books. Soon a film fell over my eyes. I saw the teacher waving his hands but saying nothing. I felt as if I were watching a movie in fast-forward and wanted to simply sit down and have someone tell me what to do.

Maybe this was why meeting Doug felt like such a relief. He was sitting on the hallway floor, working on registration, while all the chaos rushed around him. He did not even seem to notice, though his Nike-clad feet had tripped more than one passerby. There was something about him that looked so *familiar* and comforting, being able to sit alone in the swirl like that. Not to mention he looked like the Six Million Dollar Man, with chlorine-bleached feathered hair and tanned skin in a bright red muscle shirt.

One day, I pointed him out to Cheri. "Isn't he adorable?" I whispered.

"Oh, I know him," she said, and pinched my arm. "Don't you worry. I'll take care of it." In short order, Doug was at my dorm room window throwing rocks, which was how we all courted at Cal Baptist since men were not allowed in the women's dorms. The goal of all women at CBC seemed to be getting thrown into the Spanish fountain and engaged. Your dorm mates would form a circle around you, holding lighted candles and laughing as you, dripping wet, struggled to get out. It was a ritual.

Soon I was taking long walks around campus with Doug, a swimmer who said he had almost made it to the Olympics but had torn his shoulder instead. He was a "born-again" (not "grown-up-in") Christian like my dad, which made him more intriguing. Even though Doug said this volleyball player was the prettiest girl at Cal Baptist, I thought being second choice was better than being last.

Doug was not self-deprecating like my family or Ronald Reagan, who once said, "No matter what time it is, wake me, even if it's in the middle of a Cabinet meeting." Doug would never admit his foibles. Doug spoke without hesitation. He was a go-getter.

A year later, he asked me to marry him on top of Mount Rubidoux as we were leaning against the giant white cross that dons the top. First he said, "Watch out! They like to get tangled in your hair," and pointed at the bats hovering in the darkness. He said he could whistle to call them to us, then he did, making me cower against his chest while he covered my hair. Then he suddenly said, "Will you marry me?" By then we had already made it to second base on the sultry, smoggy Cal Baptist lawn, while my Bond boyfriend's letters sat on my dorm room desk, unopened.

"Yes," I said. Doug had had sex before he was born-again, so he knew what he was doing, even though he could not do it anymore since he was revirginized. His plan was to buy a ranch outside Grand Junction, Colorado, and take me there with him. My dad had taken us to his yearly aerodynamicists conference at Snowmass, Colorado, so I was ready to pack my bags. I loved Snowmass. No smog.

Though he worked the night shift as a security guard for Chuck E. Cheese's, Doug said he had a "business" that would soon bring in enough money to set him up for life. "Millions," he said, though he was very secretive about it. I assumed he was coming into a trust fund and did not want people to know he was rich. Soon we would not need college or Chuck E. Cheese's. If I did not like Colorado, he said, we could buy a house in St. John. He had already picked out several lavish "dream houses," which he showed me in his *Island* magazines. I thought I could live there. Definitely.

"You'll be barefoot and pregnant before you know it." He smiled and rubbed my belly. This made me uncomfortable, though I did not say so. Babies? I thought I needed only a husband.

Now, for a Southern Baptist man to acquire a wife is quite complicated. First, he has to get the father's permission. Then he has to get the church's permission. Pastoral approval is often more difficult than parental approval, since the rule-setting arm of the church, the Southern Baptist Convention, states that ministers can "unite in marriage only those who are biblically qualified." The husband has to prove he will love his wife the way Christ loves the church. The bride has to prove she will "submit herself graciously." Convention rules are not clear about whether the wife can work outside the home, so the pastor ultimately decides during intensive premarital counseling.

I was not feeling very biblically qualified, having made it to second base. I knew from church that premarital sex was wrong, but I was entering some limbo, an in-between zone that no one talked about. Then there was the problem of Doug's past. In a confessional moment at John's Pizza, I asked my mom what she thought about marrying a man who was not a virgin. "Do you think it could cause problems?"

"Yes," she replied, leaning in to whisper to me. "Your father was not a virgin."

This was more than I wanted to know. I knew about backsliding, or falling back on your pre-Christian ways, and hoped it would not happen to Doug. What if he ran into his ballerina ex-girlfriend and just happened to have sex with her? My friends told me that once you did it with someone, you might do it again if you ever saw that person. "It's just easier," they said. I knew it was harder with virgins like me.

Before long, I was mostly staying at Doug's house, a Levitt-style brown ranch house with a brown lawn under the brown sky of Riverside. Every night, Doug and I would kneel down by the bed and pray for strength against temptation. He led the prayers because, unlike me, he was not shy about praying aloud. It seemed to work because we did not have "sex," which meant that "nothing" really happened, or nothing that counted as sex for a Baptist. I think.

Then he left for Chuck E. Cheese's, propping up a sawed-off shotgun beside my bed before he went. I felt full and warm inside, listening to the LA helicopters chasing bad guys with spotlights. Doug liked to say there were a lot of "scumbags" in the world, quoting Police Chief Daryl Gates, who spoke of the "deadly plague invading our shores," the Crips and the Bloods and drugs and Communists. He even asked for volunteers to help fight them all. Reagan had also declared a "war on drugs" and we were to be his soldiers.

Doug and I signed up as volunteers, taking a police training course in preparation to defend the city when the plague reached us. The police teacher put a drop of mace beneath our eyes so we would know what to expect; he taught us how to handcuff and spray people. Gates also created SWAT teams and a "Red Squad" to infiltrate Communists. He believed casual drug users should be shot for "treason," so Doug taught me how to shoot too. We shot at quail in the foothills, which were too fast for our handguns, and at human figures at the range with .44s and .357s. In the backyard, we shot .22s.

Doug had his own police-issue handcuffs and also took ninja certification classes at an army base in San Diego on the weekends. So our bedroom was full of handcuffs, nunchakus, ninja stars, and guns. He liked to practice with them all, twirling his nunchaku naked by the bed or throwing knife-edged ninja stars into the walls. He also liked to practice with his handcuffs on me, and they felt so secure.

The only problem was Doug's business. I noticed that if he was asked about it, sometimes he would say he was in "real estate" and other times that he was "coming into money." If not for the danger-filled nights and fun-filled days lying out in the foothills naked for all-over tans, I might have been more concerned. But Doug knew how to give a good massage with his Hawaiian Style Coconut Tanning Oil and could find more places to massage than I even knew existed. He said a lifeguard needed to know how to give a good massage, and he had been a lifeguard in high school.

So I was already wearing a ring when Doug finally phoned my dad, and we headed home to get my father's approval. I still had not told my ex-boyfriend Phil and hoped he would not see us there.

Doug took my dad into the same room where my dad and Phil had talked about sex. But this time, Doug came out beaming. I knew then that the answer was yes. The hitch came later, when Doug discovered my father's little black book, which sat as it always did on the built-in oak wood divider bookcase with colonial-style banisters at the top that kept the living room and dining room apart. When Doug spotted the book, he took it and would not give it back.

"What are you doing?" I tried to grab it as he flipped through the pages.

"Who are all these people?" he asked.

"Mom and Dad's friends. People they work with. I don't know." I lunged forward as he tucked it behind his back. He loved games like this.

"Let me handle this," he said, and moved out of my reach.

The next day, while my parents were at work, Doug started making phone calls to people from my church. I was mortified, especially since he said he wanted to talk "business." Before I knew it, we had been invited to Mr. Porter's house for coffee and cake. Mr. Porter was the test and evaluation director for the whole base by then, after he had built the Shrike missile and run the HARM program, the "High-Speed Anti-Radiation Missile." Mr. Porter liked to call it the "Happy Armageddon Rabbit Masher." He was also a deacon at church, like my dad, and so they did deacon things together, such as carrying the offering trays and making the church rules. My mom would bristle that she could not be one. No women. I knew that since Mr. Porter was more important than my dad on the base, my dad would not approve of us asking them to feed us coffee and cake for no good reason. But what could I do?

On the ten-mile drive to their pistachio and horse farm in the desert, I shrank back in the front seat, arms crossed. "What are we even doing?" I asked, trying to pout my way into changing his mind while thinking about jumping out of the car.

Doug slapped me on the thigh and said, "Cheer up. We're celebrating our engagement with your friends. We have an announcement, right?" But something in me did not trust him.

Mrs. Porter, a demure thin woman with coiffed hair, greeted us at the door with a simple smile and "Hello." Behind her smile, however,

I thought I saw suspicion. Walking in, I saw that she had set out her good Royal Doulton plates and the same kind of flowery teacups that my mom had. "I baked a cake for us." She suddenly beamed. "Congratulations, Karen!" I sighed, and my shoulders slumped a little.

Though the property was large, with a horse corral outside, the house itself was a simple ranch like ours. The dining table, the place settings, and the cake all looked familiar and safe. Like a church picnic, with Mr. Porter serving cake instead of communion wafers. But when the cake was done, Doug pulled out a piece of paper and started drawing circles. My back stiffened slightly. "Let me show you something, sir," he said to Mr. Porter, who was still chuckling at his last desert joke. "Tell me where you would live if you could live anywhere in the world." He looked ready to write it down in one of the circles.

Mr. Porter hesitated. "Actually, we're pretty happy here."

"Okay, that's fine, sir," Doug said, not moving his pen. "So then, what would your dream house be if you could have any kind of house?"

Mr. Porter leaned back against his chair and looked around the room as if he were wondering what was wrong with it. "Actually, I really like this house," he replied.

Doug was caught off guard, thinking everyone had a "dream house."

"Well, let me tell you, sir," he continued, "the house I'm going to build is on St. John in the Caribbean. I've already picked out the plans and now am looking for the right architect." Then he wrote "St. John" in one of the circles, switching tactics.

"Well, that's lovely for you!" Mrs. Porter said brightly. I proudly grabbed Doug's arm to signify that I would be going with him.

"How would you like to live a life like that, where you don't have to worry about money?" Doug continued. I dropped his arm. It was impolite to talk about money.

"You know, we're not too worried about money," Mr. Porter replied. "My job—"

Doug reached across the table and grabbed Mr. Porter's hand. "Sir, your job . . . your *job* has obviously made you stop dreaming. I want you to start dreaming again. Think of a life without that job, think of what you would do. . . ."

Mr. Porter pulled away his hand. "Are you trying to sell something?" he asked.

"Just a dream," Doug said, "just a dream."

When my parents found out Doug had tried to sell Amway to Mr. and Mrs. Porter, they were mortified. "You were selling them *soap*?" my mom asked incredulously.

"It's a pyramid scheme," my dad said. "They get one person in, then take a cut of what he sells, and so on down the line." It sounded like Police Chief Gates talking about drug dealers on TV. "You should have told us you were coming here to sell Amway."

"I, I . . . we weren't," I stuttered.

On the way back to Riverside, Doug said, "Your mother is the most negative person I've ever met."

Before that day, I thought I was lucky not to be marrying into the military like my sister, whose soon-to-be husband, Mitch, had joined the ROTC as soon as he could. He was studying to become an engineer, commuting to college in San Bernardino, and ultimately planning to work at China Lake. He was smart and Fred Astaire tall but had vitiligo on his face, white splotches that left him lacking in confidence and looking down all the time.

They were high school sweethearts, destined for each other like an arranged marriage. Good families, same church, same ideals, same career plans. I could predict the rest of their lives. Doug had been my ticket out of that sameness, the trap of Ridgecrest, but now he had ripped up the ticket. There was no trust fund, only soap, and now he said he wanted me to sell it for him. *It is easier for a camel to go through the eye of the needle than for a rich person to enter the Kingdom of God*, I kept thinking. *What had I done?* Dream houses? The Department of Defense, which we called the DoD, always taught me to be frugal and nonmaterialistic like Jesus or my Depression-era parents. We were not supposed to waste taxpayer money. Amway wanted the opposite. What was I supposed to do now?

I already had the ring.

Like every teenage couple that year, Doug and I thought we were in Diana Ross's "Endless Love." Star-crossed lovers, living in sin, virgin with nonvirgin. In reality, we were on our way to becoming Queen's "Another One Bites the Dust." Perhaps it was fitting that, at the end of my freshman year, my dorm mates had given me the Most Gullible Award, a framed certificate with a ditzy-looking lion lounging by a pool with a cocktail in the background. I was supposed to be that lion. Only now did I feel I deserved it. I had thought that life would be more authentic, more certain, outside the socially engineered world of China Lake and ICS. I had thought I was finally outside the cage and in the "real" world, but I had merely run straight into another cult. I had felt afloat outside of China Lake, swimming in a sea of senses, and had latched on to a lifeguard to keep me from drowning.

But now he was pulling me down too.

Chapter Sixteen

"Universities Teach Poverty"

Before I knew that Doug was in Amway, I had been ready to give up everything and follow him. I even failed my final exam in sophomore sociology because, as Doug always said, "universities teach poverty." I did not realize that this was an Amway line. The professor had asked a question about Karl Marx, whom I had refused to read. I knew Marx taught poverty, or communism. He did not have a dream, or money, like Doug. They were trying to brainwash me. "How do you tell a communist?" Reagan had said. "Well, it's someone who reads Marx and Lenin." Unwilling to succumb to the teachings of the Evil Empire, I simply handed my exam to my professor on the way out the door. I told everyone I was moving to Colorado. Who needed school? I believed in trickle-down, in Reagan.

Doug approved. "Right is right," he said.

At Doug's recommendation, I had already gone to work at a Christian dude ranch in Colorado at the end of my freshman year. There, I was supposed to learn how to co-manage the same kind of

ranch with Doug outside Grand Junction. That was his dream. I told
the dude ranch owner's wife I was there only to learn how to run a
ranch. I would soon be building one, I said, with my fiancé in the
Uncompahgre National Forest. "It's going to be a million acres," I
announced. "What do you recommend I learn first?"

"Well, you need a lot of money first," she said, looking at me oddly.

"That's okay," I replied. "My boyfriend is rich."

They assigned me to cleaning the toilets.

Now what was I supposed to do? Amway had sabotaged my college career. I had a D in sociology and so had lost my scholarship for
the following year. Nevertheless, I stayed with Doug that last semester of my sophomore year and tried to make Amway, and my life,
work. I was already engaged, and Amway sounded like "trickle-
down" to me. Reagan even spoke at Amway rallies. So I got a job at
Ben & Jerry's scooping ice cream while I tried to learn "the business"
and finish the school year.

Ben & Jerry's was my back-up plan.

Doug immediately inundated me with "motivational tapes" to listen to on the freeway. "You really have to listen to them all the time
for them to work," he explained. I promised I would. On one of them,
Amway legend Bill Britt said that all you had to do was "work the
numbers" to succeed. In his preacher's voice, he explained, "I simply
showed the plan to twelve hundred people. Nine hundred said 'No,'
and three hundred signed up. Out of those three hundred, only
eighty-five did anything at all. Out of those eighty-five, only thirty-
five were serious, and out of those thirty-five, eleven made me a
millionaire."

But as much as I listened, I only got to the number two: my parents bought soap.

I only tried to sell "the business" once, in Ridgecrest, where Lorinda
and a couple of my sister's friends listened politely, sitting on card table
chairs in the piano room. They stared at me as if I were a cute poodle

performing tricks. Nevertheless, I did my best to draw circles on
Doug's $200 whiteboard, which you had to buy from Amway. As with
Mr. Porter, no one seemed to have a dream, so I started describing my
"dream house"—a two-story house with floor-to-ceiling windows on
a lake in the Uncompahgre. It would have sixteen rooms. My mom
interrupted. "A house that big would be very hard to clean," she said.
"Are you sure you want one that big?"

I ignored her, stating that I would also have a Lamborghini. My
mom turned to my dad and said loudly, "No point spending a lot of
money on a car if the gas mileage is no good. Remember those gas
lines ten years ago?"

"I can hear you, Mom!" I complained.

In the end, no one signed up besides my parents, and only because
they felt sorry for me. I knew from the motivational tapes that you
had to "believe" or it would not work, and even I did not believe what
I was saying. So I quit.

Soon after that, I found out that Doug had only one person
"under" him, his roommate, Harold, who was from North Dakota
and looked like a farm boy in a dirty magazine. He wanted to be a
model or movie star so was always worried about whether his nose
was too big or too small rather than about his grades at Cal Baptist.
He also thought his hair was too curly and his eyes were too wide, so
to compensate, he left his eyes uncovered in the tanning booth to be
sure his eyelids got tanned. We had to take him to the emergency
room when his eyes started bleeding in the middle of the night.

Though we were all the same age, Doug and I were like his parents, as well as his Amway "sponsors." When it seemed clear that I
was a failure at selling Amway, Doug gave me the job of "motivating"
Harold instead, though I was hardly motivated once I found out there
were no houses in St. John or ranches in Colorado. Mostly, Harold
and I sat on the couch and watched TV. We were the Amway de-
fectors.

One day, Harold sat down next to me, leaned close, and whispered, "You know, you don't have to get married if you don't want to." I looked down at my hands, which began to fidget until I could not control them. I burst out in tears, then sobs, everything collapsing into emptiness.

"How did I get here?" I sputtered. "How, how, how?"

Gently, Harold put his arm around me, pulling me close and leaning his head on mine until, as if suddenly changing his mind, he jumped up off the couch and ran to the kitchen. "I know the cure for this!" he said when he came back, carrying an apple wine cooler like a precious jewel. It twinkled a lovely light greenish blue in the sunlight. I had never tasted alcohol before.

"Now, you have to drink it really fast for it to work," he explained. I followed his instructions and soon started to feel warm and relaxed. In the background, Marvin Gaye's "Sexual Healing" was playing on the radio. I giggled, singing along, "Baby, I'm hot just like a bla bla bla." I did not know all the words.

"I want sexual healing," we both shouted at the chorus. Then Harold stood up, pulling me up to dance, which he was good at because he practiced in front of his mirror. Baptists were not allowed to dance, drink, listen to rock music, or have sex. Yet here I was, breaking the first three rules all at once.

"I can't dance!" I laughed, pulling back.

"Just hold on to me," he insisted, and drew me into the living room, closer to the music. "We'll just slow dance." So I stood up next to him and swayed, noticing how tall he was—more than six feet, taller than Doug.

"Sexual healing, baby," he sang quietly. Suddenly, I realized I did not want to give up these three things—the rules I had just broken—in order to be "barefoot and pregnant."

"I'm marrying a cop," I whispered. "I'm going to have little cop children."

Harold laughed and leaned close. "You don't have to get married," he whispered in my ear. It felt like an opioid to me, as though we were on the verge of a mutiny, losing the wars on drugs. We both knew the trouble this could cause yet stood there with Harold's legs against mine, pushing rhythmically, pulling me closer. I closed my eyes, giddy with the wine cooler and his soft silk shirt.

We knew Doug would be gone all night.

The next day, Doug must have known something was wrong because he insisted we go to an Amway rally. Harold looked reluctant. "Uh, see, Doug," he almost stuttered, "I have an audition in Hollywood this weekend." He never had auditions. Doug looked suspicious, then brightened up.

"Looks like it's just you and me, babe," he said, kissing me on the cheek. I knew that according to Amway, you were supposed to go to a rally every three months to stay motivated.

This particular one was held in a stadium-sized auditorium with an American flag–covered table on the stage. Amway superstar Dexter Yager's wife took the stage first to introduce her husband. "When I look at him, I see Jesus," Birdie said with a gleaming face. "I want you to listen to him—I know that you'll see Jesus too." People cheered as Dex walked in, while I wondered how Birdie could get away with saying such a thing when the Beatles could not. All my mother ever remembered about them was that they said they were more popular than Jesus. Dex looked like a Harley rider or Hells Angel to me, with a long graying beard, receding hairline, beer belly, and American flag baseball cap.

I did not see Jesus.

Dex was an "upline," which meant he was above us in Amway. Only Amway founder Richard "Dick" DeVos was higher than Dex Yager. Dick was one of the wealthiest men in America, a fortune he would pass on to his son, Dick, Jr. His daughter-in-law, Betsy DeVos, would one day become U.S. Secretary of Education and push for funding schools that use Accelerated Christian Education in order to, as she said, "advance God's Kingdom."

On stage, Birdie was saying that being loyal to your upline was like being loyal to your husband, your children, or God. She seemed sure that Jesus was right in that room, but all I could think about at that moment was Marvin Gaye.

"Are you guys tired?" Dex yelled. "Do you want to give up, or are you going to get up? Get up! Get up!"

"Let's make love tonight," I sang in a whisper as the crowd of ten thousand cheered, stamping their feet on the bleachers in unison.

"Read the story of Moses," Dex continued. "God kept saying, 'You're my man, pick up the rod.' And Moses kept saying, 'I can't, I can't, I can't.' I'm telling you today to pick up the rod. Your rod is a Magic Marker . . . and you're gonna start leading them people into the Promised Land." He was talking about drawing circles, but I wondered if our whole board would ever get covered in circles. We only had Harold, whom I had just kissed, making the circles a mess.

Dex switched to talking about Jesus, calling him the very first Amway salesman. *What about Moses?* I thought. I knew enough about metaphors by then to know that they were mixing them.

"There's one, two thousand years ago, that sponsored twelve," Dex said. "The first one recorded in the history of the world. Someone said, 'I don't want to hear that.' Well, get a job. You won't hear it. Be broke, you don't need to hear it. He sponsored twelve, he discipled twelve. Isn't that what our business is really all about?" People stood and lifted their hands, grabbing a neighbor's hand above their heads. Reluctantly, I took the hand next to mine. My hand swayed, crushed inside another, in the air.

"O Lord," Dex was praying, "let us now renew our commitment to You, to serve the way that we know is Right."

"Amen, amen," people in the crowd chanted, becoming more excited.

I could not help thinking of Harold grinding up against me. Doug was straight and commanding and did not believe in dancing. Harold moved in a way that Doug never could, his whole body yielded to mine. His right leg would gently pull back when mine came forward. His arms would pull me closer only if I had moved into him. Every movement I made seemed to make his body move too.

"And Right is Right, we know that, Lord. Remember, that's how we vote!"

"*Amen!*" The crowed began whistling and "woo-hoo-ing." Someone close to me began to cry. I glared at Doug, wanting this to end, but sometimes these meetings went until three in the morning.

There were rumors that Ronald Reagan would be at this rally, since he had been at other Amway rallies during his campaign for governor. I waited for him to come out, wondering what he would say. Sometimes the Amway men sounded a bit like him. They said things like "A hippie is someone who looks like Tarzan, walks like Jane, and smells like Cheetah." (Reagan said that.) Or "It's easy for gals to be submissive to a man that's a man, not a wimp and a whiner." (Amway said that.) Everyone in Amway thought Reagan was God, but Amway was having the inverse effect on me.

It was making me doubt Reagan.

"We come forward now to renew our commitment to building our families, our country, and our business as a place to celebrate You. We thank You for the freedom to do so," Dex concluded right when Dick DeVos stepped out on the stage. People started screaming. Dick was a Diamond, above even Emeralds and Opals in the Amway chart of wealth. Diamond meant millions, maybe even billions. A band started playing quietly at the back of the stage as Dick took the mike, urging us to come forward. His wife sat proudly behind him, beaming like Jesus.

What was I supposed to confess this time? That I was always broke, running out of gas, and having to hitchhike on the LA freeways? With the Zodiac Killer around? Should I confess that Cheri, Harold, and I had spun out on the freeway just last week, stoned on peach schnapps? Once we realized we were not dead, we got out of the car, knelt in a circle, and prayed. Then we drove on to the male strip club.

I was done confessing.

"Get up, get up, get up, get up," Dex was saying. At least half the crowd had gone forward while "Sexual Healing" was still playing in my head. Then Doug grabbed my arm and yanked me down the aisle to renew our faith. There were too many men yanking my arms.

I decided I was done.

I told Doug on a hot day in the burned-up backyard as we stood next to Harold's archery target. "I could keep the ring and wear it on the other hand, as a sign of friendship. To remember us," I suggested. But I knew he needed the money as much as I did. By then, Harold had skipped out for nonpayment of his rent but had mysteriously left his archery target behind. He had once wrapped his arms around me in front of that target, teaching me how to aim a crossbow. Now he was afraid of Doug and his guns, so the archery target sat there, color upon color inside one another. I wanted to be anywhere but here.

"No, the woman has to give it back if she does the breaking up," Doug replied. Doug always knew the rules. We both were staring at that golden ring as if we were in some living tableau where neither of us could move. Trapped by the heat and sparkle of that gold, neither of us wanted to turn away to a cold and uncertain future.

I had nowhere to go but back to China Lake.

Chapter Seventeen

The Salt Wells Flood

I started work at the Salt Wells Propulsion Laboratory as a Clerk II in the summer after my sophomore year. This time, I thought I might stay forever. I tried to repair the damage from the bombs I had thrown when I left Ridgecrest, particularly with my old boyfriend, Phil. Instead, I found myself sitting in his brown Toyota Corolla while, one by one, he threw all the letters I had written to him back in my face. My dating prospects did not look good. At least my parents were surprisingly unruffled by my failed engagement. "It's for the best," my mom said. "I always thought Doug acted like a used-car salesman." I was no closer to knowing what "my destiny" was but was not sure I wanted to get married anymore and definitely did not want to be pregnant. I thought I would try to make a living in the DoD.

At least I liked Salt Wells, built for the atom bomb, though now more famous for its bobcat kittens. Every summer, a mommy bobcat would plop her kittens in a tree near the entrance to my building. Apparently, the facility's age and isolation guaranteed the best and only cottonwood trees around. The kittens would mew at us every morning as we walked through the front door. At lunchtime, they made soft noises while they slept, like babies breathing. After work, when the whole family was waking up, we would snap photos for the base-wide contest. If we won, our photograph would be printed in a book given to retirees along with a framed picture of bighorn sheep with F-16s flying behind. We watched their kitten fur blowing in the wind while their little perplexed faces stared down at us. Were we friend or foe?

The whole facility had been built in less than four months during World War II and was located thirty miles from Mike Lab in case of a Big Explosion. The first bombs were packed in boxes marked "One Kit, Bomb Assembly." They included everything from fuses to Quonset huts to steel-frame buildings complete with air-conditioning. The kits were then sent to Iwo Jima to build the bombs for Nagasaki and Hiroshima. It was a portable nuclear bomb town. We made the bomb boxes, but not the uranium or plutonium.

After those bombs were dropped, Salt Wells switched to making missile warheads, which are the explosives packed into the missile nose, called a "payload." Sometimes missiles were packed with ammo and then taken to be blown up in the rocket sled, which looked like a roller-coaster rail laid out flat for miles across the desert. It was called SNORT, short for Supersonic Naval Ordnance Research Track, and could launch missiles at Mach 6. Other times they were shot from airplanes or rocket launchers.

We called the explosives "insensitive munitions," not because they were insensitive to the people they killed—though they were that too—but to the heat and bullets that might threaten them. When missiles were "sensitive," you could blow up a navy warship simply by hitting it with sniper fire. All the missiles on board would combust from that one bullet. Now, there were plenty of other ways you could blow yourself up at Salt Wells, but not that one.

Unlike the folks at Payroll, who handled only paperwork and pay stubs, the people at Salt Wells had to be comfortable handling explosives. Every code on the base has its own microculture because of differences like this. Salt Wells felt like an auto repair shop, where people loaded explosives like regular union laborers and walked around with dynamite residue on their hands. I hated that my desk was crammed in the middle of a room that looked like a mechanic's lobby, but I adapted. The secretary next to me, Sally, was big and loud, wore overalls every day, and used any excuse to smoke outside with the guys. Throughout the day, men and women would wander through the room with soot on their faces, wearing giant padded gloves and machine shop clothes.

Yet secretly, every person in that shop was waiting for lunch. That was when they could watch the kittens from the picnic tables in front of the building. Apparently, the mom stashed them up there to keep them safe from predators while she hunted, since they were too little to survive on their own. She must have thought it a miracle to find those trees so far from anywhere, a blessing from the atom bomb. During the day, she slept up there, too, while we watched her kittens for her. If a wobbly kitten fell to the ground while she slept, it could wander away and get picked off by a great horned owl or coyote. So we were the de facto babysitters while mom got her rest. Smoking reached near epidemic levels, so important was it to keep an eye on those kittens. An injured kitten could make an explosives man cry.

Once, a kitten did fall out of the tree during the night when no one was there. In the morning, we found it scratching at the base of the tree, meowing in desperation to get back to its siblings. An RDX specialist ran for a ladder as if his feet were on fire, then ever so gently lifted it back into place. He sighed afterward and shook his head. "What if we hadn't been here?" he asked no one in particular.

A buddy patted him on the back and said, "It's okay. We were."

At Salt Wells, the bobcats were friendly and the munitions "insensitive." The only danger we took seriously was flash floods. Salt Wells had flooded the previous year, knocking out the Melt Cast Explosives Loading Facility with its giant tubs for melting TNT or RDX (research department explosive). Employees had to drop everything and dig the facility out of the mud. What bothered them most was that a wall of debris and water had broken through a chicken-wire fence, which would have killed them if it had happened during the day. Nevertheless, having survived, people seemed to think a big flood would not happen again.

But disasters are not like vaccinations.

One day, Sally looked out the window and noticed a storm coming. We all went outside to watch. In the desert, you can see a storm coming for miles and gauge its power from the darkness of the clouds. First, it will dance on the hills, changing the scenery in dramatic shifts from light to shadow while pouring rain in the distance. Next, it will hit you with a *boom* as lightning branches out across the sky. For me, there is nothing more glamorous than a desert storm. But on that day, something went wrong with the formula, the usual slow approach of thunderclouds from the west.

Someone pointed to the east and said, "Hey, check it out. The clouds are coming from both directions."

"That's, like, totally weird," I said, having picked up Cheri's dialect. None of us knew what was in the east, so oriented to the west were we. A fierce wind kicked in and the sky smelled of creosote bushes, that musky electric smell, which meant it was raining nearby.

When lightning cracked too close, we hurried inside. There, peering out the glass doors, people began to fret about the kittens. They did not seem to know to get out of that tree.

"Get down!" I heard someone whisper.

"Do you think they're okay up there?" the RDX specialist asked.

No one answered. Then my phone rang.

"Salt Wells, this is Karen," I said.

"Karen, are you okay? You need to head home—" My dad was talking fast. "Did you get the announcement out there?"

"What announcement? It just started raining!" I protested. My dad was a worrywart.

"Stop worrying about me, Dad," I said firmly. He drove me crazy.

"Karen, the streets are running with water down here," he insisted. "Hurry."

Minutes later, my boss said the same thing. "Remember last year," he warned. "If the road washes out, they'll have to helicopter us out. Be careful."

We all started running out into the rain, which felt like hailstones on my back. I tried to recall my desert safety training, from both school and work. Stay in your car, which is safe in a lightning storm as long as you do not touch the metal. Lie down in a ditch if you are stuck outside. Watch out for flash floods. In the desert more people die from floods than heat. A two-inch flash flood can flip your car in seconds and trap you inside. An electricity pole can fall in the water and fry your brains. While a rattlesnake will normally strike only if you happen to step on it, a rattlesnake in floodwater is adrift and frightened like you.

I jumped in my car and sped away, soon realizing I had forgotten to say goodbye to the bobcats. Later, I would come to regret this, but now the wind was threatening to flip the car. I could barely see out the windshield through the downpour, which fell like buckets of paint, obscuring everything.

The illogic of driving to the bottom of a valley was not lost on me. Nor was the irony of naming the town Ridge*crest*. I still like Crumville better. The town apparently got its new name because someone had visited Ridgecrest, North Carolina, and liked it there. They wanted a town like that, even though it was located at the opposite of a crest. The base was built on the valley floor because the navy did not know about desert flash floods when they picked this spot to settle. They simply needed a long enough, flat enough spot for a B-29 to take off with an atom bomb weighing ten thousand pounds.

No one really thought they would stay.

As I passed the turn to Echo Range, I contemplated finding Mitch, who had a Jeep with an elevated intake valve that would not stall in a flood. He was supposed to be working out there that day. I hesitated at that lonely desert intersection, not knowing if I could even get on the range. With boulders now washing over the road, I stepped on the gas.

At the time, it never occurred to me then that I might be leaving Mitch stranded and not the other way around. My family was scattered across the whole base that day, miles from one another. My mom was at Area E, my dad at Mike Lab, my brother-in-law at Echo Range, and my sister God knows where. All I could do was hope the pieces would find a way to fit back together somehow, safely.

As I approached the valley floor, the water began to slow and pool into a giant lake, though it was not as deep as I had feared, not enough to stall the engine. So I drove into it until, turning the corner to our house, I was relieved to see that only our lawn was flooded. I called my sister's house first, which was easier than getting someone on the base with all its extensions, party lines, and operators.

"Oh, good, you're home!" I said at the sound of her voice. She had been married almost a year and was living in a ranch house much like my mom and dad's, except with fewer trinkets.

"Is Mitch there?" I asked.

"No, but he's on his way."

Next, I called my mom, but the phone went dead while it was ringing. I could not reach my dad, either, and was afraid he would start walking home through the napalm-filled floodwaters, trying to beat his old time while avoiding the swirling snakes and scorpions. I called my sister back and soon we were both talking that old familiar twin-talk, our voices singing in perfect harmony: hers soprano and mine the alto. It helped to pass the waiting time as the water slowly crept into the house like a thief.

Finally, Mitch showed up. Christine put down the phone but forgot to hang up. I heard Mitch say, "The Jeep went off the road into the water and—"

"You drove through a flash flood? You idiot!"

She was right to be mad. He had ignored our desert survival training.

"But the Jeep didn't roll," he said defensively, "and I got a ride home. I'll deal with the Jeep tomorrow."

"How many times have we been told *never* to cross a flash flood? Huh, Mitch, how many?" she shouted. "Were you not listening?" I felt a little bit glad to not be married. If I'd almost died, no one would have been there to yell at me afterward, which was something.

I hung up the phone and tried my mom's office again. Still dead. I remembered how crazy the phones were when we first moved to China Lake. When you picked up the phone, there might be people chatting on the line, and you could either wait for them to hang up or try to outshout them. Now, in a crisis, the phones were useless. *What if we got nuked now?* I thought.

Then I heard the garage door open.

Mom walked in, the carpet squishing where she stepped. "Oh no!" she said, looking down at her feet. No one had flood insurance. It was the desert, right? So new carpeting was out. Instead, people shared shop vacs to suck the water out of their houses.

"Where's Dad?" I asked.

"He's right behind me," she said, looking relieved to find me there. "The main gate was flooded," she explained. "So they told us to stay at work."

"You mean you were trapped out there?"

"Some tried to get out, but their engines stalled. There wasn't much I could do," she said. "When I heard Mike Lab was flooding, I decided to at least get your dad. I found him in a trailer behind Mike Lab, sitting on top of a desk. The simulations lab." She took him back to her office, where they waited for the floodwaters to recede at the gate. It took almost two hours, and then the sun burst out like nothing had happened.

"You should have seen the water pouring into Mike Lab." My dad walked in and said. "I left when the chairs started floating in the hallway. It's a good thing your mom knew where to look for me."

Later, when I saw the photos of water pouring through the front doors of Mike Lab, rushing past all the security checkpoints, it seemed miraculous that my mom and dad had walked through the force of that water. They could have been swept off their feet and died. But my mom would not let my dad go without her, would not let him be towed into that dark swirl all alone. Past the front doors, the water had headed straight for the basement, pouring like a waterfall down the steps to where all the base's historical records were kept. Later, the base would try to freeze-dry the papers to salvage them, which didn't really work.

The flood also stirred up toxic things that were meant to remain buried, like depleted uranium out at Salt Wells, as well as TNT, RDX, and chloroform. The navy still blows up or burns tens of thousands of pounds of hazardous waste every year at Burro Wash, since it is both too dangerous and too secret to send off the base. We were stuck with it. There is also a large area on China Lake's map labeled "Open Air Biodegradable Hazardous Waste Experimental Area." I assume it translates, "Where the Navy Dumps Shit on the Ground and Hopes it Disappears." Maybe the navy scatters its experimental metal-eating microbes over the hazardous waste there. Hopefully those microbes do not blow away and eat us instead.

At Salt Wells, I learned a whole new set of acronyms: RDX, CFC, TNT, HMX, PBXC-129, and more. I never once considered that all those acronyms might flow down the mountain into our house. Yet in a place where things are constantly spilled, mixed, and blown up, it made sense that they had to go somewhere. After the flood, the Environmental Protection Agency got involved and ultimately declared Salt Wells a Superfund site in 1994, claiming the chance of "inhaling explosives" and thus contracting cancer was too high for anyone to work there. The EPA said it was dangerous to touch the dirt or to drink the well water, which was laced with chloroform. I wondered if your lungs could explode from inhaling explosives.

After the "Great Flood" of 1984, base employees were asked to volunteer as "muckrakers" to dig out the base so we could focus on defending the country again. Mitch volunteered and dug around in all those toxins. Of course, no one really knew the dangers at the time. As for me, after shoveling horse poop the summer before, there was no way I was going to pick up a shovel.

I took it as a sign instead. The desert did not want me there.

Reporters at the *Rocketeer* tried to make sense of what had happened. One of them wrote, "The Aug. 15 flood of Michelson Laboratory has raised a number of questions such as 'Why was the laboratory placed on a floodplain?'" Indeed. He explained the navy's reasoning: "The possibility of flooding at China Lake was not a consideration in siting the Naval Ordnance Test Station in January 1944. . . .The primary concern of that time was winning a war by the quickest means possible."

I heard the bobcat tree survived, which meant the kittens probably kept coming back, with no one to tell them they were inhaling explosives. No one to tell them they should leave. Unlike the kittens, I knew to go. I found I actually missed the habit of entertaining myself with books—as long as it was not Marx. This time, I chose a college for the scenery. It had to be a Christian one, of course, but also one with a view. So I left for Westmont College, in Montecito, four hours away. They had forgiven my D and even given me a partial scholarship. I fled the way I wished those bobcat kittens could.

PART THREE

Dynamic Instability

Missile Guidebook:
Notice its faults, such as how often it fails to fire.
Tell this to everyone. This will take away some of
its power, since a missile does not want to be
shamed.

Chapter Eighteen

Astral Projection

I would drive the narrow, windy roads of Montecito with the ocean in my driver's-side window, whizzing through junglelike foliage that smelled of eucalyptus, down to the waterfront city of Santa Barbara. Someone said Michael Jackson kept giraffes in his yard in Montecito, but most of the movie stars' houses were in well-guarded compounds with high walls and trees blocking the view, so it was hard to say. I knew that Oprah Winfrey lived next to campus. I drove by her house every day.

I was a poor person living in a rich man's world.

In the coffee shops lining Santa Barbara's State Street, people talked about "astral projection," which means catapulting yourself into the stars to meet aliens. Since I still felt that edge of invisibility, I gleaned most of my information from eavesdropping. In fact, that was primarily how I learned to behave in each new world I encountered: eavesdropping and mimicry. I should have been a spy. If you sat still and listened, I found, you could learn most anything. At the

State Street Bookstore, a wall was labeled "New Age Books" and dedicated to Zen, Wicca, *Jonathan Livingston Seagull*, and astral projection. It seemed everyone wanted to get out of there, if only in their own minds. I could relate to that.

Westmont was not at all like Cal Baptist, though the doctrine was nearly the same. At Westmont, trust fund kids went sailing on weekends, carried their parents' credit cards, and dined at the finest restaurants. The campus library lawn looked out over a lush, forested sea of celebrity estates, which took up whole blocks and ended abruptly at the Pacific Ocean. If not for the sea, it could have been the Amazon. Since the estates were walled in, gated, and overgrown, you never saw the celebrities inside. They came and went in cars with tinted windows. Westmont's campus used to be one of these estates until a rich old lady dreamed of a Christian college among the celebrities.

At Westmont, students signed up for spring missions to Mexico to help the poor and fall semester trips to Europe for shopping. (I did both.) Tuition was as high as Harvard's, though average SAT scores were not. I could afford to attend only with the combined help of a partial scholarship, my parents, and a twenty-hour-a-week secretarial job. That was the price for this piece of heaven.

As one of the "scholarship kids," I was relegated to a particular niche with the foreigners and atheists, which suited me fine. The international students were working hard to assimilate, as I was. They were some of my first friends to whom I felt I really could relate. In the evenings, we would dance to David Byrne, U2, and R.E.M. at someone's house-sitting gig. Unlike at Cal Baptist, at Westmont dancing was ecstatic but asexual, as if we were whirling dervishes in some mystical David Byrne–style trance. My signature move was uncontrolled jerking followed by falling on the floor and spinning in circles. Or I would twirl through the air and land on my sturdy flat black boots. I discovered I liked this much better than putting dollars down Chippendales dancers' pants for a kiss.

Westmont was "ecumenical," and though it was in a distinctly Protestant way, it was enough to give many of us a whole new sense of freedom. We started by debating Methodists versus Lutherans, but before long, we were wondering if we should be Protestant or Catholic, Christian or non-Christian, Jewish or Buddhist or Hindu. Maybe we could try them all. It became a slippery slope, but a slope to freedom, not Evil. When R.E.M.'s "Losing My Religion" came on, my dancing hive of Koreans, Brazilians, Italians, and poor folks went wild in our collective dancing joy.

Then I met Garett, a self-identified Santa Cruz "skateboarder" with a shock of sandy-blond hair over his eyes. He was popular so not really my type, but we had been teamed up in art class and ordered to dig up Westmont's lawn together in the middle of the night. Our art history professor had long curly hair and wrote letters to the college paper signed "Abbie Hoffman." Though none of us knew who Abbie Hoffman was—and certainly never suspected he was an anarchist, icon of the anti–Vietnam War movement, and member of the "Chicago Seven"—we followed Abbie's directions and began to dig a lawn that was succinctly edged and mown once a day. The idea, Abbie said, was to create an "art installation" out of "found objects" and thus a "happening," though none of us knew what that meant either.

But digging up a rolled-in lawn is harder than it looks. I could barely get my shovel to break through the layer of sod that clung to the earth. Garett saw me, rested his arm on his shovel handle, and laughed. "Don't laugh, help me!" I said. Garett's father worked in construction, so he knew what he was doing. Soon we were both giggling and rolling around heavy rocks, wondering what we were making.

"I don't think it matters." Garett laughed. "Just push."

Garett was also in my modern poetry class, and I saw him in chapel once a week, since he was our campus prayer leader. He prayed into the standing microphone with more sincerity than I was used to. I liked that sound. He was also co-leading Westmont's mission to

Mexico, called Potter's Clay, along with a girlfriend who played volleyball, wore Gucci to class, and talked a lot about her "daddy."

She was about to leave him because he was poor, though neither of us knew that at the time.

Two days after our midnight adventure, Garett and I were sitting around an oak table in a Tudor-style house with picture windows: the English department. I had just finished reading aloud: "'The world is charged with the grandeur of God. / It will flame out, like shining from shook foil; / It gathers to a greatness, like the ooze of oil / Crushed. . . .'" "Crushed" felt like ecstasy to me. Just that word. I don't know why.

That was when Garett leaned over and said, "Give me a swig." *Busted*, I thought. But when I looked sheepishly up at him, he winked. I handed him my paper cup, realizing that the perfectly concealed wine in my cup must have had an odor.

"Thanks." Garett winked again and covertly took a sip.

The fact is that I was still terrified of people, particularly of speaking in public, and in a small class like this, where we went around the room, I knew it was inevitable. I thought wine might help, though it actually only turned my face red and made me more self-conscious. After that class, Garett invited me to continue our poetry reading over another glass of wine downtown. That was when I discovered we were both in love with Emily Dickinson, Seamus Heaney, Yevgeny Yevtushenko, and E. E. Cummings.

Maddeningly in love. His girlfriend was not a poet.

After working our way through our favorite poets and going to readings all over town, we turned to Russian literature, immersing ourselves in all-night debates about the relative merits of Ivan, Dmitri, and Alyosha from *The Brothers Karamazov*. In Garett's attic apartment by the sea, I became Ivan, the intellectual who refuses to believe in a God who would condemn people to Hell. Ivan instead believed in spring, saying, "Though I do not believe in the order of things, still the sticky little leaves that come out in the spring are dear to me, the blue sky is dear to me, some people are dear to me, whom one loves sometimes, would you believe it, without even knowing why." Garett did not agree.

"Cold fish," he muttered. "Ivan doesn't *feel*, he analyzes." Garett saw himself as a cross between the mystic Alyosha and the drunken sensualist Dmitri, who said of love, "A thunderstorm struck, a plague broke out, I got infected and am infected even now, and I know that everything is over and there will never be anything else." Garett added, "Now that's passion."

"Dmitri is irresponsible," I said.

"Ivan is paralyzed by his thoughts," he replied.

"Impetuous," I said.

"Heart of ice," he replied.

We argued like this for days and weeks until we found ourselves kissing instead, parked in his white Toyota pickup outside his attic rental in the quiet cove of Summerland. Garett's roommate, a red-bearded Argentinian who planned to return home as a missionary, lifted his head from his bed behind the stairwell, looked at us, and shuddered when we walked in.

"Get a room," he said.

"This is a room," Garett replied.

I fell in love with Dmitri-Garett, and he fell in love with Ivan-Karen. As in the book, we were still not compatible, but our characters had dug down into a whirlwind of emotions that we did not know existed. I know I did not. We felt the horror, together, of hearing Elie Wiesel say, "Never forget," at a talk he gave at the University of California–Santa Barbara. I thought Elie Wiesel looked like a corpse, a vision that has never left me. We heard Yevtushenko speak of his parents, killed by Stalin, then read his poem together: "It seems to me that I am Anna Frank, / Transparent, as the thinnest branch in

April, / And I'm in love, and have no need of phrases, / But only that we gaze into each other's eyes."

Garett was the first person I knew intimately who let me play whatever role I wanted, trying new identities on like hats—or characters in books. Garett thought they were all me and liked them all. After a lifetime with only the Bible, my invisible rabbit, and lizards for company, I suddenly had a real human being I could talk to. It was, in truth, too much to take in whole without shattering.

And then there was the matter of the girlfriend. Because of her, Garett and I seemed eternally poised between friends and lovers, like sister and brother in love for a while. When she left him, like Dmitri had with Gretchen, Garett howled into the night. It was not what I expected. He said he would never love again, even as I thought he loved *me*.

Slowly, I retreated into my bookish-Ivan nature and he into his Dmitri-dissolute one until I finally found a new great love: the philosopher Søren Kierkegaard. Kierkegaard wrote, "Since my earliest childhood a barb of sorrow has lodged in my heart. As long as it stays, I am ironic. If it is pulled out, I shall die." I decided he was the only person who really understood me and obsessively read everything he wrote, ignoring Garett when he chased me after class.

"Dad, I'm in love with a dead man and don't want to be with anyone else," I said one weekend at home with my father. "Do you think that's okay?"

He thought for a moment, then said, "The dead are as real as the living. I don't see a problem with that."

"We'll still visit," Garett said in the library overlooking the shiny Pacific, between the books that had both separated and created us. We were graduating soon.

The way I acted next surprised only me. Garett knew all about crying and screaming from his family, so it did not bother him as I sobbed through desperate words about not wanting to part, not wanting to live, until Garett began to hit his head against the metal end of the bookshelf. I stopped and looked at him.

"Don't!" I said, but he hit his head again. It made a hollow, hurtful sound.

"I want to hurt like you," he said. *Bang, bang, bang.*

All I could do was stop crying to make him stop.

Afterward, we went outside and lay in the grass, holding each other. In the sunlight, the grass turned all kinds of impossible new colors: bluish then yellow and white. Finally, I said, "I am going to live for the color of grass. I'm going to keep living because of that." I felt as if I were astral projecting into another world as he kissed me on the head, understanding as only he could.

At my graduation dinner, Garett sat next to me with my sister, mom, and dad. He looked confused and stiff in his white shirt and tie, as if he were shocked at my family's happiness, our seeming normalcy. Once again, I had no idea what I would do next, but at least I had made it that far, accompanied by Elie Wiesel, Yevtushenko, Kierkegaard, and Garett. Maybe I would be a secretary forever next.

But I got to have all this, all the sticky little leaves of spring.

China Lake duplexes, 1948

Earl Piper, 1941

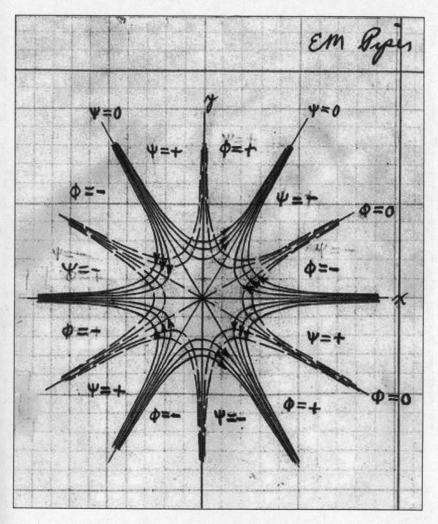

Dad's engineering sketch

Boy playing with old bomb at China Lake

First base pass

Dad in New Mexico, where he often traveled to use the wind tunnel

Me in an A-4 Skyhawk jet, circa 1971

Mom at China Lake

China Lake Boulevard, 1975

Christine and me with Patches

Salt Wells bobcats

Mike and Christine, 1984

Mom's missile, the Tomahawk

John F. Kennedy at China Lake, June 7, 1963

Dad at Cannon Beach

U.S. Navy rock art

PART FOUR

The Cold War at Home

Missile Guidebook:
Simulate a missile explosion in your own backyard.
Take between $500,000 and $3 million. Throw it
on the ground, pour gasoline on it, and burn it. Do
this until you are cured of your infatuation.

Less Lethal Encounters

"Careful walking home tonight," said my office mate, Sam. "Cops out." He had dreads and smelled of patchouli and a meld of other odors that the patchouli was meant to cover. I let him move into the office when he could no longer pay rent, though I did not know he was going to bring his black Lab too.

"What about showers?" I had asked, wondering how this would work.

He laughed in his pretty, white-dreadlocks-boy way, then said, "I don't believe in them. Capitalism is obsessed with hygiene to make us buy soap products." He also had a near religious obsession with eating five cloves of garlic a day. "You'll never get sick," he argued, and since every rain shower seemed to give me bronchitis, I even tried the cure. I thought I would vomit.

You may ask how I got here.

After graduating from Westmont, I spent a year in Santa Barbara working two secretarial jobs: one for a law firm and the other for a structural engineer. But I missed reading books and remembered what a Westmont professor and saxophone player had told me once: "Eugene, Oregon, is utopia." I imagined tasting wine, listening to jazz, and talking about books while gazing at snow-capped mountains. So I applied to graduate school for the scenery, again. In my application to the University of Oregon, I wrote, "I type letters all day long as a secretary, but live in the margins, dreaming of the books I will read at night. I hope you will give me a chance to jump off the page into those margins, to write my own story and fly."

I'm still surprised I got in.

Eugene, however, was not *my* utopia. It was a town of "primitivists," pranksters, and anarchists who wanted the downfall of civilization. There were teenagers and schizos living in the streets and frat boys who threw snow-covered rocks at cop cars when drunk. There was mayhem leading to suicide in a city of one-story buildings sprawled without rhyme or reason, where people either could not afford paint or did not believe in it. There were auto-parts stores, *taquerias*, tattoo shops, and head shops. And a view was nowhere to be found. The Cascades were more than an hour away, and you could not see them even on a sunny day. Then there were the claustrophobic-making clouds, which constantly hung over the city like a hat. Even the giant trees towering over me made me feel enclosed as they perpetually drooped into my private space. People wore Gore-Tex rather than carrying umbrellas, so were always wet. Mold crept up the walls of my apartment even though it was on the second floor. I felt like I had gone through the looking glass.

In the desert, water seeped up from the ground in artesian wells and desert springs; but here, there were no underground reservoirs, no secrets. Everything happened aboveground, out in the open. My friends said they would fuck right in front of me if I wanted them to. I was still a virgin and wanted love, not fucking in public. I wanted a mountain resort town like Snowmass. Instead, I hovered like a floating leaf above it all, confused, damp, and feeling slimy in my Gore-Tex.

Like all English graduate students, I taught Composition 101, which covered my tuition, though I hardly knew what I was doing. I was given an office in the basement of Prince Lucien Campbell Hall, a five-story concrete modernist structure with sealed windows, which had the notoriety of being the only place on campus high enough to jump from. To die, I mean. I once passed flowers on the sidewalk where someone had landed and wondered who it was. A woman, someone told me.

My office was an eight-by-five room with two metal desks and a window looking out over people's feet walking by. In one half of the office, there was Sam's futon and a perpetually panting black Labrador. In the other half, I had a desk and chair where I met my students to talk about their grades. Truth be told, I got used to that odd mixture of garlic, patchouli, and Labrador retriever. I got to love seeing that dog.

Still, I was skeptical when Sam told me to watch out for the cops that night, since I considered the police to be my friends. To me, "cops" meant the cute marine ushers at the base theater, who had helmets and special lightsaber red flashlights, and were there to protect you. Then I remembered my mom, who had warned me not to stop for the highway patrol back in California—or at least to be careful—because one of them was actually the Hillside Strangler. He dressed like a cop, then dragged young women into the hills with him.

"Why?" I asked Sam, hesitating between versions in my mind.

"They're out in force," he replied. "Just be careful walking home."

"Okay." I shrugged. Outside, the fall leaves were sticking to the sidewalk in all their smushed glory. I followed the colors as I walked: bright red, smushed red, bright yellow, smushed yellow, and brown. I was wondering how long it took for the colors to smush out when I heard the sound of a laughing crowd and looked up. A hippie crowd was crammed onto a wooden front porch so tight that a few were spilling out into the alleyway. They looked comfortable and easy-going, arms around one another, men and women, ponytails and torn blue jeans. Talking. I was tempted to merge with the crowd, a rare feeling for someone who was usually running away. They looked like they would give anyone a giant group hug.

Maybe I was starting to like Eugene after all.

Then, in a split second, police cars started zooming up, lights flashing.

"What the heck?" I said aloud, stopping in my tracks. Men in black space-suit-like uniforms jumped out of the cars and quickly lined up, facing the partyers, beating clubs against their hands, and looking ready to swing. Feeling as if I were suddenly in a scary robot movie, I stood there, mesmerized.

What happened next surprised me even more.

At first, the partygoers all came out on the lawn, blinded by the cop lights. Then, as if with one mind, they spread out into a single long line, linking arms and facing the cops, stringing themselves across lawns and alleyways like Christmas lights. A few began to sing, tentatively, "My country, 'tis of thee, / Sweet land of liberty . . ." Then everyone was singing, first quietly, then with gusto.

That was when the tear gas hit. People started running, their faces covered in bandannas. Cops started surging. Seeing me standing there like a deer caught in the headlights, someone shouted, "Go! Go!" and pointed me in the direction to run. So I ran, soon realizing I was hacking like crazy, wishing I had a bandanna. My lungs were burning. I believed in God and Ronald Reagan. How could this happen to me?

"It's a party!" I shouted at no one in particular.

My parents seemed so far away.

In the morning, I saw the headline of the *Register-Guard*: "OUT OF

CONTROL" PARTY RESULTS IN RIOT, ARRESTS. I was outside Espresso Roma, where a man known as "the Frog" was selling homemade joke books that he kept in a bicycle trailer weighed down with a rubber chicken. Next to him, a large homeless man sat on his flowerpot with his pants hanging down so you could see his butt crack. He sat there for years. My friends said he would shit in that flowerpot, though I never saw it. They said Ronald Reagan was to blame; he had closed down the mental institutions, leaving only flowerpots for toilets.

Inside, the beige-tiled floors were dirty with mud tracked in on hiking boots while flies buzzed all around. Sitting down at a flimsy card table with my café au lait, I began to worry about my safety for the first time. At China Lake, I would never be tear-gassed. In fact, we had *designed* tear-gas bombs and grenade launchers, which we lobbed at the Vietnamese to flush them out of the jungle. We also made chemical weapons like the Weteye, a bomb packed with sarin gas, and the Bigeye, full of VX nerve agent, similar to the ones Saddam Hussein dropped on Halabja. We made flash-bang weapons, smoke bombs, rubber bullets, Tasers, and "sticky slicky" weapons— sprays that either glued you in place or made you fall down. These were called our "nonlethal" weapons, until the name was changed to "less lethal" because they sometimes killed you. But all those were meant for other people, not me.

Once again, my world began to spin and turn upside down. In my Native American history class, my teacher, Winona LaDuke, talked about nuclear waste dumped on reservations, Native lands seized for military bases, and the VX nerve agent poisoning Goshute Indian territory in Utah. In my American imperialism class, my teacher taught us about CIA support for coups in South America and elsewhere. It was starting to be confusing, what was true or not true . . . but no one had told me about the riot police.

I later found out that house parties spilling onto lawns were illegal. You had to stay inside the house. Soon after that episode, I found out it was illegal to sit in trees too. People had occupied the trees in the city park to keep them from being cut down. One man's shorts were lifted up so the cop could spray his genitals with tear gas, and he still would not get down. Tear-gassing seemed to be a regular occupation for the Eugene police. At Café Anarquista, a sign warned about the intensity of "police occupation." On some days, the arrow would point to "thoroughly agitated (fight back)" and, on others, "ominously quiet" or "omnipresent (carry rocks)." It was often pointed at ominously quiet, which is how the world began to feel to me. It felt like a riot about to break out.

And I still did not know who was in the wrong, who was first to start this crazy, local war. Maybe it was the hippies and their stupid, staring dogs. Maybe we had to beat them into changing the way they dressed and talked. Beat them into taking showers. Maybe they were all drug dealers. Who was I to say who was friend and who was foe? Someone else always made those decisions for me. Suddenly, I missed my mom and dad. But then when I walked in my office and saw that trusting Lab face, panting and licking his lips at the sight of me, I had to take it all back. Immediately.

"I'm sorry, baby." I patted his head. "I know it's not your fault. You can stay as long as you want."

He nodded his head up and down and gulped in the musty air.

Chapter Twenty

The Soviet Union in California

After the first year in Eugene, I was nearly as broke as Sam and had to go home to earn some cash. Though I would have been mocked in Eugene if I'd called myself a "hippie," I was certainly no longer a Republican by the summer of 1989. I started to feel as though I were living a double life in a place I could never explain to my parents. Or admit that I liked. It was hard to go home that summer.

Yet something happened that immediately changed my mind once there. At first, I was shocked when I saw that glimpse of yellow in my manila envelope—a "Secret" clearance!—after picking up my badge at work. I was still only a Clerk Typist II, which I assumed warranted the usual blue for "Classified." "Secret" would allow me to get past gates and open files. My red Plymouth Duster with a white racing stripe like the one in *Starsky & Hutch* could tear up the desert all over the base. I could even open the "burn" drawer at the bottom of every file cabinet and finally see what was inside.

Maybe the answers would be in there.

To get to my assignment at Echo Range, I passed the wild horse and burro facility, where these animals were dumped once a year after being rounded up by the navy. The navy used to hire professional marksmen and just shoot them but had to stop when the story broke in *The New York Times*: "381 Burros Are Slain by Marksmen to Clear Naval Center on Coast." After that, the navy started to hire professional "cowpokes" to round them up. At the wild horse and burro facility, they were held until adopted, though not that many people wanted a burro. Horses were more popular.

I was tempted to stop and pet a baby burro, but I was running late. It was a thirty-mile drive into the southern Argus Range and the entrance to Echo Range. I pushed the speedometer past seventy, tapping the horn to say "hello" as I sped by my lonely long-eared friends. Work started at six thirty rather than seven thirty a.m. at Echo Range so we could have Fridays off and not go stir-crazy out there.

The road to Echo Range separates two giant chunks of the base—the North and South Ranges. The South Range was initially acquired by the navy just to keep brothels and saloons from lining the road for navy men. Straight ahead was Trona, a chemical-company town where they mined the surface of a dry lake and turned it into fertilizer, grocery carts, rayon, sugar, Pepsi bottles, and even Pepsi. My sister worked there for a while, but since the whole town stinks like rotten eggs, she didn't last long.

I turned right, avoiding the sulfur bubble, into the South Range. Crossing over a small pass, I saw a familiar-looking man with a gun standing beside a white coffin-sized box. He was guarding "the gate," perhaps an odd term since there was no real gate there—just a man, a box, and a gun in the middle of the road. You could find that sort of thing all over China Lake.

He waved me through when he saw my "Secret" badge, which was when it first occurred to me that maybe the whole place was "Secret." Maybe that's why I got the badge. Ahead, I saw three double-sized mobile homes plopped down at odd angles in the desert next to a parking lot. One brick building stood in the distance. After identifying my new trailer home from the crude map I was given, I walked in to find a hallway with green indoor-outdoor carpeting, looking like a putting green at an abandoned miniature golf course. Strangely, there seemed to be no one around, though I caught a whiff of something—coffee?—from a slightly cracked door. I knocked quietly, pushing a little.

"Excuse me, uh, I'm the new summer hire?"

A man about forty with patchy blond hair jumped up from his computer so fast that I thought he might knock it over. "Oh, I'm sorry," I said, taken aback. "I didn't mean to startle you."

"No, that's okay." He held out his hand. "I'm Russ, the division head." He wore a pastel plaid shirt and Dockers, and his face was empty and kind like a Methodist preacher's. I noticed a paisley fabric–covered button with a diagonal red slash pinned to his shirt, which people wore years ago in support of our technical director, Burrell Hays. In 1986, Hays had been fired by Assistant Secretary of the Navy Melvyn Paisley. I assumed my boss must be a Hays devotee, not realizing the battle was ongoing. Though he was no longer the head of China Lake, Paisley was still free.

"Somehow I forgot you were coming today," Russ said apologetically.

"Well, here I am." I had worked on the base enough summers to know it required a lot of standing around while people figured out what to do with you. I was the foster kid in a new family every year.

Russ grabbed my sack lunch to put in the trailer's shared fridge, then showed me to an office that looked like my dad's: standard government gray with a giant school clock. At least I had a door that closed. The "burn" drawer at the bottom of the file cabinet caught my eye. Of course, I could handle only yellow files, not red for "Top Secret," but it was a start. "Top Secret" people still got yellow badges, since it was supposed to be secret that they were "Top Secret." But they walked around carrying red files, which kind of blew their cover.

After showing me my office, Russ took me on a tour outside, stretching out his arms as though he owned the place. "So this is Echo Range. . . ." He waved across the horizon.

"Okay," I said. "But what's it for?" Every area on the base has its own specialty, like the Atom Bomb Area (Salt Wells), the Rocket Sled Area (Supersonic Naval Ordnance Research Track, or SNORT), and the "Experimental Air Center" (Area E). He looked down at my badge, thinking.

"Yes, it's Secret." I nodded proudly.

"We simulate Russian radar here," he said simply. "Our planes fly over, and we check to see how well Russian radar can track them."

"I see," I said. "So that's all you do out here?" He nodded, looking slightly disappointed.

"But why are the buildings scattered around like that?" I asked.

"Ah, you noticed!" He brightened up. "That's the trick out here. The buildings are supposed to look like ships at sea from the air."

I laughed out loud and said, "Shouldn't we be swimming now?"

"I suppose so." Russ chuckled. "You have to imagine that we are in Russian waters. You work on the Russian patrol ship." He pointed toward my office. "That is a Russian torpedo ship, over there." Then he turned again. "And there you have our aircraft carrier."

"So if I see a periscope pop up from the desert floor, should I let you know?" I asked.

"Definitely," he replied seriously, then leaned over slightly and made a faint sneezelike sound.

Laughter?

Straightening up, he lost his smile and said, "The buildings are called Sea Site One, Two, and Three. We're in One. We're Sea Site One."

"Will the Americans that fly over actually shoot at us?" I asked.

He shrugged. "Haven't so far."

We walked by the Rattlesnake Control Office, the only brick building, and he warned me to watch for rattlers inside our trailer and report them to the people in that office. "We had an incident with a Mojave green recently," he explained, "which was blocking the door to the office." I shuddered, knowing that this kind could kill you in a few hours, unlike most, which took a day or two. "People had to wait outside until Rattlesnake Control came and got it." I wondered where they put that snake. Was it in that brick building, waiting to be adopted?

"So they wait for snakes, and we wait for planes," I said. "It sounds like we do a lot of waiting around out here." He shrugged.

"Have you had any more trouble with rattlers?" I asked.

"Oh, nothing major. No bites," he replied nonchalantly. "Scorpions are a bigger problem. The woman you're replacing was bit by one when she was on the toilet. It was in a newspaper on the floor, and she picked it up. We had to medevac her out." I was surprised a scorpion bite would make her sick all summer. They could kill children but usually only made adults sick for a few days, at most. If we had a scorpion in our house, my dad would put a drinking glass over it and take it outside.

"How's she doing?" I asked.

"Oh, that was nothing," Russ replied. "She has cancer."

I was relieved that, here in the faux USSR, I would not have to type in Russian or wear Russian uniforms the way they did at Fort Irwin. There, at that army base adjacent to ours, soldiers were flown in from all over the United States for two-week intensive war games against the "Soviets," who were actually American soldiers, in heavy green uniforms with red stars. There was even a Russian town with a bakery and other shops that was used to train soldiers, not to shoot civilians in a firefight. It was strange to think that a soldier's two-year stint could be spent working as a baker in the Evil Empire.

By then, I was carrying around Karl Marx wherever I went, having read his work in my sociology class taught by Professor John Foster. Marx's Jesus-style communism with everyone sharing sounded a bit too utopian for me. In Eugene, I had watched experimental "back-to-the-woods" utopias turn into ego-driven wars, leaving me thinking that when left to our own devices we were more *Lord of the Flies* than *Walden Pond*. That said, I liked other parts of Marx's writing quite a bit, such as his ideas about "alienation" and "commodity fetishism." Marx said "alienation" occurred because we had no connection to the products we made anymore. Instead, we elevated the things we could buy to the level of religious fetishes without knowing the conditions in which they were made—such as Chinese sweat shops. As someone opposed to the eternal gobbling up of the land to make ever cheaper shit, I concurred.

My dad was not so happy about me and Marx, however. "But there's nothing even *about* Russia in it," I said at Arby's one night. The town had grown up with the Soviet Union but never grew out of it.

"Yes, but he is an atheist," my dad replied. "See, it says here—" He flipped through a book he had bought on Marx, a Christian book, of course. I suddenly realized that I was the Mormon. "'Religion is the opium of the people,'" my dad quoted Marx. "He thinks religion is only a drug."

"Okay . . ." I paused, aiming my roast beef drippings away from his book. "But my teacher at Westmont said Marx believed opium was a good thing because it helped you forget your troubles. Like religion. So he's for it."

"What kind of college did you go to?" My dad tapped his foot wildly beneath the Formica tabletop.

"Ecumenical," I replied.

Unlike my dad, Russ did not care what I read at work. On one of our desert walks, I even hinted that I might be a Communist. "I mean," I corrected, "I think capitalism may not be all it's cracked up to be." The desert "pavement," fine pebbles that stay in place when the sand is blown away, was easy to walk on but reflected back the sun like a satellite dish. It was hot, and the rocks sizzled. Everything was hiding.

"That's interesting," he said. "I don't know that much about it."

"But I thought we *were* Russians?" I asked. "Aren't they Communist?"

"Technically," he said. "But things are changing. Communism may be over." He confirmed a suspicion I had since the prior year, when I first saw a magazine on base with a story about "looking for a new enemy." There was also an edginess on base, a panic in the way people walked. Russ had it now.

My mom talked about a possible RIF (reduction in force), which was the only way you could get fired at China Lake. Technically, not "fired" but "reduced." I knew then that the collapse of the Soviet Union could really be a disaster for us. Hadn't Reagan promised to "spend them into oblivion" by building more weapons than they could keep up with? It sounded like the years of plentitude were ending.

Maybe Russ wanted the Communists back. Something had gone tipsy-turvy on base. It seemed only my dad was still mad at Communists. Then Russ added, looking over his shoulder, "Just remember to keep the door shut when you're reading. Some important people are coming by today."

As we turned around to head back, we both stopped short at the sight of all the black cars in the parking lot. No one from the desert would ever buy or even rent a black car. Only white.

"Who's here?" I asked Russ, surprised.

"Oh, they're early!" he said, and darted back. Looking down at my shorts and tank top, I knew why Russ wanted me to keep my office door shut. Washington had come.

Back in my office, staying out of sight, I fidgeted. I paced. Finally, I leaned my ear against the door, trying to interpret the sounds outside while hoping no one would notice the shadow my feet made. Nothing. Laughter. Then suddenly a burst of commotion exploded in the hallway. I cracked the door and saw a lot of Washington types milling around, sporting blue suits, ties, fancy watches, and shoes that looked as if you could fry an egg on them.

The door suddenly hit me in the face. It was Russ, pushing my door open. "Quick, come with me," he said, looking a bit too pleased with himself as he led me to the radar room, crowded with these foreigners. It was dark, with a wall of television screens showing perfectly still blue desert sky. Underneath the TVs was a black radar screen like you see in the movies, the ones that go *blip, blip, blip.*

"Brrr, it's cold in here," I whispered, rubbing my arms for warmth. Clearly, the air-conditioning had been turned up for these guys. "What are we waiting for?"

"The B-2 bomber is coming," Russ whispered. "It's the maiden flight."

"Wow," I said, suddenly realizing I was watching history. I had seen these planes, lauded as our new "wonder weapon," in magazines, but no one had seen them in the sky. They cost $1 billion each, and the air force had already bought a hundred of them. "This is so exciting," I said, now understanding his change in mood. Russ turned and smiled at me as though I were the son he'd never had, proud to show me our new gadget. Stealth bomber.

"July 17, 1989 . . ." I tried to remember the day and thought I'd better write it down. All eyes were glued to the TV screens, waiting for its debut. Finally it emerged in all its glory, looking to me like a Batmobile. It was silver on top, black on the bottom, and thin as a calculator.

"Wow," I whispered, watching $1 billion fly by. I looked around, hoping to meet the excited eyes of a stranger and thus to share and make real this sacred moment. The Batmobile's premier.

That was when I noticed no one else was smiling.

A man in front of me whispered, "Isn't it supposed to be invisible?"

"*Blip, blip, blip,*" I heard, and looked down at the radar screen.

Blip, blip, blip . . . I saw.

It seemed we were all frozen then, as though time had stopped . . . until, in slow motion, the man in front of me turned around and pointed at me like someone straight out of *Invasion of the Body Snatchers.* His eyes became the size of saucers as he screeched alarmingly, "What the hell is *she* doing here?" Everyone slowly turned to stare. I was afraid they all might jump on me and eat me.

That was when I learned a yellow badge was sometimes not enough.

Russ quickly ushered me outside, where he took me by the shoulders and looked at me like an interrogator. "You cannot tell anyone what you saw in there," he said. "Please." His face was so close to mine that I thought he might kiss me. "Okay? Don't tell anyone that I brought you in there."

Only then did I think of the questionnaire I'd had to fill out to work on the base, with strange questions like "Have you ever taken LSD?" and "Have you smoked marijuana?" I'd always checked "No" on those, although I suspected people did even if their answer was "Yes." But then I remembered another question: "Will you protect the secrecy of China Lake?" I had no particular sense of loyalty to China Lake, but I did to Russ. So I kept my secret.

Two years later, the same stealth technology entered the field on the F-117 during the Gulf War. Still I said nothing. I sometimes wonder what happened after I left that room. Maybe they took sides between those who wanted a cover-up and those who wanted to tell the truth and report what they saw. Maybe they duked it out until they all ended in a giant, exhausted pile on the floor with nothing resolved but with ties askew, blue suits ripped, and clumps of hair around them.

Years after leaving Echo Range, I read that a Tornado fighter plane crashed into my building, Sea Site One. The crash instantly killed two German pilots, whose plane had inexplicably nose-dived while they were testing their radar-jamming equipment. Six people in the building received injuries ranging from smoke inhalation to broken bones. I wondered what happened to the secretary I had replaced, who may or may not have survived cancer *and* a scorpion bite by then. I wondered what she thought when a plane crash-landed on her.

As for the Cold War ending, it turned out there was nothing to fear since weapons outlive wars and even states. Soon we would be fighting Soviet weapons in the hands of non-Soviets. We would be fighting American weapons in the hands of non-Americans. At Fort Irwin, the soldiers would simply take off their red stars and become jihadist terrorists instead.

Chapter Twenty-One

Countdown to Confrontation

And so I went back and forth between worlds, back and forth, until the whole world was twirling. Was the enemy in there or out here? *The Saturday Evening Post* once called China Lake "the Navy's Land of Oz." But sometimes Eugene felt like Oz too. Meanings collapsed around me like the Berlin Wall. I did not have the language to talk to my parents about what I was experiencing. I knew they worried, but assumed it was because I continued to study literature. No one was getting jobs in *that*. Frankly, I was worried too.

Back in Eugene, I switched to carrying around Virginia Woolf, who claimed every woman needs a room of her own. To write. I certainly wanted a room alone where I could be whomever I wanted to be. I felt pulled, this way and that, by too many cults, too many people with answers for me. I wanted to know what other women had done, how they got out of this. After my friend Virginia Woolf, I turned to Marguerite Duras and Hélène Cixous, who wrote, "We must kill the false woman who is preventing the live one from breathing." That was what I was trying to do, find the live, breathing woman. Cixous also wrote about war, lamenting "what fierceness we have to work every day in order to reattach living importance to the very delicate things which we are constantly torn away from by the forces of war." The first article I published was about Hélène Cixous in *Cultural Critique*.

In turn, that article would help me land me a job, against all odds, as a tenure-track professor.

War began to expose itself to me. In my Fascism class, we watched Nazi propaganda films and learned how Adolf Hitler mocked the free press until no one believed them anymore. Then he set up his own media and reality as he rose to power. There is a picture of him as a "gentleman" and nature lover at his country estate, laughing at a newspaper. The caption states he is amused by its "fables." In reality, he was nothing more than a thug and barroom brawler who forced the world into a war. My dad's war.

In another class, we learned what happened after the war, when a secret U.S. program called Operation Paperclip brought Nazi scientists to the United States. Wernher von Braun, who headed the *Apollo* mission, came over that way, smuggled up from Tijuana, Mexico. In Germany, he had overseen labor at a concentration camp where one-third of the population of sixty thousand people had died building V-2 rockets. They worked in tunnels where they were methodically starved to death, one after another. After the moon landing, survivor Jean Michel said, "I could not watch the *Apollo* mission without remembering that that triumphant walk was made possible by our initiation to inconceivable horror." Meanwhile, in von Braun's Alabama home, residents carried him on their shoulders while church bells pealed and fireworks filled the sky. He had chosen to live in the South because, he said, plantation life appealed to him.

After much digging, I later found out that China Lake had its own Nazis. According to the *Rocketeer*, Wolfgang Noeggerath was "brought to America in 1945 as part of 'Operation Paperclip.'" We also had Hans Haussmann and others. It was not even a secret on the base, though their immigration files were classified for fifty years. Once they were not, I would send away for Noeggerath's file, where he stated why he wanted to move to the United States. "To stop the communist threat," he wrote, which is the same reason he gave for becoming a Nazi. He said he admired the Nazis due to their "extensive program of social reforms," which could have meant Hitler's weapons industry, credited with halting unemployment, or could have meant the concentration camps. In China Lake, he was just one of "the Germans," part of a social club that made schnitzels and drank beer.

It was Noeggerath and von Braun who inspired me to travel to the tunnels where the V-2 missiles were made. There are still the rusted remains of V-2s inside, but no one speaks highly of von Braun and his "wonder weapon" there. Yet Nazis spread like a virus, all over the world, after World War II. They're still around.

Back in Eugene, our last remaining war-free days were posted in big numbers on TV screens every night, under the heading "Countdown to Confrontation." It was a bit unnerving. President George H. W. Bush said we would invade Iraq on January 15, 1991. CBS changed its eye logo to an image of planet Earth with a green radar detector flashing across it, making the world look like a target. Tick tock tick. No one I knew even had a TV, but the university bookstore put one in the window so we could watch. Bars pulled out old TVs from their back rooms. CBS kept us glued to the screen.

Saddam Hussein had invaded Kuwait, and we were about to retaliate.

In the middle of my Composition 101 class, a student poked his head through the open door and said simply, "It's started." Then he ran on like Paul Revere. It was eerily quiet. Then, one by one, my students stood up and walked out, looking shell-shocked. In the courtyard outside, a sea of zombies emerged from every building, interrupting the ultra-Frisbee players on the dazzling green grass. Blue-yellow-white grass. Students wandered around in a daze as if bombs were falling down the street and not on the other side of the world. Some hugged each other and cried.

The crowd began to flow like a river toward the regular "march" route—from campus to the downtown Federal Building. It was a spontaneous, silent, mourning march to a building where a crowd was already gathered on the steps, waiting for something to happen. On the other side of the street, a handful of agitators had also showed up, shouting angry slurs across the street. One of them carried a sign that read "Kill Hippies."

I saw Sam standing on the street, holding a sign that was blank. I ran over, happy for a familiar face. "What the heck does your sign mean?" I asked.

"Where is the media?" he said. "Why aren't these protests on TV? No one sees us. No one hears us. The media is silent." It was true: there were no cameras around.

Suddenly, someone shouted from a megaphone, "What about taking over the interstate?" People cheered and then a chant started, at first only a few voices but soon almost everyone: "Take the I-5. Take the I-5." There were at least a thousand people there.

"Take the I-5. No more oil," someone added to the chant. I turned back home, thinking, *Fuck the war and getting killed for it on the I-5*.

Instead, I wanted to see the weapons. I headed to Max's bar, one of many grimy all-wooden places of darkness near campus, where CNN was playing on an old TV. It was the first time anyone had seen war live, twenty-four-hour streaming, reported by terrified reporters holed up in a hotel in Baghdad. Bombs were dropping all around them. The world was mesmerized. A new thing took over the media that night: cable news. People wanted a twenty-four-hour view of war.

Goodbye, Tom Brokaw and the evening news.

I asked for a shot of vodka, hoping to see my mom's Tomahawk emerge from its shipboard chute. At a cost of $1.3 million each, the Tomahawk had been advertised as "One Bomb, One Target."

Suddenly, CNN cut to George Bush. "While the world waited," he said, "Saddam sought to add to the chemical weapons arsenal he now possesses, an infinitely more dangerous weapon of mass destruction—a nuclear weapon." Rumors flew that the Iraqi military was bigger than we had expected. Some said we would get bogged down in a "quagmire" we could never escape. But Bush was reassuring. "I've told the American people before that this will not be another Vietnam," he said, "and I repeat this here tonight. Our troops will have the best possible support in the entire world, and they will not be asked to fight with one hand tied behind their back." I drank another shot and went home.

In the morning, I picked up a copy of *What's Happening?* (now the *Eugene Weekly*) and found there was already a name for the I-5 incident. The "Northwest Shutdown," it was called. One woman said, "All I remembered was running down an embankment toward the interstate and hearing one of the local anti-war leaders cry, 'Lay down!' 'Lay your bodies down!'" So she did. She continued, "I can recall the smell of oil, the exhaust from the trucks that we had stopped, the feel of rough pavement against my cheek and some strange hippie's hand being way too close to my butt." For those few moments on the freeway, she said, it felt as if life had stopped. Afterward, she said, "I could not get that man's voice out of my head. It made me want to scream at random people in random places just to see if they'd do as I asked."

Lay Your Bodies Down. Die.

"War makes its stupidity reign over the world," Cixous had written.

Soon afterward, my girlfriend BethAnn, Sam, and I went to a "Women and War" conference, where we put balloons around our panel's room and labeled them "Clean," "Strike," "New, "World," "Order," "Nuclear," and other things Bush was saying on TV. One of us planned to read their paper on Shakespeare (BethAnn) or Marguerite Duras (me) while the other went around the room and popped the balloons. The point was to scare the audience out of complacency. BethAnn said it was a "happening." Finally I understood what "Abbie Hoffman" was asking for when I was rolling rocks around the Westmont lawn.

After the conference, we took mushrooms in the hotel room and, in the middle of the night, climbed the hotel marquee and changed the letters to "STOP BLOOD GORE NOW." BethAnn, the woman who finished all her PACEs by age nine, was also a Scrabble genius and had figured it out. She probably remembers what it originally said. If not, I'm sure she could reverse engineer the original wording. Today, she works on Wall Street and is known for her predictive stock market skills. Twiggy, redheaded BethAnn, who wore tight velvet red pants and a T-shirt that said "Sexism Kills" in dripping red blood. The next morning, when the manager knocked on our hotel room door and told us to change the sign back, we were grateful that he did not have us arrested. We dutifully climbed up the sign once more.

Back at school, I burned an American flag in my Composition 101 class. It seemed like something interesting to write about since the U. S. Supreme Court had recently declared it a form of free speech. Even Antonin Scalia agreed.

Not surprisingly, a student complained to the department chair, who called me into his office one day. "I just want to know what to tell his dad," he said to me. "He's a lawyer. Do you have any ideas?"

"Tell him it's legal," I replied.

The war lasted six long weeks.

On my birthday, BethAnn wrote "GET LAID AT 25!" in red lipstick on my apartment door. We had become fast friends after we found out we both shared ACE. Her school was started by her father at his commune in Washington State, and she had to wear long braids and denim dresses like the kind they wore on *The Beverly Hillbillies*. Her dad was the guru ACE leader of a place that sounded strangely Amish.

Now she liked to dominate the men she dated.

I looked up to her, and when I saw her lipstick message on my front door, I realized I could no longer think of a reason not to. Get laid. In my Composition 101 class, my student Reber had been writing me notes bordering on romantic for his "journaling" assignment. He taped in pictures of his home in Sitka, Alaska, wrote lyrical paragraphs about sea otters and Sitka spruce, and said he wanted to take me there.

Now that class had ended, I decided to give him a call. "I don't know about your boyfriend, Reefer," my landlady would later say. "He looks like a hippie." I tried not to laugh.

"No, I don't think so," I replied. "He's just from Alaska."

I remember seeing waterfalls flowing upside down when we first had sex, made of rainbow-hued colors. I thought sex was transcendental, better than LSD. I assumed he thought so too, and that we would bond forever in our shared ecstasy. I did not know a thing about the world.

He did take me to Alaska with him, for two consecutive summers, which is where I met his other girlfriends. While I was working the "slime line" with Filipinos at the fish plant, he was banging one of them in the mudroom. Back in Eugene, I went to therapy and peeked at the book my therapist was scribbling in. I saw, "She is growing up." Was that all it was and would it ever end?

I realized I was still caught between two worlds. I missed the idealism and even the *redundancy* of home, the little routines of my father's, like throwing his keys in the air, and the way my mom's smile could make the whole world forget its worries, if only because hers were buried so deep, locked away in secret boxes. I missed the twin language my sister and I spoke. But now I associated all those things with the DoD and I no longer believed in it, or in God—the two things that had supplied the stability and routines for my entire life. There seemed to be no place I could fit in. So I went back and forth, back and forth, searching the world and then coming back home— lost and confused, with books as my only constants. Books were faithful and reliable. You could pack them up and put them in a box, run your hands over their spines, flip through their pages full of memories. They always came with you, wherever you went.

When I left Alaska for the last time, BethAnn only said, "What a schmuck."

Sam's black Lab gave me a paw hug, which helped.

Chapter Twenty-Two

Death of a Salesman

When the war started," my dad said, "a TV was rolled into Mike Lab lobby so people could watch it on CNN." He was sitting in the wooden rocking chair in the piano room, the place for serious talks. There were chairs to rock away your anxieties and a humming-bird feeder outside, which made it easy to change the subject. "And when CNN showed a hit, people started cheering," he said. "After that, there was a big party for a week at Mike Lab. Everyone was watching CNN."

Surprised the Department of Defense turned on the TV like everyone else to see if their weapons worked, I said, "That's funny." Then added, "Like funny odd, I mean. Not funny 'haha.'" I was home for the summer, once again, but this time had not applied to work on the base. I would make do somehow.

"Then I noticed that CNN was showing the same missile strike over and over again. What does that tell you?" he asked.

"Oh," I said quietly, looking out the window, knowing that eye contact or sudden movements might make him stop talking. A ruby-throated hummingbird was buzzing outside, its beak with perfect aim.

"People cheered every time General Schwarzkopf showed that footage of a Tomahawk entering an air shaft," my dad continued. "But it meant nothing." He shook his head with a defeat I had not seen before. Though I was still watching the hummingbird, I could see my dad in my peripheral vision.

"Those birds sure can fly." I pointed out the window, watching two hummingbirds dive-bomb each other for air supremacy.

"Oh, I don't know . . ." My dad seemed flustered, not looking at the birds. "Maybe I'm not thinking so clearly anymore. It's become a business now. They want me to be a salesman, and I'm just not a salesman." We sat in silence, powerless. "Sell, sell, sell," he said, staring at his feet. "Our missiles are flying off the shelves now, thanks to CNN. But I don't even know where they're going."

After a fourteen-hour drive down the spine of the Cascades and Sierras, I sat with my father talking about missiles. That road had a way of clearing the cobwebs in my brain, taking me from wet to dry through every transition along the way. It pulled pieces back together again between here and there. Fir and lupine and sagebrush. Brittle-bush and desert marigold. I stopped for petroglyphs along the way, the ever-present markers from here to there. What were they trying to tell me?

For the first time, I noticed that my dad did not seem like himself. Something in the country was shifting, and Gulf War veterans were coming home with vague symptoms such as fatigue, joint pain, fever, respiratory problems, headaches, and memory loss. They could not get a diagnosis. People called them crazy. One professor argued it was "mass hysteria." Others said they were crybabies. The DoD said they were fine. But their symptoms would not go away. It affected over one-third of returning vets, the highest number of people ever permanently disabled by a war. Eventually, doctors called it a "syndrome." First, there was the Vietnam syndrome. Now there was the Gulf War syndrome. Even when a war went your way, when people celebrated in the Mike Lab lobby for a week, it seemed like war was always followed by a syndrome.

What was my dad's syndrome? I began to wonder, seeing something incalculably different.

One evening, my dad stopped in front of the colonial-style Ethan Allen wooden mirror with an eagle carved at the top. He stared at his face, then said, "Do I look the same to you?"

"Yes, everything looks the same," I said automatically. "You look normal," wondering vaguely if he'd bumped his head or something.

I was watching TV and did not want to be bothered, but then I took a second glance. His face reminded me of something, someone else.

"Sometimes I feel like I'm looking at someone else," he said. "Sometimes it seems like I'm getting further away. I recognize myself, but I'm further away." Then he shrugged his shoulders and turned away. "I must just be tired," he said. "Like Old Man River, tired of living but scared of dying. You just keep flowing along."

Who was I to say what was normal and not normal? I barely recognized myself in the mirror, particularly that time on LSD. At home, I saw Eugene-Karen trapped in a lie, a pretend little-girl face meant to please. Back in Eugene, I saw China Lake–Karen in the mirror, hoping to get out, wanting to be a little girl again.

Only later did I realize who my father had reminded me of: Ronald Reagan. On Reagan's face, there was a certain blankness, an erasing, just around the corners of his eyes. I noticed it during the Iran-Contra scandal, when the media was obsessed with what he did or did not know about the Hawk missiles sent to Iran. Everyone watched his face closely for signs. Did he know Ollie North was secretly selling these missiles to Iran, an enemy nation, and laundering the proceeds so they could reach the right-wing Contras in Nicaragua? Iran was on the list of "terrorist" states. Congress had passed a law that forbid supporting the war in Nicaragua. "What did Reagan know?" was the common refrain. Reagan said he knew nothing about Ollie North's money-laundering business. If he had, according to former national security adviser John Poindexter, "you would have a demand for impeachment proceedings."

Nixon's Watergate seemed poised to strike again. Could we stand it?

But no one looked too closely at Reagan's face. Maybe it was just too hard to admit that the head of your country, or your family, might not really be there. Then you would have to wonder who was taking care of you. People looked away, while I became obsessed with watching Ronald Reagan.

Meanwhile, my mom encouraged my dad to ask a doctor. The first one put him on antidepressants, saying depression might make him say the same things over and over again. But it was not depression. The next one gave him a B_{12} shot and sent him home, saying it was a deficiency. But it was not a deficiency. Then a doctor said he had "transient global amnesia," which meant it would go away in time. That one would have been a relief if it had gone away in time. My dad declared he would not retire until he hit the twenty-year mark, when he would get an extra $200 a month—unless he got a terminal diagnosis. The word "terminal" made me shudder and look away. I watched Ronald Reagan instead.

Reagan was forced to testify in 1990. Most were too worried about Iraq to watch. I noticed that when he climbed into the wooden witness box, he had that old Reaganesque charm on his face, but that gradually it began to fade. I noticed that when he was handed a piece of paper, his face would scrunch up in a struggle as if he could not read. I could tell that Reagan was fake reading. His face would change from confusion to light, then back again. At the same time, my dad's handwriting was starting to change and sometimes his letters would be reversed or left out.

Reagan seemed happy only when he remembered the script by heart, when he said things like "Contras were freedom fighters such as we had known two hundred years ago." It was clear from the way his eyes lit up with that old Reagan sparkle that he knew those lines usually worked. He looked surprised when no one applauded. He was in a time warp, blaming the press for foiling his covert operation, saying that if he ever got his "hands on the people who are doing the leaking," he would "hang them by their thumbs in front of the White House." He chuckled and thought the world would chuckle along with him in those last months of his presidency. We did not.

In Eugene, people called Reagan a liar. Stevie Wonder wrote a song called "Skeletons," which spoke of Reagan's "stinkin' lies" while the voices of Ollie North and Ronald Reagan played in the background. Earth, Wind & Fire wrote a song that opened with a newscaster asking, "The biggest unanswered question is: Where is the money?" The money from the missile sales.

Only the *Chicago Tribune* thought that maybe he was sick, noting that he said "I don't recall" or "I don't remember" eighty-eight times in those eight hours of testimony. I would watch his face for years to come, watch it keep time, step by step, with the dawning blankness in my father's face, the slipping into nothingness. Little by little, they went together.

In 1992, Reagan was forced to testify one last time. By then President George H. W. Bush had pardoned almost everyone involved in

Iran-Contra, and a successful war had lifted the mood of the country. Only I was still watching, along with prosecutor Lawrence Walsh.

My dad had still not received a diagnosis. My mom said he had stopped trying to learn new computer programs at work. Eventually, he would stop trying to remember his password to even get on the computer. He would go to work and just stare at the blank screen, taking breaks to pace around. Slowly, he turned into the seventy-four-year-old man who used to work across the hall from me.

"Don't tell your sister," my mom whispered conspiratorially to me. "I don't want to worry her. Besides, Mitch works on the base and might say something. Your father really wants to get to twenty years. He wants that pin. I'm trying to help him by writing notes for him to take to work." Her first note said "transient global amnesia," so he could remember what he had, then his passwords, then the day of the week, then his boss's name, and finally his own name. That front shirt pocket became very useful.

During Reagan's last testimony, Prosecutor Walsh slowly came to realize that he could not answer questions. He tried to refresh Reagan's memory by reading from his diary, but even that did not help. Reagan said, "I'm not fooling when I say that when I started reading the diary the other day, I couldn't even remember writing the things that I was writing about." The prosecutor put the diary down.

"I'm very embarrassed," Reagan admitted. "I'm sorry. . . . It's like I wasn't president at all." It was clear there was no way Reagan was going to remember what he had done with those weapons. It was possible not to remember whom you sold missiles to, or how to make them fly straight, or how to fix anything anymore. At some point, you had to let the weapons go, even if they were broken.

Finally, Prosecutor Walsh asked Reagan if he remembered a particular secret meeting in Geneva where the weapons sales took place. Reagan lit up. "No," he said, "but I remember another meeting in

Geneva." It was the one in which he'd first met Mikhail Gorbachev. The meeting, he said, was "in a big home along Lake Geneva and at a table like this only a little longer with he and his team on one side and me and my team on the other to deal with the weapons." Reagan kept talking, sinking into the memory. "As everybody started to sit down, I looked across the table at him and I said, 'Why don't we let our two teams start this discussion about the reduction of the weaponry and all, and why don't you and I get some fresh air?' He was out of his chair before I finished that sentence." Reagan was smiling wistfully, clearly back in Geneva. "So he and I left and we walked about a hundred and fifty yards down across the lawn to the lake where there was a beach house. It was cold, a real wintry day, and that beach house had a big roaring fire going in the fireplace. . . ." And he smiled, deep in that meeting, looking as though he had taken a walk in his mind and would let those in the courtroom stay to sort out the weapons.

"Sell, sell, sell," the people around him could keep shouting, but Reagan would turn to my dad and say, "Why don't you and I get some fresh air?" Reagan would wink and take my dad's arm, and they would walk, arm in arm, down the lawn to the beach house. Maybe they both wanted someone to finally acknowledge that they were, quite simply, sick and that there was no getting around it. All you could do was hang on for the ride, not put yourself back the way you were before, which is what everyone wanted you to do. Reagan would not have cared if my dad repeated himself, and my dad would not have cared where the missiles and money went. They could have had a moment of peace before they had to pull themselves back together to go out into public and look blank. Then they could prepare themselves for people like me telling them how normal they were. They did not want to be normal anymore, which only they knew. All they wanted was a roaring fire, a beach, and a wintry day with a friend.

My dad retired with his diagnosis in hand in July 1994, the same year Ronald Reagan announced his disease. In a handwritten note, he said simply, "My fellow Americans, I have recently been told that I am one of the millions of Americans who will be afflicted with Alzheimer's disease." After retiring, my dad actually seemed happier, content to be given a boxed pen-and-pencil set, a bobcat photo, a framed bighorn sheep, and, especially, that twenty-year pin because it took so long to be diagnosed.

After years of doctor-led wild-goose chases, my parents had gone to the Mayo Clinic and accepted that the best possible fit was Alzheimer's. Through neuropsychological testing, the doctors said they could be about ninety percent sure. Ninety percent was enough. Only I could not say the word that started with an A. It was still transient global amnesia to me, because the other one went with "terminal."

"It's terminal," my dad had said when he announced his diagnosis. "I'm going to quit my job." We all knew and did not know. "I thought you should know," he said to his shocked children.

"But you seem fine," I lied. "Everyone forgets things. Maybe they're wrong."

"No, I'm worse than you think," he said calmly. Between us, we could not say the word, nor did he want to carry it in his shirt pocket. "Anyway, with all this new technology at work I'm feeling pretty useless."

Only my mom could say it, maybe because that was now her full-time job, his disease. Ironically, my mom seemed to rally as my dad went downhill, maybe simply because someone had to. She still got cross when she found five new cups of coffee in the house, knowing my dad forgot he had already poured them. But she also started to laugh more often. Maybe knowing was a relief for them both.

Their children, on the other hand, scattered like mice into holes.

"He's relieved to have Alzheimer's," my mom said one day. "He was ready to quit work, and he thinks it won't be painful." I think he was happy to be retired and ready for the slow decline.

"But I'm not!" I wanted to shout. The part of my reality that was contained inside my father's head was going to pieces. I was going to pieces.

Over time, I came to think of his disease as a kind of flood, gradually filling up parts of his brain and making them unusable. For us, it was definitely an unwelcome visitor. But for him, it may have felt like walking on a beach in Cornwall every day, watching the stars.

Chapter Twenty-Three

Near-Death Experiences (NDEs)

Perhaps my sister got pregnant because my dad had Alzheimer's. It is hard to say, but I was not particularly pleased. I had seen how babies took over women, like in the movie *Alien*. Those babies turned the women into something else. I did not want to lose the sister that I knew. I wanted her the way she was, with only me and Mitch. *We* were the kids. The addition of a husband had been hard enough, and now I felt I might lose her. She had been changing along with me, covertly, drinking wine but hiding the wine bottles when our parents came to visit. We had *strategized* together. Then, suddenly, she betrayed our covert quest and decided to become our parents instead. She was going to *settle down*. How could she?

My mom once said of having kids, "That's just what you did back then." Since it was not "back then" but *now*, I took this to mean that I did not have to have kids like she did. I assumed she had not wanted them either. I thought we were all in it together, but we were not. Even my mom later said I had completely misunderstood her. "No, I always wanted kids," she corrected me. "Ever since I was a little girl. I thought you would want to be a mom too. You would be such a good mom."

I wanted to throw a glass across the room.

"But, but, the future!" I stammered. "Why do people keep having kids when things will only get worse? Climate!" I shouted, too riled to add "change." My mom looked at me like I was two, with the kind of smile reserved for little kids.

"Ah, but you were such cute kids," she said. Then, "Don't say that. I had you!"

I was alone in the universe.

Nevertheless, I adapted. When my sister called me from the hospital, I still recognized her voice. She reached out from her antiseptic room to my mold-filled one. I had put my futon in the tiniest attic cubbyhole room, where black tentacles crawled across the walls, not realizing it could make me sick. By then, I was what people called a "professional student," used to the various discomforts. I once told my mom I had calculated how to survive on $5 a week by eating only lentils. Afterward, she sent me a $5 bill with a note attached: "For a week's worth of food." I found out lentils had their disadvantages.

My sister got pregnant the year of Reagan's first testimony. Around her due date, I got antsy, staring at the mold on the walls and seeing terrible pictures and prophecies in it. I stayed at home waiting for the phone to ring. Cell phones had made their appearance—big, brick-sized things with antennas—but I was a decade behind being able to afford one. Same with computers. Instead, I typed blocky yellow letters into the soft brown screen of my $100 word processor. After a lifetime of manual typewriters, I thought it was miraculous.

"Hello," my sister said when I picked up, then made a deep, low-pitched groan.

"Are you calling me from the toilet?" I asked. "It sounds like you're doing a BM."

"No, no, that's just a contraction," she said.

"Are you having your baby?" I replied. I started to pace as far as the cord would allow. "Should I hang up? Do I need to call an ambulance?" I did not even know that women could talk while in labor.

She laughed, more relaxed. "No, it's okay. I'm already in the hospital. Labor takes a long time, and it's so boring here. I thought we could chat."

So we did. I told her all the things I could not tell my parents, knowing she was a vault, knowing that we would never spill the secrets that might disappoint them. Then the pain got too bad, the contractions too close, and she had to go.

I waited by the phone for good news after that, but it did not ring. All night.

In the morning, I knew something was wrong when my mother said hello. "Karen," she said next, "there's been a complication."

"Where are you, Mom?" I heard clanging in the background.

"I'm at the hospital and your sister . . . well, she's unconscious." Her voice was too quiet, swallowed up by the clanging hospital and moldy walls.

"What?" I asked. "What's going on?"

"The doctors say she's barely hanging on. Her bilirubin is 5.1." My body went numb. I had no idea what 5.1 meant, but I knew that when my mom starting pulling out the numbers, it was never good.

"But where's the baby?" I asked, suddenly afraid there was no baby. Just 5.1.

"She had the baby, and the baby is okay," she said. "He's a boy. It's just that, afterward, Christine did not get better. The nurses kept saying she would, but she was hurting so they gave her something to sleep. Then she woke up in the middle of the night and was rocking in pain and crying. By the time the doctors got her into testing, her bilirubin was too high. Extremely elevated."

"Is she going to die?" I asked, cutting her and her numbers short.

"They don't know yet. She's on anticonvulsion medication, and she went into a coma around seven this morning. They say all we can do is wait."

I hung up the phone, sat down on the floor, and stared at my carpeting. I had a nephew, but all I could think about was the crappy carpeting in my crappy apartment. I needed my sister. To have a sister, even one who beat you up as a kid, is to have someone who shares the grief of being a woman, which may be precisely why she beat you up. Even while I was at grad school, she was sometimes jealous and angry about my freedom. I would explain that not being able to afford food was not so wonderful. Then she would say, "It's not so wonderful to be married sometimes too," and we would call a truce. My mother always said, "It's a man's world," but only a sister learns what this means with you as you are growing up. My sister held my memories in her brain. Even though she fought with me about what had or had not happened, without the fighting, no one would even care about those memories, what was true or untrue, what was mine and what was hers.

I went into my bedroom and began to scrape away at the mold, first with my fingers and then with a knife. After a while, I got out the bleach. I did not leave the house or go to classes. I just kept scrubbing.

A week after she went into a coma, when the walls were polished white, the phone rang again. "I'm okay," Christine said, though she sounded barely conscious. "I'm awake," she said. "They say I'll make a full recovery."

"Good, good," was all I could say, afraid another word might kill her.

Then she said something I could never have expected. "No one is here. I have to tell you," she said, gasping for air between words.

"Okay . . . ?"

"It was wonderful, Karen," she slurred. "I died. I have to tell you." She drew out each word slowly, almost painfully, in a whisper.

"You rest," I said, assuming the morphine was talking. "I'll talk to you soon."

But even when she was feeling better, she insisted that she'd died. She called me secretively to tell me about it. I worried about her brain but did not say so. She sounded beatific as she explained, "Don't tell Mom, Karen. She's pretty upset right now about the whole thing. But Karen, it was just like you hear about. There was a white light and then it got bigger and I was in a white room full of people that I didn't know, but I wasn't scared. They were standing there waiting for me. I walked into the crowd and felt enveloped in all this love and bliss. I know it's all going to be okay now. I want to go back there again."

She would never change her story. During her slow hospital recovery, her voice reminded me of how she sounded in labor, when she was grunting and then gasping for air with each contraction. But this was a weird labor of death as she spoke in short bursts before stopping from exhaustion on the phone.

She was diagnosed with HELLP syndrome, which stands for hemolysis, elevated liver enzymes, low platelet count. Everyone just calls it "Help." It's a rare disorder triggered by pregnancy that causes your enzymes to elevate and destroy your liver. HELLP might as well be a person who rips your liver out in front of you and starts chowing down on it. By the time they caught it and stopped it from its munching, my sister had only a quarter of her liver left. According to her test results, she should have been dead. My mom said later that even the doctor had said her chance of surviving was not good.

Luckily, I learned that livers grow back, so we waited for that to happen.

My mom was with my sister then, while I was stuck in classes. She said Mitch had tried to go home and rest as soon as Christine stabilized. "So he asked the nurse when he could visit the baby again," she said, "and the nurse said, 'That baby's going home with you. Nothing wrong with the baby.'" So Mitch learned how to take care of an infant full-time while Christine dreamed of being in Heaven. My mom and dad refused to leave her side. Just in case. So baby Jonathan became his daddy's boy. Oddly, he developed a fear of touching the floor as he grew. He wanted to crawl but would put his hands on the carpet and start to scream instead, holding them up for someone to wash. He wanted someone to fix it all.

When I was finally free to visit Christine, I noticed she had a moony-eyed glow to her, though it went away slowly over the next year. I knew it was the glow of death. It seemed as though aliens had taken over her body, not *Alien* aliens, but the happy kind. Still, I did not trust them. They wanted to take her away.

In the end, being a mom did not change her as much as I had feared. She was still my Christine, the same witty, sassy, angry girl. She just had a baby now and a ticket to Heaven too. It actually seemed like a pretty good deal to know where you were going next. Not many people got that.

The doctors told her not to have more children, in case it happened again. We all assumed, of course, that that was the plan. Then one day, she said to me, "Don't tell Mom and Dad."

"What?" I whispered conspiratorially.

"Labor is addictive," she said. We were eating at a rooftop café, I believe in Los Angeles, though in retrospect it is hard to imagine how we got there. I remember the rooftop railings were white, and that we were eating crab, and that she still had that moony-eyed look to her.

"What do you mean?" I asked, even though I knew.

"I want that feeling again," she said. I knew she was not talking about labor. She wanted to go back again to the place where it was all over, where it was safe, where it was better than Prozac.

Could I blame her?

PART FIVE

Anything Can Be a Weapon

Missile Guidebook:

Follow its money trail. A missile will have a money trail that often leads to someone corrupt at the top. Find out who that person is. Have him fired, or impeached, if you can.

Follow its blood trail. A missile's blood trail will lead to those at the bottom. Find them and talk to whoever is still alive. When you get back home, tell everyone what they had to say.

Anything Can Be a Weapon

Chapter Twenty-Four

Eco-terrorism for Fun

I noticed Keith at Espresso Roma when he was talking about blowing up the Columbia River dams, all fourteen of them. I recognized the tenor of this coffee shop conversation immediately. It was the one about "How far should we go?" or "How much are we willing to risk?" For example, how far would you go to keep an old-growth forest from being logged? Would you stand in front of the logging truck or would you blow up the truck? It was a test of your moral boundaries, which sometimes deteriorated into "Would you throw your dog off a cliff for a million dollars?"

I knew this was the "Would it be worth it if you killed one person" quandary.

In Eugene, I came to realize, friends came and went in complex combinations, building new realities while tearing down old ones. My friend Lydia Yuknavitch joined a lesbian separatist commune in the woods, only to return because there was no plumbing. "You put down an outhouse, fill it up with shit, and then move it to a different place," she said. "But eventually, you're falling through into shit as you walk around." To me, Lydia was a fearless, braless beast with her long blond mane, cargo boots, and patchwork Depression-era-looking skirts. Other friends of mine went to live off the grid in "sustainable" communes. One or two built cities in trees and dropped out of school to keep those trees from being cut down. Some people in that crowd poured cement in holes they had dug in the ground with one side of a handcuff stuck in the cement. Then they would put a hand in the other. To block the bulldozers.

But I was too shy for that sort of thing and so just kept reading books, wide-eyed at all the transmogrifications around me. Inside, I was transmogrifying too. I had switched from English after my MA to get an MA in environmental studies and then a PhD in comparative literature. I wanted to read everything, get degrees in everything. Until I maxed out my student loans, that was the only plan I had. I stayed eight years and met Keith in my last.

At that coffee shop, Keith was wearing a blue Gore-Tex jacket, a wool plaid shirt, and blue jeans that were clearly ripped because they were old and not because it was trendy. He looked as if he had just come from a fish-packing plant. With dark thick Eastern European hair, enormous blue eyes, and pale skin, he was smoking with the nervous apprehension of someone who looked as if he might get caught. Sitting across from him was a friend with curly grayish hair, cargo cutoffs, and an old denim satchel, nodding as if taking directions. Next to them, a woman in plastic flip-flops, two skirts, a wool scarf, and a corduroy jacket was sitting with a man in a "Free Leonard Peltier" T-shirt, vigorously engaged in a political discussion.

Keith kept looking over at me, nervous that someone was listening.

"All you have to do is dynamite the hillside above the reservoir and the water will overtop the dam," he said. "That would be enough to topple the first dam, and none of the other dams would have the strength to keep back the flood of water. The rest would come down like dominoes, all fourteen, starting in Canada but gaining enough momentum to take out the big dams in America." As I listened, I shook my head. While you might eventually forget that dog you threw off a cliff, I knew you would never forget the person you killed.

It was not that I had a problem with sabotage. For my Composition 101 class, I had assigned *Ecodefense: A Field Guide to Monkeywrenching,* which teaches techniques such as spiking trees, building smoke bombs, and putting sugar in gas tanks to disable logging equipment. I had taught *The Monkey Wrench Gang* by Edward Abbey, a novel whose heroes blow up the Glen Canyon Dam. So I knew about blowing up dams. You did it to save the ecosystem. Perhaps we all contemplated it, at one point or another, as we watched tender Oregon firs plowed down and carted away in Weyerhaeuser trucks, or when we saw newly dead trees sticking out of reservoirs. We all wanted to do *something* to stop it.

Keith continued, "I've devised a system for warning the people in Portland, but even if a few die, I say it would still be worth it, eh?" The rhythm of his voice was quiet and reassuring. Only a Canadian could talk about killing and make it sound like a polite proposition. His friend still said nothing, as Keith continued, "The Columbia dam system is blocking salmon that are trying to get up the river to spawn. It's destroying our fishing industry, people's livelihoods." *Our* fishing industry, he said. "We've got to help the salmon. . . ." His friend kept nodding. "Don't you think? I'm serious."

I found out Keith was also getting his master's in the environmental studies program. We often sat next to each other in the graduate student lounge, working at our respective white plastic boxy computers. Keith was Canadian-shy so never spoke to me, though I would look up and watch him working on the computer. Every now and then, I would find him looking at me, not as invisible as I thought I was.

One day, an email showed up on my computer, green lines on a black background. "Student lounge is dreary, isn't it?" it said. I looked around the room, and he waved. I introduced myself—on email. Before long, our emails turned into missives, manifestos, and declarations, which we kept writing even after we started going out. I still have a box full of them.

I asked about his hometown, Vancouver, British Columbia. "Isn't it dreary?" I wrote.

"Even this summer in the worst rain of my life it wasn't dreary because of all the life," he wrote back. "It was like moving through one large living thing, like being inside of a whale. . . . Sure some days were raining like hell and others were equally hot, but the word 'dreary' never came into my mind. 'Alive' certainly did."

I shared an essay I had written about the Oregon woods, and he responded, "To have language that can circle something living, like a relationship, like putting your arms around a big cedar, feeling its life and power, while allowing the roots and stems to continue to grow. By holding something living like this, the language becomes equally living. It makes us alive. Your essay does this, these things." I watched him typing, his fingers moving so fast, so freely, unlike mine. I watched his brain working as he typed.

No one had ever written to me like this, like someone who knew me. Even then our transactions occurred only on email, as if there were a wall down the middle of the student lounge. On my side of the wall, he reached me in my place of isolation.

One night, we ran into each other at the gay bar, the only disco in town, where we had each been invited by mutual friends. A big sign at the entrance read "No Overt Heterosexual Activity." A friend of mine had been thrown out for such activity. Now I sat across the table from Keith, a disco ball spinning overhead, while one of my girl-friends flirted with him. We looked at each other, secretively, every now and then. My blood boiled a little when Keith touched her neck for a moment after she asked him to put on her neckleace. He spoke with her all night and never to me.

The next day, fearing he'd gone home with her, I found an email in my in-box that had been sent after we'd left the bar. Keith wrote, "You are hard to read. You don't have a jacket that you didn't give up after leaving the Hells Angels. You don't dance like you studied ballet for 20 years (you dance better). I have never seen you eat so I can't tell which hand you use for a fork. I am curious because you hint of things not right although what I see looks very well adjusted indeed."

I wrote back, "Let's get a shot of tequila."

I watched him, fearfully, when he finally came in and opened his email, but he replied, "Tell me where you live and I'll bring the tequila."

Is this how love begins, in fear, and glances, and encrypted emails?

Keith was a spy into my life. He captured my love of furry animals and desert wanderings and wrapped them up inside his brain. He found my secret backyard.

That night, we made love on the roaring banks of the McKenzie River. The rocks poked into my back, even though he laid out his Gore-Tex for me, but the pain did not matter. Nothing did but this. After that, we had sex in hammocks, on beaches, on mossy forest floors, anywhere. We were in love.

He felt the waterfalls inside his head too.

Our only problem was that we'd met too late, or so it seemed at the time. After eight long years, this was my last year of funding at the University of Oregon. The thought of what came next was terri-fying to me, with professors hardly in demand. My friends ended up working in chocolate factories, starting nonprofits, or becoming waiters or waitresses. One friend said he planned to hold a sign on the freeway that read "Will Interpret Novels for Food." So when I started getting phone calls about job interviews, rather than that dreaded letter in the mail, I was shocked. Where would I go, and was I ready?

It turned out it would be the University of Missouri, where I was finally hired. You must understand that we have no real choice in the matter as to where we go. It's a national job search, and at the time, hundreds of literature PhDs were getting rejected for every tenure-track job opening. Many ended up teaching at below poverty wages with one-year or even one-semester contracts. Some of them still do, wondering every year if that job will be there for them the next. For decades. Others worked at the nice restaurants in town, offering a little conversation on Proust with dinner. Hoping smart people walked in.

I wrote to Keith, afraid to tell him in person. "I got a job in Missouri," I wrote.

Surprisingly unflustered, he wrote back, "Maybe living there will spur you to write more, to reminisce over lost land, lost home. . . . Maybe you will take root there, find yourself going to church, gossiping, picketing abortion centers, quilting, polishing silverware, watching evangelists, darning socks, looking for UFOs in cornfields . . . and then again maybe you won't." He did not mention what this might mean for us. We had been together less than a month.

I felt unmoored, and each time this happened, the pain seemed to be worse. Maybe this was because I was finally inhabiting my own skin . . . but my skin hurt. Ever so slowly, Oregon had become home to me—the chanterelles that popped by the bucketful in the forest, the mountain huckleberries I ate until I was sick, and the wild winter ocean. Even the rain. Again, I wrote to Keith, "How am I supposed to leave the West Coast? I keep saying that but no one takes me seriously. I've won the lottery, gotten a job—and everyone is screaming congratulations—and it is happy, I do deserve it. But then this other thing starts to nag . . . how am I supposed to leave? This place, all of it, has made me who I am. And now I feel I've been consigned to exile in some foreign land, where I have no identity or history, where there is no picture in my head." At the time, it truly felt like a disaster, and that disaster would keep growing.

So when Keith asked if we could hike up Mount Pisgah to see the "super" moon and have a "talk," I expected the worst. *We'll still visit*, I pictured him saying, as Garett once had.

It was a pitch-black night as we started up the hill, passing a bottle of tequila back and forth. The moss beneath our feet was dark and squishy. At the top, we leaned against each other in our Gore-Tex jackets, saying relatively little. His black and gray jacket was patched, and mine, navy, was second-hand. Then the moon burst over the horizon, huge and red and glowing like a spaceship rising, ready to suck us up and take us somewhere.

"Wow," I said. "That's cool."

"So American." Keith laughed, pulling me close. "'Wo-o-w.'"

"Had enough of that, e-e-h?" I playfully swatted him.

As I did, he grabbed my hand and started to suck my fingers, one by one, and it looked as if he were trying to tie a knot in a cherry stem with his tongue at the same time.

That's a bit odd, I thought before I realized what was happening.

He pulled away to reveal a ring on my left ring finger. I stared at it stupidly, thinking the stone looked black. He asked, "Will you marry me?"

"How did you do that?" I replied, impressed, then, *"Yes!"*

I screamed and hugged him, laughing. "You were freaking me out!" I said.

In the moonlight, the gem was so dark that he had to tell me it was a ruby, though I did not care if it was onyx, or black diamonds, or a piece of lava. He was my love.

It never occurred to me then that perhaps I was rushing into things. I was desperate for something to stabilize me, thinking I could not handle entering a whole new world alone, not this time. Missouri may as well have been another planet, so far from home. What would I find there?

The moon was the color of Agent Orange.

Chapter Twenty-Five

American Woman

Let's do a tour of Karen's past," my mom said excitedly when I brought Keith home. We loaded into the back seat of their new white Toyota Camry to take a tour of Ridgecrest with its one main drag, China Lake Boulevard. There, teenagers loved to "cruise" at night, shouting to one another out their car windows as if it were any ordinary small town. We drove past "Rocket Park," with its rocket-shaped slide, and the post office with its navy, army, and U.S. flags. Keith sniggered, "Canada has child care, and you have rocket slides!" He elbowed me while I cringed. No one laughed.

"I heard you're Canadian," my dad said politely from the driver's seat. That was before they took my dad's license away, when we were only at the stage of occasional blank stares, repeated phrases, and lost coffee cups. There were still plenty of good times to be had ahead. "Mary and I love Vancouver Island," he continued. "We had our honeymoon in Canada." At least he seemed fully "there" that day. Nothing *too* weird was happening yet. After passing the main attractions in town, John's Pizza and Cerro Coso Community College, we headed for the base, where my dad got his usual salute at the main gate.

"Always nice to see that," he said as we drove through. He was crisp and happy. *Maybe it* is *transient global amnesia*, I thought. We drove past Kennedy's Forest to a roundabout with an A-4 Skyhawk in the middle. Once used in Vietnam, the plane had been spray-painted a solid gray. Past the A-4, my dad took the exit to the armaments museum, one of the few places tourists could visit.

At the entrance, my mom pointed and said, "Hey, that's my missile. I made that!" I didn't recognize it. More than six feet tall, it was planted upright in front of the door. As with the airplane, its markings had been painted over, this time in basic red. The paint was faded and old. Keith stopped but said nothing.

"Inside there's a better one," my mom said, "straight off the factory floor." Then I noticed that my dad had already gone in, wandering off on his own. A very old man who looked as if he might have been dozing sat next to a guest book in the lobby. I peered beyond him, looking for my dad, as he lifted his head, startled. "Wel-wel-welcome to China Lake," he said. "Please sign in." He looked like an older version of my dad in the same white short-sleeved shirt and gray tweed pants with a black leather belt. He even had a pocket protector for his pens.

Keith signed in with a fake name and address before the old man led us forward. I looked at him quizzically, not having seen him do that before. He shrugged as if he didn't know either.

"Okay, we usually start with the Sidewinder room and work our way around to the exit," the man began as we followed him into a room full of missiles in glass cases. My dad was there, staring at the AIM-9 missile, the one we used in Vietnam. "This looks familiar," he said.

"Did you work on it?" I asked.

"I'm trying to remember," he said.

Keith had already rushed into the next room without stopping to admire the Sidewinders, and the guide seemed confused by our party splitting up. My dad refused to be herded past the AIM-9L Sidewinder, which he was examining intently.

"Ah, there it is!" my mom exclaimed, seeing a Tomahawk in the next room. She moved on, walking up and touching its nose like the face of a familiar friend. Leaving Dad behind, I followed her. "This nose is where my computer chips are stored." She pointed. "That is where the guidance system goes." The missile was enormous, about eighteen feet long, far larger than the sleek and friendly Sidewinder. I never knew they came that big and shuddered at the thought of one dropping on me.

"What are these?" Keith shouted back at the guide, who must have felt he was herding cats.

"Videos about base history." The old man shuffled over to Keith. I suspected he already wanted to go sit back down, unable to keep up with my fractured family. "Want to see one?" he asked politely. "How about the Kennedy visit?" Keith was staring right at it.

"No, I think I've seen enough," Keith replied. It was not the right thing to say. I worried about the impression he was making.

Back in the car, Keith began to quietly sing, "American woman, stay away from me." Everyone was silent. I froze.

No, no, no, I thought. All the things I had hid from my parents seemed to want to burst forth in that song. "I don't need your war machines," the song went. Yet my parents *were* the war machines. Keith sniggered and elbowed me, clearly thinking I was in on the joke. My parents must have thought he did not want *me,* not knowing the lyrics. Was it possible to separate me from China Lake—or them?

My dad started his own song to drown out Keith. "Oh, I like Jim Hill, he's a good friend of mine. / That is why I am hiking down Jim Hill's main line. / Hallelujah, I'm a bum . . ." It brought back memories of all the folk ditties we had sung on family road trips, mostly old union songs my dad had learned from his parents. This song was actually about "*Joe* Hill," a union organizer executed by firing squad after being framed for murder. My dad changed his name to Jim Hill, my high school principal after Mr. Crackling left. Everyone loved Jim Hill, who was not creepy like Crackling.

I joined in loudly, "Oh, I like Jim Hill, he's a good friend of mine. / That is why I am hiking down Jim Hill's main line. / Hallelujah, I'm a bum, hallelujah, bum again. / Hallelujah, give me a handout, to revive me again."

"All this singing today!" my mother said pleasantly. "Oh, there's Ridgecrest Heights." She pointed at some houses. "That's where another one of Karen's boyfriends lives." It was my high school boyfriend Phil's house. "Are you still in touch with Phil?" My mom turned to look at me.

"Mom, I went to Sunday school with him when I was sixteen!" I took Keith's hand firmly. I was on his side on this one.

"Well, you never know. I hear he still asks about you. . . . What does 'dating' mean to young people these days, anyway?"

"You know, holding hands, that sort of thing," I replied. "Going to the movies." Keith and I smiled slyly at each other.

Like the roll moment for a missile, when does a relationship begin to go astray? Was it when I realized that blowing up the Columbia River dams would kill Americans and not Canadians? All I know is that at some point our relationship began to circle around the "which side would you fight for in a war" quandary. Canadians or Americans? What was really meant was, "Are you on my side or not?" Or, "Will you fight for *me*?" But when did it start, the cups thrown and insults hurled? If only I could capture that moment, examine it, and turn it around. Could we have stopped that moment if we had caught it then?

All these questions, but no way to turn back, to stop.

All of us were committed to our own trajectories. Keith had committed to following me to Missouri. I was determined to marry while my father could still give me away. My father was headed to a place none of us could understand. I somehow wanted my dad to know I was taken care of before he was gone, even though "being taken care of" did not even fit who I was anymore. Maybe that was the problem. We were all veering off target at the speed of flight. There was no way to stop us now.

It was really just a question of where we would land.

Chapter Twenty-Six

The Weather Is a Weapon

On the day of my wedding, fifteen people sat inside the chapel at my old alma mater in Santa Barbara. It looked like the magazines, surrounded by vine-covered pathways, Spanish fountains, and ocean views from every spot. I decided to wed in this chapel at Westmont College because when I had been feeling at my lowest, a sense of grace had overtaken me there. I do not remember what had upset me. Perhaps it was the existential crisis of Kierkegaard or perhaps it was Garett. But I had been crying in the chapel when suddenly light flooded through the stained-glass windows. I felt full of colors and bliss. Eugene was too frenetic, too sex-as-enlightenment-driven, to capture the moment of innocence I had once felt here. Besides, it was simply not a marrying kind of place. Eugene had *orgies*.

I wanted something else. I needed it to be like the magazines, which only my sister understood. I wanted to get married while my dad could still perform his duties. More than that, I needed my dad to say that I was doing the right thing. I needed to hear him say that it was going to be okay, to say, "Go marry him. Your mother and I approve."

Unfortunately, it had not started as a good day for my father. "I need to get the . . . ," he had said that morning, looking at my mom with that familiar helplessness. He shook his fist, repeating, "I need to get the . . . you know, the . . ." Then he gave up and walked away, not knowing how to say he had lost his cup of coffee, not knowing where it was. My mom chased after him with his coffee cup at a plush bed-and-breakfast with more than enough room for someone who did not know the word for "coffee."

Now heat lamps protected the patio from the sixty-five-degree weather outside, while inside my sister had covered the wooden benches in white bows. She had started saying that marriage was "mainly a convention," but she still loved the fabrics and the flowers. She said she believed in Montaigne, who said marriage was for friendship and not passion, which could only exist outside of marriage. At the altar were bouquets of tall purple delphinium, almost completely concealing the cross behind it, which had been the plan. We were not there for Jesus that day.

But something still was not right.

More than a year ago, Keith and I had loaded up our U-Haul truck to move to Missouri, taking the scenic route over Yosemite Pass, which was where we had our first argument when our brakes caught on fire. We were heading down a narrow road hanging over a cliff when blue smoke started coming from the front wheel. Keith pulled over as I dangled over the cliff, terrified of heights. We did not have a fire extinguisher, so I wanted to call a tow truck or someone to give us a ride into town. But Keith used to be an auto mechanic and said it was no big deal, that the cold would put it out. So we continued on, even though I didn't want to. Was that when I should have just gotten out and said, *You go on without me*? But we made it down, which I guess proved he was right.

After that, our arguments seemed to follow the same pattern. For instance, we ran into a bear sitting on the trail while hiking in Yosemite. I instinctively said, "Stop. Let's back up slowly," while Keith instinctively picked up a rock and threw it at the bear.

"It's not a dog to shoo away!" I yelled.

"I'm not trying to hit it!" he yelled back. Only the bear seemed unconcerned. Failing at dislodging the bear, Keith then ran up to it and kicked dirt in his face.

"Are you crazy?" I shouted. "You don't run *toward* a bear." But it worked. The bear ran away, and Keith thought he was proven right again.

These were the little arguments.

Our big argument happened when we got to Kansas, and in Kansas, there is no way to end an argument. It spreads out before you, on and on and on, a flat plain without interruption. There are no forests or bumps in the road or distractions. Just argument. We were supposed to get married as soon as we reached Missouri, but we had postponed it for a year before we even arrived.

Being a new teacher was stressful enough, I decided.

In Columbia, a college town of one hundred thousand with a campus built by slaves, Keith could not find the kind of work he wanted, with an environmental nonprofit. Surprisingly, that was not really a *thing* in Missouri. We found only one such position, and it did not pay. Then he looked into working at the Department of Natural Resources but found it focused mostly on hunting and fishing, not ecosystem management, which was his specialty. Eventually, he settled on the fisheries and wildlife PhD program at Mizzou, even though he complained it was not "*fish* and wildlife," as they had at other universities. "Fisheries," he said, means protecting fish so people can eat them, not for the fish themselves.

He wanted to save salmon for the sake of salmon.

Even so, we were delighted that he got into the program on such short notice, with a tuition waiver and an office in the Natural Resources Building. We laughed in the hallway of his new building, which was lined with stuffed animals in glass cases.

"Hey, a bobcat!" I pointed at one. The taxidermist had made it look *mean,* as if it would tear you to shreds, which I found hilarious.

"It's like some kitsch *Twin Peaks* set in here," I said, laughing. The building was new and entirely corporate looking aside from these scary dusty displays.

"Can you believe it?" Keith said, then grabbed my hand and led me down a staircase. "You've got to check *this* out," he said. In the basement, we entered a dusty locked storage room, which he had discovered earlier that his key would open. Inside, he pointed to something that looked like an elephant's foot.

"What the hell is that?" I asked. There was a glass table on top, covered in a sooty dust.

"Someone made it into a coffee table." He laughed as he tried to pick it up.

"Oh, my God," I said. "I teach about this kind of shit! I can't believe that's here." I had been hired to teach postcolonial literature and theory, including the history of the British Empire. I knew about the use of elephant feet from Africa as coffee tables in London in the Victorian era. But why was it here, in a basement in Missouri? It could not get more *Twin Peaks.*

"Lots of taxidermy specialists in Missouri, I guess," Keith said.

We went to his grad student "orientation" on a day when the sassafras and dogwood were starting to turn and the limestone blocks in the old stone buildings sparkled enough to make us relax a moment. The barbecue was held in the courtyard outside a more picturesque building than Keith's.

As we approached, I noticed that the meat on the grill looked eerily squirrel- and bird-shaped. I assumed it was tofu, knowing that tofurkey can be shaped to look like a turkey for Thanksgiving.

I asked a man in a Mizzou T-shirt, "What's cooking?"

"Oh hi!" He seemed bright and friendly. "That's mine there and this one is Sheila's—" He touched the tofu squirrel with a stoker. "They're almost done." Then he turned to Keith and said, "Did you bring your animal?"

"No," Keith said abashedly.

"What are they talking about?" I whispered to Keith as he pulled me to the side, while the friendly man turned back to the grill.

"Excuse us for a moment," he said to Mizzou man. "We need a drink."

Then he whispered to me, "They called it the 'Missouri Beast Feast' and said we should bring the animals we were studying to eat. I thought they were kidding!" I looked back and saw there were squirrels on a stick, turtles on the shell, and lots of tiny songbirds. Even a river otter. Growing up, I had been haunted by *Ring of Bright Water,* a movie about a Londoner who lives with a pet otter until a neighbor ignorantly hacks it to death. *Not Mij!* I thought. I was mortified.

Back at the grill, I asked who brought the otter.

A bookish-looking blonde perked up and raised her hand. "Aren't they endangered?" I asked.

"Oh, they fly in the frozen carcasses from somewhere else," she replied. "For research."

"Yum," I said sarcastically.

Keith never could pick an animal after that. He briefly worked on the deer vaccination program, shooting birth control pills into deer with a bow and arrow. In Canada, he said, they would just bring in some grizzlies or wolves to eat those deer right up. Problem solved.

In the midst of all this, we were getting married, and weddings do not stop to give you more time to contemplate beast feasts or deer vaccinations. The date had been set and the date would arrive. My sister offered to meet me in St. Louis to shop for wedding dresses while Keith went home to visit his parents and clear out the last of his things at an apartment in Eugene. In Columbia, the only options I found looked like ruffly prom dresses. I wanted a bigger city, an LA-sized city with LA style.

I really had not intended to end up in a tent off the freeway in East St. Louis, but Christine and I were, respectively, thrifty and broke, so we stayed at a sketchy urban KOA campground filled with the sound of truck traffic. It was clean and cheap, at least, with motorcyclists in tents and older folks in RVs.

"I want something chic, simple, and not white," I told my sis. "How hard is that?" She was living in Indianapolis at the time, where Mitch's company had moved.

After a full day of shopping, however, it turned out it was hard. "We'll try again tomorrow," she replied.

After gathering a sufficient number of quarters, I tried calling Keith from the campground pay phone hanging on the KOA office building in the mosquito-filled night. He was supposed to be at his old apartment that night, which he had shared with a roommate and was still using as a storage space. First he had visited his parents in Vancouver, but he had called me on the way home to Eugene. No answer. Disappointed, I left a message: "I'll call you in the morning."

If I had not had that dream, we might still be married. It was as vivid as a hallucination. Keith was standing on a bright ocean dock with the sun behind him, holding out a bunch of daffodils to me. I felt this peaceful bliss as I walked toward him, ready to take them. Then, out of nowhere, another woman appeared, walked right past me out onto the dock, and took the flowers.

I woke up in a childhoodlike panic, then realized it was a nightmare. I wanted to hear Keith's voice, to be sure. Out I crawled to the pay phone once again. No answer. It was two a.m. and his old roommate was out of town. Then I remembered that Keith's ex-girlfriend lived halfway between Vancouver and Eugene. After that, I could not sleep.

"Oh, thank goodness, where were you?" I asked when he finally picked up the phone the next day.

"Yeah, I got tired and slept in my truck on the way," he said.

"Oh my God, I was worried! I thought you'd been in an accident!" I said.

"No, everything's fine," he said.

I slumped in relief and exhaustion. "Thank God," I said. "I had the weirdest dream last night. . . ."

After recounting the dream, he said nothing. Then: "I . . . uh . . . yeah . . . okay."

"Did you meet Barb?" I asked as the temperature seemed to suddenly drop.

A pause, then: "Nothing happened. We just talked."

By then, I very well knew what "nothing" could mean. I had done a lot of "nothing happened" or "just making out," after all. He was talking my language now.

Once he was home, I interrogated him until he finally fleshed out all the nothingness of that night. At first, he said they only "made out" for a few hours, but I knew a few hours was time for a whole lot of "nothing." Later, he told me about the parts of her body he had kissed or not kissed, the places that he had rubbed and not rubbed, and the sites that were naked or not naked. Blow by blow.

Surprisingly, Keith's repentant, desperate recoiling from his own actions made *me* feel guilty. I did, after all, torture him into every single painful detail for weeks on end. I broke us both, but still wanted more. I could have left it alone. It was "nothing," after all.

First, he said it was because of Missouri, not me. Then he said it was because she accepted him for who he was, while I did not. This meant it was my fault, not his. In some ways, he was right. I had wanted him to be happy in Missouri, to be happy with me, but he never was. I had wanted him to get a job.

"There's something else," he said, and stopped. "When you turned on me in Kansas because I had lied about some little thing from my past, I felt I could never tell you the rest. I thought you would never accept me. That was *nothing*." He was talking about the women he had loved and the children he may or may not have had with them. A whole life before me of things that scared me, some of which had been changed because it scared me. Keith had a crazy drug-filled youth.

"What else didn't you tell me?" I asked, calmed by his solemn, sad tone. It was his childhood, he said, a story as long as Kansas, and he slowly began to unravel it for me.

Because he was afraid of his father as an adolescent, he said, he ran away from home and was taken in by men who were not good to him, men who offered drugs and more. By the end of his tale, we were both curled in a ball on the floor crying. "I've never told anyone this. It feels like a basketball floating to the surface inside me," he said. "A huge weight has been lifted." That weight was transferred, then, from him to me. I had no idea such things happened in the world. How could I not love this poor, fearful, abandoned boy, this son?

After that, I carried in me the PTSD from the war that was his life. I froze up in his sorrow and let the train keep rolling, all the way to the altar. If I had not had that dream, I would never have known any of this. Would that have been better?

Suddenly, in a panic, I ran out of the wedding chapel and into a nearby mansion where the college president's office was. Leaning over a marble bathroom sink, I tried to catch my breath, which was failing me. I cringed at my reflection in the mirror, seeing the burn mark on my face from the hairdresser's curling iron. "Oops," she had said, as if this were any other day. "Oops." There was a two-inch red welt next to my eye. I had tried to cover it with makeup, but that only made it look like a bruise, as though Keith had hit me.

My mom walked in and stood by me quietly. "You don't have to do this," she said. "Not for us. The money doesn't matter. We can cancel the whole thing right now."

"No, I'll be okay," I lied. "I'm just upset about the burn. I can't seem to hide it."

The truth is I felt I was in a vat of Jell-O. The Valium was kicking in.

As we walked outside, it started pouring rain. I cursed Santa Barbara's weather modification program, which made it rain more, keeping it lush and green. China Lake had designed that cloud-seeding program, too, where you drop silver iodine into clouds to make them rain. It was impossible to get away from them. "We regard the weather as a weapon," China Lake scientist Pierre Saint-Amand once said. "Anything one can use to get his way is a weapon and the weather is as good a one as any." After they used it to cause landslides in Vietnam, they brought it to Santa Barbara. To fill their reservoirs. To ruin my wedding day. I started to cry.

"Can you get my umbrella, Mom?" I looked away to hide my tears.

"Of course, baby," she said, and ran out in the rain.

Suddenly, everything was falling apart. My hair had been done up and the flowers had been done up, but I could not stop the rain. I could not make it perfect, could not erase the past. I was wearing gold brocade Vera Wang and carrying French tulips, but everything started wilting under the weight of the water.

Inside the chapel, Keith stood in the front in his tuxedo, which I had made him wear. He dealt with his discomfort by making "look at me I'm a snob" faces, lifting up his nose and looking down on our guests. Had I made him do this? I thought. As he stood there, our childhood photographs flashed on a TV screen in front thanks to Mitch, who had set our photos and home movies to my favorite Rachmaninoff concerto.

As I started down the aisle with my dad, I began to hope that, as in *The Graduate,* someone would bang on that window overlooking the ocean to stop us. I pictured a man pounding on the pane behind the empty cross, yelling at me to go back. I wanted shocked guests looking on as we drove crazily and forever away while *Sounds of Silence* played.

"Who gives this woman away?" asked the minister, a woman who had been ordained online before everyone was doing that. She looked nervous, this internet minister, knowing we were suddenly her responsibility.

All I needed was one sentence from my dad, which I had patiently coached him on. "Her mother and I do," I kept repeating. "Her mother and I do." Now was the time to say it, and then he could be done acting normal. Forever. "But you *have* to get it right," I had said. I wanted to be released, to be allowed to make all the mistakes I knew I would make when he was not there to watch.

In this moment for which I had waited so long, I suddenly realized that I was furious. I hated my dad for being sick and not being there for me. I hated him for never being able to look me in the eye and say, *I know who you are, and it's okay. You're okay with me.* I hated him for everything he had concealed, for all those feelings I would never know now, and for a sickness that seemed sometimes like the last manifestation of a life of secrecy. Now he was going even further away than I could ever go from him, and I hated him for that. I hated him for going to a place where I would never be able to reach him, further than a locked bedroom door.

"I do," my father said in his black tuxedo.

"No, no. Try again," the minister prodded gently.

I just knew my father would forget, but I wished the minister would let it go.

"Huh?" he said, looking flustered.

"Her mother and I do," the minister whispered to him.

"Huh?" my dad said, and I thought he would walk off in frustration as he often did, out the door to who-knows-where. Once, he walked out of a London hotel and we all had to chase him through the crowded streets. When we gave up and turned back, we found him quietly sitting in the hotel lobby, looking at us like "What's all the fuss?"

"Her mother and I do," my sister whispered.

"Oh, my mother and I *do*." My father laughed, emphasizing the last word. Then he shrugged, clearly thinking, *Of course . . . that's what I said*. Then he kissed me on the cheek and let me go, obviously glad to be done with the whole thing.

Keith and I turned to each other to say our vows. It was then that I realized I had taken too much Valium. I had said *half* a tab would be enough—but no, Keith had wanted to go all the way. I stood there, in a Valium-induced haze, hoping someone would stop me. My husband said he loved me, and I knew he did. But the man who took my hand to marry me looked at me as if I were the prettiest little virgin girl in the whole world. He loved me as though I were nine years old and promised to watch over me. He said I was his soul mate, and I was too stoned to care. I had wanted to rescue Keith from his past, but he had wanted to protect me from ever knowing that world.

"Now take these candles and light the one I'm holding, symbolizing the two becoming one," the minister said, signaling the end of the ceremony. She handed us two birthday-cake-sized candles. I was embarrassed by how small they were, as if that were all she could find around her house that day. *What are we paying her?* I thought. She also forgot to bring a match, and among a group of nonsmokers, it was hard to find one. I suspected Keith might have one stashed on him somewhere but would not admit it, since he told me he had quit smoking. Finally, my ever-ready cousin Linda came to the rescue, and the minister lit her candle. As Keith and I leaned in to light our candles from hers, a gust of wind came in and blew all the candles out. The minister laughed nervously.

"That's okay, we'll try again," she said. The second time it worked, but all I could think about was the Columbia River coming up, up, up, putting out every light, smashing down cities and towns and people. Keith smiled, a stoned smile, as my dad walked out of the room without even waiting to watch the kiss. "Her mother and I do," he muttered, shaking his head as my sister ran after him down the aisle.

Chapter Twenty-Seven

The End of the World

After the wedding, Keith and I began to live for roads: dirt roads, roller-coaster roads, long bicycle paths that made our thighs chafe, roads to Anywhere-but-Here. Roads to the Farthest-Away-Possible. Keith was like Conrad's Marlow, putting his finger on the blank space on a map and saying we *have* to go. Of course, this blank space was always in Canada. Had we stayed at the Farthest-Away-Possible place, I sometimes wonder if we would still be married. That was what Keith had wanted, after all. But I was born with a terror of poverty, of going *back*, of not having health insurance. I would not, could not, give up my job. So we traveled instead on a shoestring in a Ford F-250.

First, we biked around Newfoundland and Nova Scotia, then spent a summer in Quebec, and when we thought the world would finally end, we drove to the most remote place Keith could think of: Bella Coola, British Columbia.

At the time, everyone was worried about the giant computer

glitch. On December 31, 1999, the world was supposed to go dark because no one had bothered to program the computers to recognize the year 2000. "It's not like you even need more *space*," I had complained to my mother. "You just need a '2.'" The world's computers were expected to all fritz out at the stroke of midnight because apparently they needed to know the *when* in order to figure out *what* they were supposed to be doing. Or something like that. Stoplights would go dark, air traffic control screens would go blank, civilization as we knew it would end. Keith and I sort of hoped it would.

At first, I assumed the giant glitch was all hype, but then I called my mom. "Mom," I asked, "what will happen when midnight comes?" I assumed she would explain it in detail to me, alleviating my fears with words I could not follow. Words about national security, backup plans, and so forth. Computer words.

Instead, she said, "Anyone's guess." She probably never knew that this was what sent Keith and me fleeing to a town of five hundred people in remote BC.

"She doesn't *know*," I told Keith, incredulous.

Keith said that when the world ended, we could settle down in Bella Coola and live off the grid. The "grid" would be a thing of the past, anyway. In many ways, we were in our element. I could build a straw-bale house, which I had learned how to do in my "Green Architecture" class. "No, rammed earth," Keith corrected. "Too wet for straw." He could identify mushrooms and gather mussels.

"If the people with guns find their way to Bella Coola," he said, "I know an even better spot in Haida Gwaii, an island off the coast of northern BC."

I remembered a story Keith once told about him and his father getting red tide in Haida Gwaii. "It was wild," he said. "Our hands started tingling and going numb, and then it gradually moved up my arms. All I could do was wait to see where it stopped. People die when it paralyzes their heart or lungs."

Keith had panic attacks that sounded like that, starting with his hands tingling, then going numb, and then the sensation moving up his arms. He had a terror of public speaking, which we shared in common, though I did not have his fear of bridges. He thought he would drive off of them but would never let me drive instead.

"Did you go to the doctor?" I asked.

"No, there are no doctors where we were in Haida Gwaii."

After that, I secretly started making my own plans for after the great computer glitch. I did not want to get paralyzed eating mussels. I wanted my mom. So I called my mom again. "Mom," I said, "if anything happens, I think we need a plan. I'm stocking up food. Missouri is a natural halfway point for all of us. Try to get to my house, and tell Christine to do the same. Stock up on gas." By then, Christine and her family had moved to Philadelphia, where Mitch had become president of his defense contracting company. It was closer to Washington, DC, and the politicians.

"Okay, I will," my mom replied. I started hiding food like assets in preparation for a divorce. I pictured my mom shoving my dad into their wheelchair-ready van and setting off, evading gunfire along the way, just to get to that food.

"Sure, I could live in Haida Gwaii," I would lie to Keith, even as I planned to steal his truck. I think we were both hoping the world would end, which would decide the fate of our marriage. It would all finally be over.

"In Bella Coola, the Indians are cowboys," Keith said on the way to Bella Coola as we passed ranches and signs for rodeos along the one road leading down a narrowing valley. Gradually, the trees got bigger and the world grew darker as giant snow-topped mountains inched closer to the road, enveloping it in night in the early afternoon.

At the end of the road, a glowing world popped out of the darkness. The enormous firs stopped before the edge of the fjord, where jellyfish were glowing white in the bluish-black waters. Mesmerized, I exited the truck to what I thought was the sound of their tentacles pushing the inky depths. The sky was pitch-black; only the stars and these bright orbs lit up what looked like a long dock extending out to sea.

Keith took my hand and whispered, "There are spirit bears here."

"What are they?" I whispered in the quiet certainty of our union, our Gore-Tex jackets pressed against each other. This was us at our best, pressed together, looking out.

"White bears are born from black bears only in this region," he said. "No one knows why. People say they will awaken your unconscious if you see one." In this luminescent sparkling world, it did not surprise me the bears would glow white as well. An orca suddenly jumped from the water, bluish white in the reflection of the twinkling sea. I gasped. If only we could stay, I thought. If only the world would end and the bears would bring us back to life.

We decided to drive along the bay to find a place to camp, and when Keith found a suitable spot, he went ahead to scout out the darkness. Soon he shouted back, "Look at this!"

I jumped out and slammed the truck door shut, rushing to see what he saw. Abruptly, my hand refused to join me. My arm yanked me back to the site of my hand, where one finger was neatly jammed deep in the truck door. This is how a wolf must feel, looking at her leg in a trap. I wanted to gnaw it off, to get rid of the problem as quickly as possible. I pulled and pulled, not caring if it broke off, but it would not budge. I did not feel a thing but simply knew my finger was no longer my own.

"Keith, I need the key to the car," I said, trying to stay calm.

"In a minute," he said, not turning to look back.

"Keith!" I then screamed. "Get over here now!" I was jumping up and down, neither in pain nor in hopes of freeing my finger, but simply to demonstrate urgency.

When is it going to hurt? I kept thinking. Shouldn't it hurt?

By the time Keith turned the key and opened the door, my finger looked white and lifeless. We rushed to the tiny Nuxalk town of Bella Coola as my finger slowly turned red in a flood of blood and began to scream and swell. "Ouch," I whimpered as we passed darkened mobile homes and government-style buildings.

Keith found an open gas station where the attendant, a quiet large man with suspicious eyes, rushed to the phone when he saw my finger. "Hey, Steve," he said. "Get over to the clinic. You've got a broken finger."

Broken? I thought. "It needs to be amputated right away!"

It turned out the gas station attendant was right. After a hole was drilled in my nail to release the pressure and my finger was nicely bandaged and splinted up, Keith and I went back to the gas station to thank the man who had helped us and buy some ibuprofen. He looked in his thirties with short dark hair, blue jeans, and cowboy boots. "Hey, you survived," he said, nodding at my finger. "You okay?"

"Yeah, it's not serious," I said, glad I had not asked for an amputation.

"A little tequila might work better than aspirin, eh?" he joked, handing me the ibuprofen. Suddenly, that feeling of suspiciousness we all had upon first meeting in the darkness was gone. "There's a party over at the Valley Inn. End of the World and all. You should come."

So there we were, with midnight approaching, jumping up and down with a group of Nuxalks who had pushed aside the pool tables to dance in the End of the World. Slowly, Keith and I realized that when they talked about the End of the World, they had two possibilities in mind. First, their world was going to end when an oil pipeline was built across their valley, as someone drunkenly said to our drunken selves: "The tankers are going to pull up into *our* bay to get oil from the pipeline. But those pipes leak, you know it? And the boats are filthy and, one day, one will crash. But what can we do?" That was the first End of the World. The second End of the World was the same as ours, but it seemed as if they kind of wanted it too. I realized then that you cannot build oil pipelines without computers. You cannot build missiles either.

Choose your own End of the World, I guess.

There we were, dancing in the celebration of the coming darkness.

"Let's go to the dock before the clock strikes," Keith shouted to no one in particular. A few men in their twenties followed us to the promontory perched on a shining sea. There, we put our arms on each other's shoulders, all in a circle, as we counted down the clock. "Ten, nine, eight," we yelled, and the mountains echoed our voices back to us, creating their own time confusion.

Finally, "Happy New Year!" our new friends shouted, and started jumping up and down hard enough to shake the old boards on the dock.

Soon we joined in the jumping and screaming, "Happy New Year!" Over and over again in a frenzy of joy at the End. We hugged in the darkness of No More World.

See, the thing is that we had no way of knowing if the computers had glitched or spat or groaned. The Valley Inn was on a local generator. Even as we crawled out of the truck in the morning, hungover heads first, we agreed we would have to drive back out of the valley to find out if the world had ended, too embarrassed to ask in town.

What if we just decided that it had and stayed?

Instead, we were a bit defeated when, hours later, we saw a commercial airplane overhead. Then we noticed the growing traffic and noise and busyness of unconcerned travelers whose faces looked blank, signifying to us that the world was intact or, at least, that a different End of the World was in store for us.

But that one still remained my favorite.

PART SIX

Off Target

Missile Guidebook:
Believe your mother when she says she has had
experience with them. She can help.

Chapter Twenty-Eight

Student or Spouse

Keith left the year the Twin Towers fell. A month or so before. The signs had been there for some time, but when it happened, I went into shock. I wanted to kill him. To attack. Trauma can do that. I started to suspect there was a problem when he said he had to take off his wedding ring to get back across the border into the United States. It turned out that he had never updated his visa status from "student" to "spouse."

"What were you thinking?" I scolded him. "You need to take care of that."

"I know, I know," he said, but we got across.

A year later, he was stopped at JFK International Airport and sent back to Heathrow after we had spent a glorious summer hiking the Cornish footpath. My parents and sister even met us there to see my dad's Cornish past, including the hotel where he was boarded during the war. In it, there were pictures on the walls of soldiers who had stayed there, but not of my dad. My mom even paid for us all to go to Sweden after Cornwall, though not for Keith. "I'll pay for him," I insisted. "I'm not going without my husband." It was on the trip that my dad wandered out into the streets of London. He returned, while Keith did not.

"I forgot to take off my ring," he said sheepishly when Border Control detained him at Heathrow. They rushed me through as he stayed behind, growing smaller and harder to reach. "Don't worry, I'll sort it out and be back in no time," his small voice shouted from his shrinking face. If the world had ended, there would be no borders.

It was only the third and fourth times that I'd had to admit there was a problem, that maybe he did not want an American visa. Or an American wife. The third time it happened, his friend had to drive four hours south from Nelson, Canada, to pick him up at the Canadian–U.S. border in a barely running VW van in the middle of the night. It had all started with syringes, which I was carrying in my luggage for my allergy shots. When the U.S. border guards found those, they proceeded to tear the car apart while drilling me about my alleged heroin connections in a fluorescent-lighted room with a government gray metal desk like at home. The whole thing took around four hours.

Outside, two Canadian border guards, who had been watching the ruckus from a distance, ran across the empty two-lane highway from their post to ask if we needed help. I politely said no, wondering what they could do. Were they suggesting I claim asylum in Canada? It was late, dark, forested, and miles from anywhere. Then I realized those nice guards were probably offering to take us in for the night. Maybe we should just have run, dropping our bags and heading back across the border for a nice cup of tea in that Canadian border post.

Finally, while still rifling through the car, the U.S. bully-guards found a bottle of Flonase nasal spray and acted as if it were a brick of cocaine. One shouted out, "Hey, where's the prescription for this?"

"I didn't bring it with me," I shouted back, cold and tired.

He huffed over, held the bottle in my face, and said, "I can arrest you for this." I started to cry, wondering what they did to brown people at the border.

Next, they found another gold mine: Keith's wedding ring. It seems his visa was still marked "Student." His ring was in the glove compartment. Of course, Keith actually was a student in fisheries and wildlife, but the problem was that you could not be both a student and a spouse in the United States. Being a spouse invalidates being a student, or at least the visa, it seems. America was too confusing for me.

The air smelled like forests as I climbed into his Ford F-250 and watched him disappear into the darkness in my rearview mirror. I wanted to be on the other side with him, even as angry at him as I was.

Keith's fourth and final border trouble came in the U.S. mail. I once thought "being deported" meant the sheriff came and dragged you away, putting you on a plane to who-knows-where. Now I know the mailman can do it. The letter, which looked so flimsy and frail, simply said he had to go. We both knew by then that a sheriff or a SWAT team was somewhere behind that letter, waiting to jump out at us.

Strangely, Keith never seemed to mind his deportations or barred re-entries, which began to make me worry. When he finally got his spousal visa, our fate was already sealed in a cycle of doubt that only the end could stop. It was too late. As I was busy adjusting to the problem of getting tenure and all the fear and work that it implies, Keith was becoming a global exile, the opposite of a "citizen of the world." He did not know where he belonged; maybe getting kicked out solidified his self-image.

"I'll move wherever you want," I once said, "but only if you find a job there first. I don't want to quit my job unless we have something else."

"Why don't you find something else? Just quit and move with me. You can find work wherever we choose to live," he replied. As my brain spiraled into a hole of incomprehension, he quietly added, "Or we can both go on welfare."

Canadians think differently from Americans.

"You want me to quit a tenure-track job to go on *welfare*?" I said.

One day, Keith said we should go to his grandfather's cabin at 100 Mile House for Christmas break. It was one room with no plumbing, electricity, or oven. Named for being one hundred miles from anywhere, 100 Mile House is actually a postal stop, not a town. There is also a 200 Mile House. I pictured that long drive back to Missouri alone again and hesitated. "I think it would be good for us to get away," Keith said. "We can use it for free as long as we want."

"I'm not moving there," I said. "I don't care if it's free." I had been there once, a spot deep in the woods where Keith's grandfather's hand-hewn cabin had sat closed up for years, collecting dust, bugs, and mouse droppings.

"It doesn't even have plumbing," I argued. "We can't live there."

"No, it does. Remember the toilet in the corner?" I vaguely pictured a toilet bowl covered in dirt with no lid or doors around it. It looked like a prison cell toilet. "It's stopped up, but Grandpa told me how to fix it. There's an outlet in the lake that can be easily unplugged. It's marked by a plastic milk jug."

"But it's December. What if the lake is frozen?" His insistence was starting to seem bizarre. Was he finally leaving me? Keith's face was unreadable.

"I always do everything you want me to do . . ." He raised his voice. I knew this was turning into the argument we always had. "Why won't you do this one thing for me?"

"There's no plumbing!" Clearly, I was not being unreasonable. Or was I? We were descending into an argument that was by then too painful to go through again, so we focused on the toilet instead. It was unfixable, but we had to go. If we did not go, it could never be fixed. That was the question of our marriage.

"Are you coming with me or not?" I did not answer.

I knew Keith was angry because I had turned down a job offer in Toronto. There had been a blizzard when I visited, the teaching load was too heavy, and I thought Keith would leave me anyway by then. I did not want to be stuck in what I imagined would be a permanent blizzard, knowing no one, and having to teach all the time. All I wanted to do, as ever, was sit in a room of my own and read books. There was too much uncertainty and cold in Canada, besides a salary cut, which sent my mind into a tailspin until finally I said, "No."

He could not forgive me for that. It was my act of treason.

Yet now that it seemed he was really leaving, I *was* tempted to simply quit my job and throw in the towel. Then would we finally be fixed or were we simply unfixable? One hundred miles from anywhere in a cold cabin, alone. Keith off chasing the bears. Not coming home. For years, I agonized over these kinds of questions. In the end, I chose myself. I chose my job. Because despite my whirlwind of marital despair, I was actually starting to like it.

There was no way around the toilet then. Keith began to pace while pantomiming how easy it would be to fix it. "All I have to do is cut a hole in the ice, dive in, and find the plastic bottle . . ." His voice was getting louder, his arms raised in a dive. "My grandfather has done it a million times. If I pull on it, it will unstop the toilet. It's a very simple mechanical fix."

"I can't go," I said firmly.

"Well, I'm going," he said, equally firm.

After he left, all I could do was wait by the phone, hoping he was not dead and that he could find a way to let me know. But the only person who called was my mother.

"What's up, Mom?" I asked a bit too curtly.

"Oh, nothing important," she replied. "I just thought you should know that Christine is pregnant again."

"No!" I said, even somehow knowing that she would.

Eventually, I got an email asking for a divorce. As we had begun, we ended in cyberspace.

Touché.

After that email, Keith would not pick up the phone or respond to my panicked questions online. For ten years. I simply got the divorce papers in the mail with an ultimatum to sign. "I'll take the house," he wrote on a Post-it note, "if you do not sign. The settlement arrangement is fair."

For years, I kept having this recurrent dream in which Keith was reaching for something underwater that I could not see, something he was trying to untangle from a fishing line. Slowly, he realized that the fishing line was my hair, and the more he struggled, the more his entire body was entangled and unable to move. Slowly, he grew still as algae swirled around him and his blank eyes watched a carp swimming by. In my dream, I do not know if he is alive or dead in the end.

In real life, it was only my dad who died, not him.

It was after the Twin Towers fell.

Chapter Twenty-Nine

Falling Buildings

When the World Trade Center was hit, my first thought was that it was a missile. I could not imagine a plane, but no one knew what to think at first. It was like when people get lost in the woods. They will bend reality, trying to fit it into where they *think* they are before accepting they are lost. Someone might insist that the sun sets in the east rather than admit being lost. We could fit anything into those first few seconds after the plane hit. A multitude of nonsensical thoughts emerged simultaneously in people's minds for those first few seconds. For me, it was that a missile had gone off course.

It was only when I saw the plane on TV that I accepted the facts. Others, to this day, refuse to accept them, insisting it was an intentional demolition, or a missile, or the many other things that people say when their minds have not yet adapted to that feeling of being lost. The sun is still setting in the east for them.

It happened in the morning as I was getting ready to go to class. My friend called and told me to turn on the TV, as so many people did that morning. Phones were ringing all over the world like that. Keith was already gone. On ABC, the World Trade Center was burning from an apparent hole in the center. I did not have time to think. I was late for class. I turned off the TV to get dressed, not knowing the whole world had stopped.

On the way to class, I turned on the radio as Peter Jennings said, "We now have . . . what do we have? It may be that something fell off the building. We don't know, to be perfectly honest." He cut to *Good Morning America*'s Don Dahler, four blocks from the towers, to figure out what was going on.

Don said calmly, as if he were in shock, "The entire building has just collapsed. . . . It folded down on itself and it is not there anymore. It has completely collapsed."

"The whole side has collapsed?"

"The whole *building* has collapsed," Don said as they were both adapting in their minds before admitting they were lost. One, two, three seconds . . .

"The whole *building* has collapsed? My God."

Two buildings burning. One gone.

All those people, I kept thinking. How many people are in there? The news said fifty thousand. It took seconds for the buildings to fall.

One, two, three, four . . .

Fifty thousand, I kept thinking. Crumbling, falling, one by one. Slowly, that number started going down since the workday had not yet started. It ended up at under three thousand: 2,753. I knew there would be more, the victims of wars to come, as well as the victims who breathed in the dust of dead bodies and buildings that day.

In class, I told the handful of students who arrived that the World Trade Center had been bombed "or something." I still did not know it was a plane. Even after I did, I had a hard time switching to "attacked" and kept saying "when the World Trade Center was bombed." No one knew how to talk about this new strange thing, how to comprehend what was happening. Then I said, "Go home."

People wandered the streets of New York City in a daze, covered in the dust of dead bodies. Vice President Dick Cheney went down into a bunker to prepare for nuclear war and later said he had wanted to ensure the "continuity of government" *after* nuclear war. At the same time, President George W. Bush was finishing the book about the goat that he had been reading to schoolchildren that morning. For some reason, he insisted on finishing that book even after hearing about the attack. He was lost. Secretary of Defense Donald Rumsfeld went missing around the same time. He was found wandering around the Pentagon lawn, trying to help survivors of the plane that had crashed there. He was lost. He had forgotten that he was supposed to save the *country*, not pull lives from the rubble. We all waited for more planes to fall from the sky. We all prepared to run. For a few hours, no one seemed to be in charge.

Later that day, I wandered the streets of Columbia in a daze, feeling the need to be outside and look at the sky. A local reporter stopped me to ask how I felt. I replied, "I'm scared, because I know we are going to bomb someone, and I don't know who it will be." I was on the news that night. I wondered if other people felt that way, or if only I was in terror of the war to come, already mourning for the victims.

No one knew who had hijacked those planes. Fifteen out of the nineteen hijackers turned out to be Saudi and the rest Egyptian, Lebanese, and Emirati. In their last nights before blowing up the world for Allah, they had been acting like a bunch of sailors: watching porn, inviting call girls to their rooms, and hanging out in strip clubs.

My dad did not care for violence on TV by then. It would make him start groaning, stand up to pace, and sometimes walk right out the door. My mom would have to change the channel to keep him at home. When the World Trade Center was hit, he began to rock back and forth while moaning, but my mom would not turn it off then. She needed to know what had happened. She needed to know if we were safe or if a war was starting.

Then we invaded Afghanistan. *Afghanistan?* I thought. No one seemed to know where it was, but everyone wanted to attack it. These were bad years for my dad, who was deep in the "wandering" stage of Alzheimer's, when they want to walk. No one really knows why. Some say it is because they have lost a sense of time and space and want to search for landmarks in an attempt to orient themselves. Others say it is because they have regressed to their childhood and are searching for something from their past.

My dad would walk to the bank and demand the teller give him milk, thinking he was at the supermarket. He would go to church thinking he was supposed to be in a committee meeting on the base. Sometimes he would simply walk out into the desert until the police found him and pulled him in. Since everyone in town knew my father, they would simply return him to my mother like a coat left behind at a party. An old man in the desert. "Oh, there's Earl again," they would say, and call my mom. One time my mom got a phone call at four a.m. from a policewoman who said she was having coffee with him at Denny's. Eventually, my mom put alarms on all the doors. The alarm would go off and she would run out in the street and drag him back inside, over and over again.

After the Twin Towers fell, people began to ask, "Why do they hate us?" But I think they meant that rhetorically. Their real question was, "How could anyone hate us?" We believed we were essentially good and were horrified to realize that others disagreed. It takes a very long time, sometimes a lifetime, to admit the things you do not know. To ask for help. To adapt to being lost.

Before he died, my dad wandered like those people covered in ash on September 11, not knowing where they were going, not knowing what to do. Around them fell mementos of their loved ones—a passport here, a sheaf of papers there. A body. A life.

And then my dad fell like the towers, crumpled up, and disintegrated.

At the funeral, an American flag was draped over the bottom half of my dad's coffin, which was open on top and lined with satin inside. My father was displayed in that same gold-and-turquoise room at church where ACE had shown all its movies, like *A Thief in the Night*, about the woman who wakes up to find everyone has left for the Rapture. That one had terrified me once, but now I did not believe in the Rapture, or in Heaven or Hell, or God. I did not believe my father had gone anywhere in particular. All that mattered to me was making it through the funeral without falling apart. I did not want that coffin to be open right then and thought I might run up and slam the lid. Later, I hoped it would never close.

I was conscious mostly of my sister's dress next to mine. Her velvety green skirt looked soft and brilliant in the sunshine streaming through the ceiling's stained-glass windows. I was conscious only of where her skirt touched mine and where it did not. I was thankful, even if she was not, that God had not allowed her to get close to Heaven again, that she and her baby had both come out fine. My sister folded her hands in her lap the way my father used to do. I realized I was doing the same. The three of us—my mother, sister, and me—held our bodies in the same stiff, tearless position, heads down, as if to show we had all agreed to the funeral's formality. We decided to be my dad so as not to scream, since he could not; with our hands and bodies, we were him.

If I focused on my sister's dress, I could stop thinking about my father's body for a few seconds here and there. I especially did not want to think about his thumb, which looked as though it had not been embalmed properly. It was thin and flat as a piece of paper, with the nail hanging on weirdly. It looked as if it had not been filled up properly with the embalming liquid. It looked like those cartoon characters that get run over by steamrollers and end up flattened on the road but still alive. In the cartoons, it is funny precisely because they are still alive, but this was not funny. All my dad's fingers were normal, but he barely had a thumb. It was the first thing I noticed.

"What's wrong with it?" I asked my mom at the viewing the day before the funeral, but she looked offended.

"Nothing," she said. "That's just how they do it." She clearly did not want to think about his thumb. Other than his thumb, his body looked healthier than it had in life. The color of his face had been artificially restored, and his hand, which was once cramped into a permanent tortured fist from arthritis and lack of movement, had been surreally straightened out. I wondered if they'd had to break his bones with a hammer to make it look like that. We could never get him to open that hand, as hard as we tried, so maybe his thumb always looked like that inside, like the way my club thumbs once looked inside my fists. Maybe he was embarrassed it looked like that.

To me, this was the thumb that had carefully run over the missile rollerons, spinning them gently. It was the thumb that used to grasp me around the waist and swing me over his shoulders. It was the thumb that used to hold sextants to shoot the stars. I did not want to see it gone. His thumb became a vortex that I tripped and fell into, a thumb surrounded by a body—my father—now a body, not a father. Yet the vortex I was sucked into, that space of death without senses, still seemed more sensible, more real, than the cardboard characters sitting in the pews. My mother, sister, and I were all arrested by that same vortex of death. Who had propped everyone else up in here?

In my dad's last months and years, his body began disappearing and shrinking all over. At first, he stopped eating but would still drink Boost. Later, he would not even do that. The only thing he would eat, in the end, was ice cream. My mother tried to keep him full of ice cream to keep him alive, but he often insisted on drinking his ice cream through a straw, perhaps thinking it was Boost, even though nothing went up the straw. When my mom took the straw away and gave him a spoon, he would shout like a child, "No! Give me the spoon!" and then take the straw back. All the while his body was shrinking and shriveling in the hospital bed at home. It got smaller and smaller even as his mind refused to die. At least the metal bars on his bed kept his body from falling on the floor, turning slowly into dust down there. Before we had those installed, the firemen would have to come and pull his cobweb-ridden body up and back into the bed. My mother could not lift him, and it seemed all he wanted to do was slump to the ground, as if getting ready to go under it, to dig a tunnel down.

In the last stage of Alzheimer's, the body forgets how to work. The stomach forgets it is hungry, the mouth forgets to swallow, the heart forgets to beat. In the end, my mom would not forgive herself for not being his all-night vigil, not being able to stay awake to keep him alive when his body forgot how to live. She had slept through his death, through the sound of his rasping breath, and now could not stop the nightmares about how it may have happened. Even though his death certificate said he'd had a "heart attack," she thought it was her fault, as she once had felt by her mother's side.

My mom said that even near the end, when my dad mostly slept, he might suddenly open his eyes and say, "You look pretty today." Because of moments like these, she had agreed to a feeding tube to keep him alive a little bit longer. In the end, that tube hung out of his belly, attached to what looked like a Slurpee machine. But we knew that it was plumping up his body again, a body that had wanted to shrink into nothingness.

Now my dad's body was artificially plumped up by embalming fluid. The death artists had even managed to close his mouth, shaping it into a peaceful smile: not *too* happy, just enough to signify rest. At the viewing, my mom had leaned over and whispered to me, "It's nice to see him looking healthy again." I imagined my mom wanted him to wake up to forgive her then, and I knew he would if he could. He would hug her and tell her that she had done a great job, that dying was its own fault. He would have said he was sorry because, even though he had made it to twenty years at work, he could not make it to fifty years with her, holding out those last few months until they got to Gold. He would smile at the sight of her in her best funeral dress and say, *You look pretty today.* But because he could not say those things, my mom compulsively pictured his death for a year, even in her dreams.

The pastor was talking as though he wanted to save someone, not realizing there was no way to save my dad now. I wanted my dad to dance on top of his coffin, to come back to life as his great-uncle had. The pastor said, "And his wife, Mary, is a true saint for taking care of Earl until the end." My mom smiled and looked down modestly. Behind her, in the stillness of that moment, someone chuckled. Her smiled vanished.

"Of course, someone had to chuckle," she said later. "I could not possibly be a saint." But she was. For years, I had watched her mind adapt to his needs and way of thinking as she soothed him back to life even as he was dying. She would always correct me when I said he was "crazy." She would say, "It's an illness, a disease, not a psychological problem." She dove into his disease with him. When he flirted with me, unaware that I was his daughter, she said nothing. "Oh, I didn't know you liked me that way," he said as I helped him put on his seat belt. She told me about the time he panicked when he could not recognize her. When he insisted that he had to find her, that she might be hurt, she had driven him around town for hours, looking for herself. Periodically, she would stop and show him her driver's license, trying to convince him of who she was. "No, not that Mary," he would say. "The other one."

"Don't worry, we'll find her," she would say, driving and crying quietly.

Even as my mom slowly moved into my dad's mind, she would try to translate his world to the world outside. She always believed what was in his mind was just as valid as the world outside—because it was *him*—and seemed slightly offended when others did not. If she had woken up in time to see my father dying, I knew his eyes would have simply lit up one last time, not caring about the dying anymore. Just happy to see her pretty face.

On a large screen behind the altar, Mitch projected a video he'd made with photographs of my father set to classical music. There were very few of his childhood, giving one the illusion that his life had started in World War II. This seemed fitting, since as my father's mind had gone backward in time, slowly erasing its recent history, it had finally decided to stop at the war and stay.

My dad stood in a field in Cornwall in his dress U.S. Army Air Corps uniform, with a silver sword by his side. He looked like a kid playing dress-up, pretending to go to war. But his thumb held that sword tightly in place, just as a living thumb would do. He was receiving the Air Medal for a heroic act he never told us about. Maybe it was for the woman who chased him with a gun in Stockholm. My sister and I never got whole stories. We could see one alleyway but not the city, one doorway ducked into but not the war.

After the funeral, we headed to the cemetery, past the wild horse and burro facility and dog pound, close to the Russians, on the outskirts of town. There, you could look out over the valley, with delicate yellow daisies punctuating the view like exclamation points.

As "Taps" was played and the American flag finally folded up and handed to my mother, I felt that my father belonged there, in the place where words were written on petals, where dogs and burros were your guardians. He deserved to leave his sanity, finally, here.

"Beyond the sanity of fools is a burning desert," the Persian poet Rumi once wrote, "Where Your sun is whirling in every atom: / Beloved, drag me there, let me roast in Perfection!" I wanted to be thrown out on the desert floor after I died, which would keep my body warm, not into a cold, dark hole. I wanted to let flowers grow all around me and coyotes lick at my flesh. I cried for my father but also for the veterans that surrounded him—and for the next war and the next, and all the wars that I knew would never end at China Lake. I cried for all the bodies.

Chapter Thirty

The Rubble of a Life

After the funeral, I found my dad's secrets buried in his box, a greenish-gray cardboard carton held together with a shoelace-like ribbon from World War II. It was the box that no one ever opened, meant to remain forever in that secret space between his bed and our beige carpet. So when, only a week after his death, I found it sitting on top of the bed, I felt as if I had stumbled upon a crime scene. My mom must have pulled it out. It looked so exposed, waiting for anyone to look inside. What was I supposed to do?

I pulled off the top.

Inside, I rummaged through stacks of letters until I came across a photograph I recognized, the one he kept in his top dresser drawer, next to his Tums and spare car keys. Only now I noticed something different about the black-haired woman in the photograph on the cliffs of Cornwall. I never knew who she was. I had asked my father once, and he'd replied, "She was my best friend's girl. He asked me to look after her when he went to the front." Maybe he was still looking after her, in his drawer. Only now did I notice that she was posed so beautifully and seductively that it was clear she loved the photographer. Was he my father or his best friend? I could see only her eyes, not his.

Thrusting my hand back in the box, I felt around as in a grab bag until my fingers met the hard edges of a U.S. Army Air Corps dog tag. It was stamped "Earl Marwin Piper." There was a story about this too. My dad told us he always thought his middle name was Marvin, and no one was really around to correct him. His parents, of course, must have told him his middle name, but then they were gone and there were no other Marwins around. So he started writing "Marvin" on his official forms until the air corps caught his mistake. Then in Newquay, a stranger noticed the name on his tag and said, "Ah, Marwin, 'Friend of the Sea.' You're Cornish?" That was how my dad found out his name was Celtic. Cornwall had given my dad back his name, a name perhaps ironic for a man who could not swim, yet appropriate for someone who flew over oceans. "Welcome home," the Cornish man had said.

From his great-grandfather, who had been a tin miner in Cornwall, to his grandfather, who had blown off his arm at fourteen in a mine, my dad must have known his family's story was buried deep in that Cornish soil. He must have learned that his sister's pasties, which my mother could never replicate, were designed to be easily carried in your pocket down into the mines. He must have realized that his small, dark stature came from Cornwall, where the door frames were rarely more than five feet tall. He must have felt he finally "fit." The mines took and took from the Pipers, but serendipity and graves and the stormy ocean had finally washed a tiny bit back up on shore for my dad. A name. A door frame. A great-grandfather buried nearby.

As my father's past must have materialized before his eyes in Cornwall, so my father's box made my memories take on a physical, tangible dimension. Then I pulled out something unfamiliar, a passport with stamps and dates inside and a photograph of my dad in a white aviator's cap with gold braid on the edge. It read "American Air Transport Service." My dad had never been a commercial pilot or navigator, so the picture looked all wrong. I ran into the living room, passport in hand, to ask my sister what it meant. Time was our paramount concern since we could not predict when our mom might return from the store.

"Where'd you get that?" she asked.

"His box was on Mom's bed, so I opened it," I confessed, hoping she would not rat me out. "Did he ever work for a commercial airline?"

"Wow, that's a spy passport," my sister said, looking it over closely. We examined each stamp to see where he had been: Leuchars, Metfield, Bromma. She had told me earlier that she thought he was part of Operation Sonnie in Sweden, which she had pieced together from his flight routes. "I knew it!" she said.

"Is this what you thought he was in?" I leaned over her beanbag chair to look more closely.

"Yes, it's Sonnie," she said. We had proof, even though we had to quickly store it back in its hiding place in case our mom walked in.

And so the spy ID was stuffed back into a box that we both knew was vulnerable to shredding, since my mom could not seem to kick the habit of shredding secret documents for the DoD. The shredder was her way of downsizing, packing up, and moving on, leaving me wondering what was real from my memories. It was destroying evidence by the day.

Yet thanks to his fictional passport, I could now follow my father into his past, piecing together a life after mine that had been torn down by his death. Each piece, I would later realize, was a brick in my own identity. Now I could pin down his movements in 1944–1945, Leuchars, Stockholm, and "American Air Transport Service." I could go there with him. The passport triggered memories of stories he'd once told, such as being chased by a woman with a gun in

Stockholm. He said she chased him because he had forgotten to take the price tag off his suit, his "disguise" as a civilian. That price tag gave away that he had bought it just for this occasion, that it was not really his. He also said the B-24s he flew in had to be painted black or green and that their bomb bays were converted to carry passengers and cargo. To me, these tales had merely been bedtime stories about enchanting faraway places, but now the facts had washed up on the shore for me.

As I researched Operation Sonnie, I discovered its purpose was to bring American airmen who had crashed in Sweden, which stayed neutral during the war, back to England, as well as Norwegian resistance fighters who had to flee German-occupied Norway. It was run by the Office of Strategic Services (OSS)—the precursor to the CIA. The operation also carried load after load of ball bearings to England. Near the end of the war in Europe, they carried a German V-2 test missile—launched from Peenemünde by Wernher von Braun—that had inadvertently landed in Sweden. It was a dud, but it was enough to start the missile race in the United States. No one had seen anything like it before. With a successful launch, it was feared, Hitler would win the war. He was that close to getting it right.

It seemed my father had followed the missiles from the start.

To understand my father's job, I decided to follow the cargo, which in this case was ball bearings. Such a small thing, but so necessary for winning a war, for keeping all the cogs and gears of the mechanical world running. In 1943, the U.S. Army Air Corps bombed the center for ball-bearing production in Germany, Schweinfurt, realizing that Germany could not win a war without ball bearings. The problem was that Swedish ball-bearing manufacturers quickly filled the void, delighted to find a market desperate for their goods. These round little gems became a gold mine. To get these companies to stop supplying Germany, the United States had to offer more money than the Germans did. They had to buy the ball bearings.

Being "neutral" was more like being a money launderer than a pacifist, it seemed. Sweden tried to get the best deals from both sides. They wanted to trade things. Internees for ball bearings. And so my dad came to carry loads and loads of ball bearings from Sweden to England—discreetly, of course.

As for that other little thing, the price tag on my father's suit, we were always told that my father ducked into a bar after seeing the woman with a gun. There, the guy next to him saw the price tag and quickly tore it off. Was he a spy too? I discovered that Stockholm was a hotbed of spies at the time, both German and American, and that the guy next to my dad at the bar must have known that that price tag meant my dad had just pulled the suit out of his duffel bag and had forgotten to remove it. Did anyone else forget to remove the tag? Did anyone die because of a price tag?

As in Casablanca, where my father also flew, nothing was as it seemed in Stockholm. In bars across the city, there were copies of *Handel und Wandel,* a German newspaper with the byline "Businessmen within the Reich." In reality, it was written and published by the OSS in Washington, DC. My dad probably carried that too. In it were tales of investment opportunities in the United States and Europe, as it explained "the willingness of Allied businessmen to work with German businessmen once the Nazis were out of the way." It was trying to turn Nazis, to flip them.

Was it in my dad's bar that night?

In Stockholm, people were changing sides every day, as people tend to do when the winning side starts to lose. My dad was there in that confusion of not knowing who was whom. After being shot at, American airplanes were crash-landing in Sweden if they could, a better place to be interned than in Germany. They crashed there by the dozens.

Nazis were also fleeing to Sweden, where they complained of not being treated as well as the American internees. They were kept on school grounds with the Norwegians while the Americans got to stay in nice hotels. Perhaps the Swedes were amazed by how quickly a Nazi could become not-a-Nazi. Perhaps not. Of course, if the war had gone differently, the Germans would have gotten the hotels and the Americans the internment camps. These were the small creepings up and down in the ladder of power. There was a price tag, or a ball bearing, that decided everything.

Then there were the people my father carried. The Norwegians who escaped Nazi-held Norway crossed the mountains in snowshoes or skis, seeking that rare German-free route into Sweden. Then there were the Jewish refugees. One particularly persistent Swede, a spy also affiliated with the OSS, Raoul Wallenberg, was recruited to hand out fake Swedish "protective" passports to every Jewish person he could in Budapest. When the Nazis caught on to this ruse, Wallenberg rented thirty-two buildings downtown and declared them Swedish territory. He put up signs that read "The Swedish Research Institute" and "Swedish Library." There, he housed almost ten thousand people at a time as arrangements were made to get them out of the country. Though he survived the war, he was arrested by the Russians as a spy afterward, sent to Moscow, and never heard from again. He was officially declared dead in October 2016.

A strange brew of companions had been stuffed into my father's bomb bays, which were converted to hold passengers. Some were headed to war, some to prison, and some to refuge in Palestine. The flights out of Sweden were allowed to leave only in bad weather so the Germans could not find them, and the crews flew without parachutes so they could not be captured and tortured by Nazis. The mission was that secret. From Stockholm, my dad would have had to navigate north, through the clouds, above the Arctic Circle. Only then, in that place where war and radar had not penetrated, could they cross over German-occupied Norway to the North Sea. They had to fly higher than the Luftwaffe planes, which meant their wings would slowly ice up while over Norway. My dad had to calculate that moment between certain death and safety, no matter who was on board, that moment it was finally safe to turn south.

Maybe my dad left me this gift, moving his "spy passport" to the top of his box, knowing I would be daring enough to open it when the time came. I still do not know what he did at Normandy beach, in Italy, or in Africa. But I had learned enough to understand, and at just the right time, that some people are willing to carry others out. That was all. Someone would always want to sell the ball bearings, no matter who the highest bidder was, and others would always want to carry those in danger to safety. To open the doors and let them in, no matter the personal risk. I learned enough to have hope again.

"When all else fails you," my dad used to say, "you still have dead reckoning." Intuition. For navigators, it means there are no stars or land in sight with which to navigate. It means you are floating free in the clouds, with no ups or downs or here or there. "Dead reckoning," he would say, "that's when you know you're in trouble."

Then you tune in to your instinct and try to fly straight.

PART SEVEN

Life without Weapons

Missile Guidebook:
Find a new language that is not written with
missiles. There are very few surviving languages
left. If you can learn that new language, you
will learn joy. It is a language that is past $E=MC^2$,
after the wrong turn, out beyond the carvings in
the rock. It is where you can find me, lying in
the sun, smiling.

Chapter Thirty-One

Petroglyph Targets

It was only when I said I wanted to visit the base petroglyphs that my mother paused. "The base petroglyphs?" she asked, and for the first time ever, her voice did not have that ready-to-go-anywhere excitement.

"Yeah, Mom, it's where you live, remember?" I replied. It had been three years since my father died. She was still living in Ridgecrest, and I thought she would be excited to hear I wanted to come home. Usually when I mentioned some new place to visit, she would reply, "I have my passport. Let's go!"

"Patagonian wilderness?"

"I'll stay in the hotel while you hike."

"Egypt?"

"We can see that mummy there. Sure."

"I want to take a drive along the Syrian-Iraqi-Turkish border, Mom. Do you want to come?" That region really got messed up by ISIS later. But at the time, I was writing a book about transboundary water disputes and water privatization, so I was fascinated by borders. I had just received tenure and a sabbatical with funding for research.

"It's always an adventure with you," she would say, though partly I think she was afraid I would get myself into some dangerous situation. She was afraid I might need her. So we would get on a plane, thinking all we needed was a credit card, rental car, and GPS. We were not rich, but we patched together my travel grants with her Social Security and our willingness to sleep on anyone's couch.

Only China Lake made her pause.

This was surprising to me. It was as cheap as it gets, after all. And it wasn't Syria.

Then she said, "I think you have to take a tour to get out there now. I don't have my badge anymore, remember. There's no sticker on the car."

"I know, I know. I looked it all up," I reassured her. "I found the tour. It's a four-hour hike in and out to the petroglyphs. I think we went there once, when I was little. Do you remember? It was back when anyone could drive right in."

"Oh, maybe your father took you," she said. "I don't think I've ever been there."

Then she added, "Remember, security is terrible out there now, since 9/11. You better be sure you have everything you need to get on the base."

"I know, I know," I replied. "I looked it up."

Then she said she thought she might go with me on the tour.

"Are you sure?" I asked. "You better think about it."

I was thinking of her shoes. I knew she did not have the right kind, which she would never concede. Besides, she was seventy-four years old and could fall and break a hip. Yet she seemed to have an endless amount of energy left in her, as if my father had simply moved into her body and given her whatever energy he had left. If she could survive the Himalayas, I figured she could survive China Lake.

We arrived at the carpool site at five o'clock in the morning, where my mom and I were to ride with the tour leader, Todd Gunnison, in his SUV. "Got your passports or birth certificates?" he asked as we left the parking lot. We did.

At the first checkpoint, we were directed to a "holding area" surrounded by concrete blast walls. It looked like Iraq. There, we handed over our passports and stepped out of the car so it could be searched. "You used to be able to drive right through," my mom said, marveling. "I almost reached for my badge and thought we would be waved through." There were no barricades back then, but there were also no "terrorists" either, only "Communists," whom we all thought lived far away. So we waited as four guards searched our cars, entered our names in a database, and finally handed us our "visitor" badges. I tried to attach the badge to my T-shirt, but it kept falling off, seemingly designed for people with lapels and collars. That had always been a nuisance. I shoved it into my purse instead.

Back in the car, Todd said, "Ready for the next one?" We drove past a sign that read "What you see here, What you hear here, What you do here, Let it stay here." At the second checkpoint, Todd turned in all our information to the military police, then said, "One more to go. It's sure not like before September 11th. You're lucky to be here at all. Who knows how many checkpoints there will be tomorrow." Nothing remained of the haphazard, devil-may-care attitude of the base, when it was a place that felt dwarfed by the desert at every turn, a kooky jackrabbit ride on a missile.

Finally, we got in line behind fuel tankers at a guardhouse with a gate labeled "North Range." Todd complained, "They've just got to count every drop in every truck, now, don't they?" I knew by then that the U.S. military uses more oil than whole countries and is the biggest oil consumer in the United States. Ironically, the Pentagon now states that climate change "poses immediate risks to U.S. national security." Another catch-22.

"Interesting hat," I said to Todd as we waited. "You like the B-2?"

"Used to work on the B-2," he replied gruffly, "out at Northrop in San Diego."

"How's the B-2 bomber working these days?" I asked.

He shrugged. "Oh, it works okay, but it's only our 'strategic option' now."

I knew that meant it carried only nuclear bombs, which meant that no one really used it anymore. In fact, the B-2s were housed a short distance from Columbia at Whiteman Air Force Base and would fly over our homecoming game every year for a little added excitement. The noise of them rattled me, as did their presence in general. When I heard they were stationed nearby, I looked up how far a nuclear blast wave would travel, since those bombers would be an obvious target. I discovered that the biggest nuke tested was the fifty-megaton Russian Tsar Bomba in 1961. It was determined that people sixty-two miles away would get third-degree burns. *Damn it*, I thought. Whiteman was forty miles away.

Those B-2s were following me everywhere.

"Didn't they find out the old Soviet radar systems could detect the B-2?" I asked Todd.

"Oh, I don't know about that." His voice stiffened. "I don't know who you've been talking to. I'm just here to show you some petroglyphs."

We soon found out that Todd was much more than a tour guide, having served in three wars before his job with Northrop. Now he was retired. He once led troops into Basra in Iraq and now led tourists into the Coso Range. "It's a hobby," he said. "I volunteered." No wonder I liked him. I tend to get along with veterans.

Todd handed each of us a brochure about the base's main points of interest, then informed us we were passing the first one: the navy's eighteen-hole golf course. He laughed and said, "You can go anywhere in the world, and wherever the navy is, there will be a golf course." I thought of what my sister once said, that she would never vote for a golfer. "It's like a men's conspiracy," she said. "You see the president teeing off with all these important people around the world, and there's never a woman there."

Slowly, I realized I was looking at the golf course I had grown up next to, where navy guys came to shoot jackrabbits at night. My mother warned me not to go there at night, but I did sneak out once to see a field of bunnies munching away under bright overhead lights. But now, in Todd's SUV, it looked backward. I'd never had clearance to drive on this road so had never seen it from this angle before. The whole base was backward, as if I were seeing it in a mirror.

On the other side of the road from the golf course were piles of scrap metal and what looked like leaking barrels of hazardous waste. All that debris, so close to my house. The brochure said only that we were driving by Lark Ramp, one of the first guided missile launchers on the base, which was shut down after a missile fired from it almost landed on Ridgecrest. Afterward, Lark Ramp clearly became a dumping site, where now a greenish pool of water held a lonely wading egret.

As we started the long drive across dry China Lake, my mom pointed to a couple of buildings that looked like heat mirages in the distance. "Hey, that's my office!" she said.

"Oh yeah? What'd you do out there?" Todd asked. "I mean, I'm curious 'cause I'm not from around here. I've always wondered what they do here."

"I etched circuitry," she said, typically circumspect.

"It's something to do," Todd replied. I remembered driving to the lakeshore when it rained to collect fairy shrimp, which would come alive by the millions when it flooded. At home, we put them in a jar and watched them swim, before realizing we could buy them in an aquarium kit called "Sea Monkeys."

Then Todd pointed to a notch in the hills. "That's where we're going," he said. "It's only a quarter mile away, but we have to go the long way around unless you want to drive through the missile-testing sites."

On our left was a simple concrete wall and a couple of railroad cars stacked on top of one another. Targets. I noticed the backside of the railroad cars had already been blown up, then turned around to shoot at again. Recycling. The logo on one side read "Hyundai." I turned to look over my shoulder again, disoriented by the view, when the car suddenly swerved. My mother grabbed her seat belt and laughed from the back seat. "What was that?" I asked, turning forward again.

"Lizard," Todd replied.

"Man, you're a softie!" I kidded. "I would never go out of my way for a lizard."

"Don't tell anyone," he whispered.

The road narrowed, heading up a canyon and finally over a ridge, where an enormous poppy field opened up in the middle of a Joshua tree forest. Black-and-white mottled horses dotted the landscape, grazing on the orange poppies. They looked like unicorns in a perfect fantasyland.

"Take a picture!" my mom said, handing me her camera from the back seat.

"I can't," I replied. "We're not allowed." Todd looked at me and nodded in approval before staring intently in his rearview mirror.

"If I see those photographers stop and pull out a tripod," he said, "I'm going to shoot them."

"Have you seen any bighorn sheep out here?" I asked. I knew the navy was trying to reintroduce them to the ranges and wondered how they kept from getting shot.

"Nope, and I hope I never do," he said. "Just the paperwork would be terrible. There are ninety biologists waiting for us to see a bighorn sheep. We'd have to shut down the whole tour and go report it."

Finally, we pulled into an unmarked dirt parking lot, where Todd gave a little lecture: "If you see any ordnance or missile parts around, don't touch it. This is a military base. Be sure not to leave the canyon."

My mom and I giggled, and he looked as though he wanted to hush us.

As we started our walk into the canyon, my mother began to worry. "I don't know about this," she said, looking down at her feet. The trail of desert rubble and rocks led down into an even rockier canyon. But I did not want to turn back.

"You can probably make it up to there," I encouraged her, pointing to a bend ahead. "I'll help you." I held out my hand, as I had so many times before, walking ahead of her like a human cane, step by step. I wanted her to see at least one petroglyph.

Suddenly, the petroglyphs jumped out at us from around every corner, white chalklike drawings on black rock in all kinds of fantastic shapes and forms. "But what are they supposed to mean?" a photographer asked.

Todd replied, "No one knows. The Shoshone etched most of them as early as sixteen thousand years ago, but no one knows what they mean anymore. And it's not only Shoshone that used to come here. There are petroglyphs here by Pueblo Indians of New Mexico, Kawaiisu, Paiutes, and Kiowa Sioux Indians too. They came from all over to this place. It's the largest collection of Native rock art in the Western Hemisphere."

"Do Native Americans still come here?" I asked. I knew they lived on tiny reservations nearby, even though technically they had never signed away their rights to this land. There are cup-sized holes in large boulders where the women used to grind acorns.

"Sure, they can come out whenever they want," he replied, "except when the road's closed for bombing. They can book a tour like anyone else—but they don't know what the petroglyphs mean either." Or maybe they do not want to tell you, I thought.

I noticed my mom was lagging behind but had found a friend, an elderly man who was helping her with the tricky spots. I heard them laughing, so I hurried to catch up with Todd. "So what happens in the rest of the Coso Range?" I asked him. "I mean, why can't we see the other petroglyphs?"

"You tell me," he replied. "Secret stuff."

Finally, we approached a rock chute that we had to slide down. My mom stopped and said, "Okay, that's it for me."

"Can you get back on your own?" I asked, worried that I would have to turn back.

"Oh, don't worry, Karen. Evan wants to go back with me." In a white short-sleeved shirt with green suspenders, Evan looked about eighty years old, even older than my mom, but he nodded happily and took her hand.

Meanwhile, Todd was pointing out the figures carved in rock, which were predominantly bighorn sheep, but also humans, dogs, and rows of people linking arms. There were also many figures that were half human and half animal and many others that looked like aliens. "Some of these animals are now extinct," Todd said. "Gone for eleven thousand years." I thought I saw a saber-toothed tiger.

"Shamans used to come here to get power from the rocks," Todd said. "They sat in rock shelters all night without food or water and smoked tobacco until they had hallucinations." Spirits lived in the rocks, it was said, so they waited for cracks in the rocks to open up and let them in. Meanwhile, women ground holes in the rocks and covered themselves in rock dust, clothing themselves in the world of spirits.

Today, some psychologists claim that the shamans were "seeing things," explaining that our minds will create patterns out of partial images to make sense of them in darkness. Blind people also see things this way. What the shamans saw were bighorn sheep with three heads. Upside-down people. Footprints of "water babies," who are mischievous newborn spirits that live in the water. People climbing out of cracks in the rocks. The spirits going back and forth.

Then, after the California governor offered a bounty in 1856 of twenty-five cents per scalp for killing Native Americans, the drawings began to change. By 1860, it was up to $5. Around then, numerous flying shamans appeared. They did not fly Superman-style but had spiraling lines in their faces to show that a whirlwind was carrying them away to safety. They had helicopter faces. There were also shamans with bulletproof shirts, provided to them by animal helpers. The spirit helpers in the rocks were practical, it seems, and adapted to the changing times. Some say the shamans' trances were caused by extreme fatigue. They called this place *pohaghani*, which means "the house of supernatural power."

Then, suddenly, the drawings ended.

"Why do so many bighorn sheep have squiggly lines above them?" I asked Todd.

"That's rain," he said. "The Indians thought bighorn sheep brought rain because they would come streaming down the mountains when there was a thunderstorm up there, which usually meant that rain was on its way." Then he shrugged his shoulders. "Of course, all these etchings were certainly done while on drugs, so who knows."

On the way back, I noticed "$E=MC^2$" carved into a rock.

"Was that done by people on drugs too?" I poked Todd with my elbow and pointed.

"Oh, that," he said. "That was done by some scientists in the early days, when they could come out here anytime. There were sometimes crazy parties, I've heard."

"Ah, so it *was* done on drugs!" I chuckled.

"Well, you never know," he said. "But that etching might be history someday, too, just as important as the others."

Before long, I became impatient with the slow pace of the photographers. Sensing this, Todd said, "You can run ahead now. You don't have to wait for us." I gratefully took the opportunity and ran, confident of the way back.

After a while, I started to notice the canyon walls seemed darker and shinier, like obsidian, and the petroglyphs were different too. A long, deeply carved line jumped from rock to rock, looking like a snake. Curious, I followed it until a bright fuchsia flowering beavertail cactus interrupted the line, clinging to a crack in the side of the wall. It was then that I knew I was lost, since I would have remembered those flowers.

Nevertheless, the contrast of the brilliant flowers, the polished black walls, and the abstract, swirling line was haunting. The colors were stunning and pulled me forward, everything seeming suddenly supernatural. This was a land of unicorns and mazes, fuchsia cacti, orange poppies, and long hypnotic swirls. Though there were only lizard-tail tracks in the sand rather than footprints, the feeling of peace was so powerful that I could not stop. I wanted to curl up in the sun and watch for wildlife. I wanted to be with my father again, peering into desert holes and wondering about the animals inside. I wanted to be on my old porch, watching the crevices of the Sierras fold into darkness. I wanted to be inside the holes and canyons of childhood. I did not want to go back. My father might crawl out of a rock at any moment and be my spirit helper, giving me a bulletproof vest. These were the moments that kept me going.

Suddenly, I remembered I was on an active bombing range.

I headed up a ridge to get my bearings before realizing I could step on a land mine out here. Missiles and mines could be anywhere. Unexploded ordnance. This was not like being lost anywhere else. Instinctively, I turned around and started retracing my steps, hoping I was going the right way, hoping nothing would blow up beneath my feet. Finally, turning a corner, I saw Todd in the distance. I stopped, leaning over to rest my hands on my knees, and realized how heavily I was breathing. Almost hyperventilating. Catching my breath, I shouted, "Hey, over here!" waving my arms.

Todd turned and, seeing me, looked as if he had just seen a dead friend. He shook his head back and forth the way my father did when I was in trouble. "You can't get lost out here!" he shouted across the desert. "You just can't."

Shamefacedly following him back, I came over a ridge and saw my mother. She noticed me, brightened up, and waved. In her face, I saw I had everything I had ever needed. It was finally clear.

Getting closer, I heard my mom happily chatting with Evan about weaponry. "We used to call burros 'warm targets,'" he said. "They would be good practice for our heat-seeking missiles. Besides, there were just too many horses and burros out here."

"I know," Mom said. "Now they can't find enough people to adopt them."

Todd stormed up to them while pointing at me. "We almost lost her!" he said. "She got lost!" He seemed to think my mom would be as upset at me as he was.

My mom laughed. "Yes, but she always finds her way back," she said, smiling at me. "She knows what she is doing."

Todd turned to me and said, "Think of the paperwork if you hadn't come back! Just think of it."

But I just chuckled. We were okay. Todd had survived three wars. I had survived China Lake.

Chapter Thirty-Two

My Hidden Knowledge Detector

For so long, I had believed that only a man could pull me out of my baby cage, my fake reality, my MK-Ultra box. I believed, like so many women, in a rescuer, someone who would take me away from China Lake. Yet men had only sent me into new altered domains, regions too difficult for me to compute. I needed to hunker down. To investigate further.

I needed to learn how to trust my own "dead reckoning."

After all, I had survived. I had held down a job, published academic books for tenure, and done all the other things women do to stay afloat. This memoir does not negate any other versions of me circulating under the name Karen Piper. You can Google them. We are, after all, multiple beings. But with this book I was building a new me, brick by brick.

A guidebook.

In this version, I doubled down. From my dad, I learned about migration routes and safety. From my mom, I learned to laugh no matter what was thrown my way—and the world, it seemed, was just starting to hurl things at us. We knew the world was changing all around us—migration routes were opening and closing as wars started and ice caps melted. The Northwest Passage opened. The Syrian borders closed. Mom and I wanted to be there before too many routes closed. We wanted to see architectural wonders before they were razed by this or that fundamentalist group set on destruction. Hindus blew up mosques. Muslims blew up temples. We wanted to see the animals and coral reefs before they went extinct.

Now there is a name for this form of travel. It's called "extinction tourism." Apparently, a lot of us want to see disappearing things, to have one last look at the penguins and orangutans and pandas and leopards that no one seems to want to keep alive. To say goodbye. And sorry. Coyote, antelope, jacket rabbit.

I was testing my "dead reckoning" in a world that seemed to have lost its bearings. I was in search of clues, of stars with which to steady myself. I bought a new house to contain all the driftwood of my memories, a place that was mine and not Keith's. I threw a bright red rug over the light hardwood floors. I bought a black leather couch and teal pillows. Cardinal and indigo bunting. I hung the Sierra Nevada mountains on the wall. My two decks, one screened in and one not, became my offices. I chased the sunlight, or fled the mosquitoes, from one to the other during the day. I watched the whole world come to my bird feeder, migrating from north to south and south to north, showing they could match the pace of my new migrations. An indigo bunting flew by my window, a fiery flash of royalty with iridescent wings changing from purple to blue in the sunlight. A cardinal stood out against the spring leaves of my forested backyard like a spot of fresh blood. A deep breath entered my lungs and stayed.

Was I moving on or settling down? I could not tell.

Nearby, the Missouri River raced down a channelized path, roaring with its own stories and changes. Sometimes it jumped its banks. A friend invited me to kayak on the river, and we fought it upstream to a sandbar in the middle, where we stopped for wine and a picnic. Then we floated back silently in the dark together. Over time, this became a habit. There was an addiction to seeing what the river was doing. Sometimes a bonfire would be raging when we arrived at our island, and our circle of friends would expand. Sometimes the island would be entirely submerged. When the river was high, we would dodge refrigerators and trees caught in the melee of its roaring waves. We were wild. I was wild again.

Still, I had some unfinished business. When I found out where all of China Lake's archives had been sent, thirty years after the fact, I knew I had to go. I had been trying for years to gain access to these files. When I first started looking, I naively thought I could just walk into the basement of Mike Lab, where I knew the records were kept. Then I remembered they had been moved, and many destroyed, after the flood of 1984. I heard the files were sent to the base's technical library, next to the commissary store. Having had been there many times before, I somehow assumed I could just walk in when my mom still had a badge and could take me on the base. Instead, I discovered the doors were locked. No explanations are necessary on the base. History just vanishes.

So when I heard the records had been moved to the National Archives in Riverside, I was delighted. I wanted to know more about what my dad did for a living. The archives are kept in a small government building on the outskirts of town, surrounded by brown grass fields for cows. My mom offered to pick me up at LAX and take me there, so I flew in from Missouri. We could get a hotel, she said, go to the mall afterward, and then head back to Ridgecrest.

Inside the archives, it was freezing cold, which is the case in many places deprived of cool air outside. "Did you bring a coat, Mom?" I whispered. A young man with black European-style square glasses greeted us at the door as though no one ever came to visit him.

"Yes, yes, yes," he said, bowing and waving us inside. "Come in, come in."

"I'm just here for the air-conditioning," my mom told him. "She's the researcher."

"Yes, well o-kay," he said, lifting the last syllable as a question. "The air-conditioning *is* good."

Perhaps my experiences in being turned away elsewhere made my mom think we would soon be at the mall. Instead, we were directed to a room with about thirty schoolhouse-sized desks and asked to sit down. A woman bent over a nearby desk, deep in thought. She was the only other person there.

"You can mark the files you want to see," the man said, handing each of us a menu as if we were ordering sushi. Then he sat down at a larger desk, facing our desks, and waited for us to decide.

After a cursory perusal, I marked everything on the Sidewinder, having no idea this meant that library-sized carts filled with files would be rolled to me, one after another. When the first cart came, my mom laughed. "Oh, Karen," she said, "what did you do now?" She knew the mall was getting further away and only then began to study her menu of options. Three days later, we would still be there.

I knew it was probably still too early for my dad's files to be there since we had moved to China Lake in 1971 and now it was 2008. Thirty-seven years. Technically, they were long past the declassification date, but the process takes a long time. Names have to be erased and files redacted. So the files stopped at 1974. I homed in on the years around 1970, where I thought I might find my father.

That was when I discovered Sidewinder engineer Howie Wilcox and first read his warnings about "idealized missiles" heading to Vietnam. The Wilcox files took up shelves, and were filled with early prototype drawings, test results, and mathematical equations for the Sidewinder. By the end of the first shelf, I felt as though I knew the guy.

Then I came across something completely unexpected, something more important to Howie than the Sidewinder. It was in a file he marked "Global Thermal Pollution" from 1973. The first thing I noticed was that much of the writing was in all caps. There were even exclamation marks, unusual for a scientist. "Global thermal pollution," as he described it, was potentially more catastrophic than smog. If unchecked, he explained, it could "melt the polar ice caps and cover the world in a steamy haze." After that, he wrote, "the tropical oceans would begin to boil," and eventually the "earth itself would be vaporized."

I had been looking for missiles, not this.

The report was written while he was working for China Lake's "Independent Research" branch, which actually appeared to support climate change research and mitigation. This was surprising to me, since even Democrat president Lyndon Johnson clearly did not understand it. In 1965, Johnson had appointed a scientific advisory panel to report on "Environmental Pollution." They wrote, "Through his worldwide industrial civilization, Man is unwittingly conducting a vast geophysical experiment . . . the climatic changes that may be produced by the increased CO_2 could be deleterious from the point of view of human beings." But Johnson said to the head of the auto workers' union that the report was about "the whole natural beauty thing" that "more garden clubs are getting interested in."

In response, he proposed a "Highway Beautification Act" to clean up the highways and said to this union guy, "We're going to have Travel USA. We're gonna try to make 'em see American, and go to Wyoming, and go to Colorado, and take their kids out on Sunday afternoon . . . and we sure want to make these places attractive to drive on 'cause we'll make more automobiles sell more." That was his solution to climate change. Maybe the panel should have written, "The tropical oceans will boil." Maybe that would have gotten Johnson's attention.

Meanwhile, the navy let Wilcox start a prototype ocean kelp farming operation off the coast of San Clemente Island. Kelp, he said, would photosynthesize our vast sunlight resources, turning them into a biofuel that could replace fossil fuels. It would also absorb CO_2 from the atmosphere. It was the first large-scale geoengineering proposal. I think the navy's top brass knew, even back then, that sea level rise would cause their ports and bases to sink. They knew it was a threat to national security.

Wilcox patiently anchored the large bulbous algae to the ocean floor with lines that could later be pulled up for harvest. There, they took root and thrived. Sea otters came to celebrate the feast.

It is all in the files, including the farm's unnatural demise.

In 1971, a navy review team came to China Lake from Washington, DC, to review their "Independent Research" programs, including Howie Wilcox's kelp farm. Other programs at the time included a portable igloo that could be blown up and filled with water, which would then freeze in the Arctic. They included a "Hidden Knowledge Detector" that could measure "covert mental processes." According to the report, these were very different from lies; they were what people did not even know they were lying about. Then there was the deep-sea jeep, a glass orb that roamed the ocean floor and was powered by melted salt. (Jacques Cousteau helped out on that one.) There was a scientist obsessed with figuring out the "quantum mechanics of H_2O." No matter how hard his boss tried, this man would not be stopped. He did not care about the money. He cared only about H_2O. He always knew he was *this* close. It is in the letters.

I laughed out loud. Igloos and Knowledge Detectors? I wanted a jeep that ran on melted salt. Finally, I got to the navy's review of Howie's project. The team concluded that while it was worthwhile, "there is at present no apparent military application of this work." The time for kelp farming and igloos was over. It was time for war. For Vietnam.

Maybe that is why Howie Wilcox began to write in all caps. After that report, Howie sought funding elsewhere with limited success. He wrote a book titled *Hothouse Earth*. He kept fighting. When he died, he left most everything to Planned Parenthood, not because he cared about abortion ethics. It was simply his last attempt to stop the planet from being vaporized. His wife said she was proud of him.

The man with the black glasses was still going to and fro when I noticed that the other person in the room was competing for the same files I had asked for. The young man was taking my files straight to her. I looked at her more closely. She looked quite professional in her brown sheath and small heels, at least in comparison to me in my T-shirt and flip-flops. She was around forty and had perfectly curled short hair and jewelry that looked like real gold. A big diamond too.

After building up the nerve, I approached her table, which was only about fifteen feet from away mine. She jumped when I said, "Excuse me."

"Sorry, you startled me." She laughed, embarrassed.

"I'm sorry," I replied. "It's just that I noticed you're researching China Lake."

"Who are you?" she asked, looking suspicious.

"I'm from China Lake," I said. "I noticed we're working on the same files."

She turned to reach for something in her purse. "You are?" she asked, acting suddenly eager. Her professionalism scared me a bit as she handed me a card. I was not prepared for this.

"I don't live there now," I said, trying to backtrack. "I just grew up there. My mom still lives there." I pointed to my mom, who was poring over an old map.

"Really?" she said, looking excited. I glanced at her card, which said something about a data research group. She explained, "The navy hired us to study the effects of radiation on people who lived there, mostly depleted uranium."

"So you mean on me, huh?" I joked, then realized that she actually did mean that.

This felt very strange.

"But I was always told we didn't work with radioactive materials," I said.

"Not uranium, but depleted uranium," she replied. It was what doctors believed caused the Gulf War syndrome. It was used as a shell casing to rip holes in tanks.

"What are you talking about?" My mother smiled and walked over, apparently thinking I had met a friend from China Lake.

"Sorry, my name is Jolie." She held out her hand. "Are you from China Lake too?" she asked my mom. "Is it possible I could interview you?"

My mom scowled. "My work out there was secret," she said.

"Yes, I know," Jolie replied. "I won't ask you about your work." My mom took her business card politely and said she would think about it. But after we left, my mom handed me the card and said to throw it in the trash.

"Don't you want to talk to her?" I asked. "For history?"

"She wants to know too much," my mom replied.

Perhaps I wanted to know too much too. Perhaps all my questions would never be answered. Nevertheless, there was one last thing I wanted to know, which I had been looking for in those files but had not found. I wanted to know why my dad had been so happy to retire, why he thought even Alzheimer's was better than the navy. I wanted to know why he said the navy wanted salesmen and why he said they "faked the tests."

So I called the former technical director of China Lake to ask him. I called Burrell Hays. I simply looked him up in the Ridgecrest phone book. I remembered that he had once been told to keep silent in the face of corruption too. Maybe he would know my dad.

Someone picked up the phone. A woman.

It was then I choked. "Uh, uh, excuse me . . . I mean, is Burrell Hays there?"

"Yes, but he's out mowing the lawn," she replied pleasantly. "Can I help you?"

"Well . . ." I did not know how to explain. "I worked on the base when he was director and wanted to ask him—"

She interrupted, "Oh, let me go get him. I'm sure he'd love to talk."

I gulped, suddenly feeling like I was driving to Mr. Porter's house to sell Amway. What was I doing? Hays was the head of everything before Mr. Porter.

Nevertheless, he picked up the phone.

"Uh, I'm Karen Piper . . . and I worked on the base when you were technical director," I stammered. "And I remember the Paisley buttons and when you were fired and was just wondering what really happened. My dad worked on the Sidewinder."

"Ah, China Lake," he said, as if he were talking to an old familiar friend.

He paused, then unexpectedly laughed. "You know, *People* magazine once called me and asked me that, twenty years ago, but I couldn't tell them. But I suppose I can tell you now. I suppose it doesn't matter." He was seventy-four years old then.

And so began a long story about one of the nation's first armed drones, which had been tested at China Lake and, like the B-2 bomber, had failed its tests. "It was a black program," he said.

"Supersecret." Assistant Secretary to the Navy Paisley was not happy with the results. As Hays explained, "When he heard that there wasn't any way this thing was going to work, he said, 'Well, change the data, so it looks like it will.'"

"Did you?" I asked.

"No, of course not," he said. "I went to the admiral that ran the black program and told him essentially what was happening, and he said, 'Well, whatever happens to you will not be as bad as if you blow the cover of this program. You can't do that.' So I essentially was left on my own." I felt for him then, alone with this secret. He continued, "I believed it when that admiral told me that my penalty would be a lot worse. He was talking about things like firing squads. You know how those secret guys are."

"Yeah, I know." I nodded, though I had never heard of firing squads on base. He was scaring me a little. Because he would not change those tests, he explained, he was forced to submit his resignation, retiring with just enough pay to support his wife and a little house in Ridgecrest, where he still mowed the lawn. A few months after he left the base, Hays would learn that Paisley was under investigation by the FBI. It seemed that even the FBI could not save Burrell Hays.

Investigations can take a long time, while the government is crumbling around you.

"I see," I said, and we were both quiet. I felt as though we were talking about my father. To finally talk about secrets like this with someone who knew, who understood, felt like an explosion in my stomach. I thought of all the grunts in the field who got the bad weapons. Like me, they never had a "need to know." I tried not to start crying.

"You know . . . ," I hesitantly proffered. "My dad once said they were faking the tests on the Sidewinder."

"Well, now you know why," he said. "Paisley didn't think this up all by himself. Industry controls the navy." We paused in silence.

Then he said, "You know, Tom Amlie, who was director before me, once said there were only three reasons for black projects. One, you're doing something that should genuinely be secret. There's only a couple of those. Two, you're doing something so damn stupid you don't want anybody to know about it. And three, you want to rip the money bag open and get out a shovel, because there is no accountability whatsoever." I chuckled with him, though I still wanted to cry.

Finally, I asked, "What about now? Did anything change?"

He laughed. "Now you just give a contractor a requirement and money and then you throw him off in another room and pray that something comes out. There are no requirements for documentation. There are no requirements for follow-up. And that's how your weapons are being built now."

When I hung up the phone, my eyes welled up, then spilled over, and finally turned into rivers. Burrell Hays had told me the things my father could never explain, perhaps because I was too young to understand or perhaps because they were "Secret." I half thought I had imagined it.

But now Hays had confirmed it was real. He had spilled the secrets, twenty-some years after the fact, right at the moment I needed to hear them.

I still do not understand why men make war, but I know that it hurts us when we kill others, sometimes irreparably. I know that the ghosts of the dead stay with us or are silenced only by amputating a part of ourselves. I know that when wars are waged for money or resources, they can become a perpetual-motion machine. I know that sometimes weapons kill the wrong people. I also know that wars are waged long before a gun is fired or bomb dropped. There are propaganda wars and cyberwars. There are wars between individual spies and cold wars between states. There are wars between oligarchs where murders happen right outside the Kremlin gates. I know that people can lie without realizing they are, and that these lies can cause wars too. I know that war is a bad habit, a habit of saying "yes" when the other person says "no."

"Yes, anyway. I will. I must. I grab."

My Hidden Knowledge Detector has finally kicked into gear.

Chapter Thirty-Three

Leaving *The Twilight Zone*

I was finally ready to visit my dad's grave. It was time. I was poignantly aware I had been avoiding it for too long, even before my mom left Ridgecrest and my visits there were regular. I could not stand to see him dead. But now that I was ready to leave China Lake behind, I wanted to say goodbye. So I flew to Los Angeles and rented a car for one last trek into the desert alone in 2016.

I planned to stay only the day. First, I thought I would visit my childhood home, not the Rowe Street duplex that was bulldozed, but the one across from the jackrabbit golf course on Shangri-La Street, named after an aircraft carrier from World War II. Somehow I thought, with a visitor's pass, I could just drive in and take a picture, even though technically both were illegal. Base visitors are allowed to drive only to the armaments museum and then back out. Photos are prohibited. But my mom was not with me, so she could not stop me from sneaking out to my house and back. The military police could, but I hoped they would not notice.

Around noon, I drove straight to the main gate to get my visitor's badge at a double-wide trailer filled with offices. Inside, I was discouraged to find all the waiting room seats taken. "What is everyone doing here?" I asked a man standing near the entrance, waiting for a seat, arms akimbo.

"Time to renew badges," he said, staring glassily ahead. I saw forms for base employee badge renewal hanging in gray metal holders on the walls. The boredom, waiting, and metal gray felt familiar.

Cutting in line, I asked a clerk behind her trailer desk if I was in the right place for tourists. "I'm only here for the day," I explained.

"This is the right place," she said. "But I doubt you'll get in today. You can take a number and come back tomorrow if you want."

"But I'm only here for the day," I repeated.

"You're interrupting this man," she said, waving me away. "It's his turn now." Her weary eyes pushed me back to the waiting room as she said, "Even if you get through the line before we close, you can't get a badge today. We need to do a background check first. And the museum closes at four. It all takes time."

"I see," I said. "It's just that I used to live here and was hoping—"

She interrupted, "This is a military installation, after all. What did you expect?"

No, it's my home, I wanted to say. I wanted to be angry. I wanted the guards to carry me out, kicking and screaming, shouting, *I just want to go home!* Instead, I left the center in resignation, feeling my exile more poignantly. All I wanted was a view of the tree I once climbed and the smell of grapevines that clung to our fence. I wanted to see that jackrabbit golf course and remember bunnies. I wanted evidence of my childhood, even after all these years. I wanted to know it really *happened*.

But there was nothing I could do.

Outside, the 115-degree heat hit me like a wall I knew well. *Don't mess with me,* it said. *Better slow down.* A heat wave was hanging over

California, and the sun burned into my corneas. I had forgotten my sunglasses. *Stupid*, I thought. My confidence was truly sagging now. Did I belong here?

I drove on to my father's grave, stopping to say hello to the horses and burros on the way, huddled around a watering trough in a dirt corral. It was the same spot I had seen them in almost thirty years ago, when I would drive by on my way to work. They must have wondered how they'd ended up locked in there as remnants of a forgotten mining history.

They looked as though they needed a nuzzle.

I got out of the rental car, and the burros perked up their long fuzzy ears, their own friend-or-foe detectors like the navy's. The littlest one approached first, its eyes full of wonder, and soon the whole herd was upon me, licking my hand through the gate. I wanted to adopt them all.

By the time I got back to the car, the steering wheel was too hot to touch. My thighs sizzled when I tried to sit down. I jumped up like those burros' ears when they'd heard me screech, "Ouch!" I pulled a top from my suitcase to sit on and carefully inched back in, placing my thumb and index finger around the bottom and shadiest part of the steering wheel. Then I drove on, barely touching the wheel until it cooled down, feeling like the stupid outsider again. In Ridgecrest, everyone has sheepskin wheel covers and seat covers precisely to avoid this problem.

At the cemetery, the graves were covered in silk and plastic flowers that, even though sun bleached and a tad unsightly, at least stood the chance of lasting more than an hour in the heat. I looked down at my fresh flowers, dismayed, while also facing the fact that nothing looked familiar. Where was my father? I had assumed you could not lose your father's grave, that it would jump out like an old wound at you. Instead, all I could do was walk from grave to grave, my flowers gradually wilting as my shirt filled with perspiration. "Dad?" I yelled. The graves were as abandoned as the burros.

Were my instincts really right this time? There was no one in sight. Finally, a brass military cross on the ground caught my eye. I looked more closely, weirdly hoping not to see his name, believing that not finding it would mean he was still alive.

"Earl Marwin Piper," it read. "Beloved husband and father."

I lay down in the grass and cried, kissing the earth that was his head. This was why I had come.

"We're okay, Dad," I whispered. "Don't worry about us. We miss you, but we're okay." The sun crept a little down the horizon in the cool of the shade trees. I finally got up to leave, but then suddenly flopped back down again, remembering my mom. She had asked me to bring the flowers. Did she want me to tell him something?

"The flowers are from Mom," I said. "She loves you."

Then, reluctantly, I drove away, feeling my dad and all my burro children tugging at my sleeves. Maybe they wanted to go for a ride too. Their faces in the rearview mirror grew smaller and smaller even as I wondered if my last words to my dad were really true.

"Mom, were you in love with Dad when you married him?" I had asked only the week before while we were antique hunting in Seattle, where my mom and I had just bought a condo together.

She thought a minute, then said, "I don't think I've ever been in love. What do you mean by 'in love,' anyway?"

"What?" I was shocked. "You stayed with him for almost fifty years!"

"He was good to me, and I appreciated it," she said. "It was more like affection."

"I don't believe you," I insisted. "I know dad loved *you*, anyway."

"Did he? What makes you say that?"

"He wrote you romantic cards and brought you flowers all the time!" It must have been clear from the tone in my voice that this was not up for dispute.

"To me, that meant he treated me well," she said, shaking her head in a way that said, "Young people these days . . ." She did not understand us.

"But you were always kissing and holding hands," I insisted while realizing the absurdity of trying to convince my mother she had been in love. What did it matter now?

"Were we? I don't remember."

"Okay, whatever," I conceded. It was not my place to say. "It's just that . . . that's weird."

I think she realized she had disappointed me, because she started looking for examples of love. "He used to read the Song of Solomon from the Bible to me," she said. "Is that what you want?"

"Well, that's romantic." I nodded, vaguely remembering something about grapes and breasts. It was the Bible's "erotic" book.

"I suppose it is. It seemed very natural to be with him."

Then she thought of another example. "Before we married, our friends secretly followed us to the park and started pushing up and down on the car bumper with us inside. We thought it was an earthquake."

"What's that have to do with anything?" I asked, exasperated.

"Well, what do people do sitting in parked cars?"

"I know you guys had sex, Mom." I rolled my eyes. "That's not what I mean. You sound like the old couple in *Fiddler on the Roof*, you know, where the guy asks his wife if she loves him after twenty-five years and she says, 'For twenty-five years, I've washed your clothes, . . . so I suppose I do.' Or something like that."

"Oh yes, your father liked that one!" She nodded and smiled. "He said we were like that. Yes, that's it." She did not realize it was not a compliment.

So maybe I told my father a lie. I hope not.

Over the next few weeks, my mom began to remember more. We were driving in the summer Seattle rain when my mom told me about the first time she met my dad, at a church party. "I remember leaning over Lydia's back to talk to him about the binomial theorem," she said. "I was learning it in class at the time. It seems so silly now. I talked about math for hours." On their first date, she said, she wore a green wool two-piece suit she had made, with lining in the collar so it would be straight. "We were more careful about most things back then," she said. She bought a green full-length slip in case her midriff showed. My dad brought her a corsage and took her to Fisherman's Wharf in Seattle. She said it was too expensive. And so they began their fitful journey.

"Come, my beloved," I imagined my dad reading to my mom, "let us go out into the fields and lodge among the henna plants; let us go out early to the vineyards, and see whether the vines have budded, whether the grape blossoms have opened, and the pomegranates are in bloom. There I will give you my love." They parked by the lake at Green Lake Park. Before long, she said, my mom started saving money for *after* he died because he was eleven years older than her. For her, this was the ultimate sign of love.

From their letters, I could piece the rest together. Twelve days before the wedding, my mom wrote to my dad, "Are you sure you want to marry me? I'm still shaking and wish you were here. . . . My doubts and fears are still present and how I wish I could get rid of them."

He wrote back, "I still love you and want to marry you, but I will not blame you if you change your mind." He ended the letter with, "Please marry me, Darling Mary."

In his last letter before the wedding, my dad wrote, "Though I may not be able to pray well yet, I believe the Lord hears me and answers my prayers. After all, he gave me you. . . . I've never loved you more." According to my mom, he was afraid she would not show up at the altar. What he did not know was that after meeting her so-called "weird bunch of relatives" for the first time, my mom was afraid that he might change his mind.

When my mother finally appeared with gardenias in her hair, thick cat's-eye glasses, and a body covered in Chanel No. 5, my father must have gasped, and she must have smiled to see him standing there, waiting for her after all. In their wedding pictures, they are both beaming. They stand with the fear of abandonment still in their eyes and the wonder at each other's presence filling their hearts.

"I suppose we did love each other," my mom finally admitted to me one day. "It's just that we were always afraid that the other would leave."

I told you I had a Hidden Knowledge Detector.

"Roller-coaster road!" the kids would soon shout from the back of the car on the way to China Lake. I would tickle my sister while she laughed in glee, wrapping her arms around me to make me stop. Full of song like a bird in a nest, I would begin to warble tentatively, "Thumbelina, Thumbelina, tiny little . . ." and my sister would join in automatically, as our voices grew stronger, in perfect harmony, through all the ups and downs ahead.

"Stepping into *The Twilight Zone*" was how the base's first commanding officer described arriving at China Lake. I wonder if he was surprised when he learned he would assume command over a vast desert city-ship rather than a real one, overseeing thousands of civilian scientists while tending a million acres of desert. Coming straight from the war in the Pacific, he must have found it hard to be surrounded by open desert rather than open water. It must have seemed as though his engine had cut out and he would have to float in that sea forever, waiting for someone to reach him with supplies. But we all learned how to float somehow. In the sky without a parachute. In war.

When I left China Lake for the last time, I turned on my engine and revved it just a bit first. I relished the power of leaving in me. I was ready to turn this ship around. I was ready to head for shore. I drove away from that missile town knowing that all of us—the burros, me, and my dad—were fighters. Even the creosote bushes refused to die, throwing out rings of protection around themselves. We would ensure that history was not erased. We would do this simply by surviving, in life as in death, for better or worse. I tipped my head back, the power of desert animals in my bones, and had the last laugh.

Then I sped away.

Acknowledgments

First, and most important, I must thank my mom and Christine for putting up with me as I wrote this book and, especially, for sharing their stories with me even though they knew I would warp them into something new. I could not have written this book without the pooled collection of resources in our brains. I could not have written without those stolen letters and notes. My mom did not know about my experiences in college and graduate school until she read the first draft of this book; for forgiving me for all my mistakes, as always, I am grateful. My sister is an expert genealogist and recorder of oral histories; many of my relatives' stories came from her, while there are many more yet to be written.

Beyond my immediate family, there are so many more that made this book happen, a whole industry of support, in fact. I will list them chronologically and ask for forgiveness from those I forgot to mention. The Sitka Center for Art and Ecology was the first to believe in this book and provided me with a writing residency at Cascade Head, Oregon. There I shared space with the artists Alex Chitty and Deedra Ludwig, whose sense of color and landscape inspired me to see the empty paper as a palette. At the time, Chitty was making woodblock prints of dead birds, Deedra was making paint out of mushrooms she had collected, and I was putting the Oregon woods to paper. It was a magical time.

The University of Missouri graciously let me have time away from teaching and provided funding so I could visit China Lake one last time. Robin Albee gave me visions of landscapes across America and encouraged me to change this book from fiction to nonfiction almost a decade ago. The people at China Lake—from Bill Porter to Burrell Hays—will forever impress me for their integrity. Composer Patrick David Clark helped me see writing as a symphony and stayed up far too late with me more than one night, talking me through the various movements of this book. Bill Roorbach encouraged me to keep writing and helped with an early draft of this book.

Steve Weinberg, who is a blessing to all writers, encouraged me when I felt stuck; his friendship, editing eyes, and dedication to journalistic integrity were irreplaceable to me in shaping this book. He also recommended me to my agent, Colleen Mohyde, who laughed with me through the dark days of a "Snowpacolypse," a conservative backlash to student protests at Mizzou, November 2016, and my near-death brush with HAPE (High Altitude Pulmonary Edema) in the Sierras. She fought to get my story out there through this all, even when I sometimes wondered why it mattered. Steve Weinberg put her in touch with Carole Desanti at Viking Penguin, who then acquired the book. Chris Russell proved an excellent editor until he was picked up by Axios to write. Emily Wunderlich then took my book to the finish line, and her Missouri calm in the whirlwind of New York City publishing made me feel at home. The whole team at Penguin—from graphic artists to my copy editor—made me realize why people call it a publishing "home."

Thanks to the English department in Missouri who left me to my own devices until "nobody knew what the hell was going on" with me. That space allowed me to write this book; while the kindness, sassiness, and intellectual strength of my colleagues—particularly my dear friend Anand Prahlad—always lifted me up. Joanne Hearne and Kavita Pillai sang ditties and Bollywood songs with me across India as we chased dreams of feminist languages, farming methods, and films. Finally, if the University of Missouri had not funded my travel, particularly to Iraq, I would not have the perspective I needed to finish the book. If my mother had not gone with me, there would be nothing to write about. I may have been too scared to go.

I also want to thank the Kawaiisu, Shoshone, and Paiutes of California. It is their space that I occupied to tell this tale, without their permission. Hopefully it does not displease. I know that my tale in the desert is only a small dot in history in comparison to theirs. In *Braiding Sweetgrass*, Robin Wall Kimmerer quotes her elder Henry Lickers, who spoke of Europeans settling here: "You know, they came here thinking they'd get rich by working on the land. . . . But the land is the one with the power—while they were working on the land, the land was working on them. Teaching them." Thank you to the land that taught me.

Author's Note

If three people all tell the same story, it will be quite different each time. So I must apologize to my family for the things misremembered or just downright wrong. For instance, after talking to my mom about the "Great Flood," I realized that I might have conflated two floods in my mind. She filled in a few blanks about what she remembered but could also not remember where I was. I have only my own faulty memories to rely upon. Dialogue between family members is also impossible to remember accurately from childhood. I tried to capture the *gist* of our conversations and the *way* we talked instead.

In contrast, China Lake's history was acquired mainly through extensive archival research, though names have been changed for some base employees (and ex-boyfriends) to protect their privacy. I did my best to be true to my own memories, particularly the emotions behind them, since this book is a record of history for me too. Memoir is a collection of impressions, memories, historical fact, and art. It is meant to be not an encyclopedia but a memory, and that's how memories work. They are partly fiction, partly family collaboration, partly gone forever—and a little bit true, one hopes.

Works Cited

Part One: Becoming China Lakers

10 **"The region surrounding China Lake":** *NWC Information Guide: Naval Weapons Center, China Lake, California*, April 30, 1971, NWC Administrative Publication 132, rv. 1, publishing division of the Technical Information Department. First printing September 1968. According to this booklet, "over 75% of the airborne weaponry in use by the free world today was developed at NWC." In 1973, NWC commander Henry Suerstedt Jr. called China Lake "the Navy's foremost research and development facility." See "Center's Impact on Kern County Economy Cited by RAdm. Suerstedt," *Rocketeer*, January 26, 1973. www.chinalakealumni .org/Downloads/Rocketeer/1973/Rktr01.26.1973.pdf.

13 **pictures in *Life*:** "Rocket Town," *Life*, February 16, 1948.

16 **"rigors of peacetime malnutrition":** Frederick Hovde of the Office of Scientific Research and Development wrote this in a letter to E. C. Watson. Quoted in J. D. Gerrard-Gough and Albert B. Christman, *The Grand Experiment at Inyokern: Narrative of the Naval Ordnance Test Station During the Second World War and the Intermediate Postwar Years*, Washington, DC: Naval History Division, 1978, 173.

30 **veered straight up:** Elizabeth Babcock, *Magnificent Mavericks: History of the Navy at China Lake, California,* vol. 3, China Lake, CA: China Lake Museum Foundation, 2008, 241.

32 **"We get lost":** Paul A. Dudchenko, *Why People Get Lost: The Psychology and Neuroscience of Spatial Cognition,* Oxford: Oxford University Press, 2010.

33 **"for eight seconds":** Ilana R. Yurkiewicz and Jack W. Tsao, "Book Review: *Why People Get Lost: The Psychology and Neuroscience of Spatial Cognition* by Paul A. Dudchenko," *Journal of the Neurological Sciences* 313, issues 1–2 (February 15, 2012): 197–98. www.jns-journal.com/article /S0022-510X(11)00583-1/fulltext.

39 **"he saw a jet three feet off":** "The Skipper Sez," *Rocketeer,* September 7, 1984.   www.chinalakealumni.org/Downloads/Rocketeer/1984/Rktr09 .07.1984.pdf.

42 **slot machines at the officers' club:** See Gerrard-Gough and Christman, *Grand Experiment at Inyokern,* 52. The authors write, "For a price, a person could get a 50-mile-round-trip ride in a battered old touring car, marked 'Taxi,' to the mining town of Red Mountain, then notorious for its ladies of the evening."

42 **"war-weary veterans":** A. L. Pittinger, as told to Virginia Pittinger, "Captain Burroughs Credited with Success of Military/Civilian Team," *Rocketeer,* April 8, 1993. www.chinalakealumni.org/Downloads/Rock eteer/1993/Rktr04.08.1993.pdf.

43 **living in three sedans:** *Before the Navy,* booklet, Ridgecrest, CA: Maturango Press, 1997, 32, 67.

43 **"an American Peenemünde":** Quoted in Gerrard-Gough and Christman, *Grand Experiment at Inyokern,* 45.

43 **"men and arms":** "NAWS Mourns the Loss of China Lake's First Commander," *Rocketeer,* October 1, 1992. www.chinalakealumni.org /Downloads/Rocketeer/1992/Rktr10.01.1992.pdf.

44 **"All service personnel":** Letter from Walter V. R. Vieweg to all departments, divisions, and branches of the Naval Weapons Center, Station Order No. 52-52, chapter 8: "Restrictive Action; Out-of-Bounds," August 15, 1952. Filed with the National Archives and Records Administration,

Riverside, California, under "Naval Weapons Center, Weapons Department, China Lake, California, Project Files 1952–1976."

44 **"Housewife to Draftsman":** Babcock, *Magnificent Mavericks*, 172.

52 **maintain a "dual reporting":** James P. Pfiffner, *The Character Factor: How We Judge America's Presidents*, College Station: Texas A&M University Press, 2004, 55.

53 **Robert Drinan testified:** "Representative Robert Drinan Opening Statement," C-SPAN TV news archive. Accessed July 10, 2013. https:// archive.org/details/CSPAN3_20140806_022200_Representative_Robert _Drinan_Opening_Statement.

55 *Lemuria: The Lost Continent:* W. S. Cervé, *Lemuria: The Lost Continent of the Pacific*, 2nd ed., San Jose, CA: Rosicrucian Press, 1935.

56 **CBS News had reported:** *CBS Evening News* with Walter Cronkite, aired October 17, 1973. See also "Mississippi Authorities Ask Federal UFO Probe," *Brownwood Bulletin*, October 17, 1973.

56 **Ohio's governor:** Brian Albright, "Ohio versus the Flying Saucers," *Country Living* 58, no. 2 (December 23, 2014). (*Country Living* has since been renamed *Ohio Cooperative Living*; the magazine is the official publication of Ohio's Electric Cooperatives.)

57 **a man named "Burro" Schmidt:** Bob Jones, "Kern Tunnel: Monument to Old Man's Dream," *Bakersfield Californian*, March 6, 1977.

59 **Charles Hickson and Calvin Parker:** Craig Ammerman, "UFO Sightings: Whatever Became of the Little Green Men?" *Brandon Sun*, October 23, 1983.

61 **They call it Operation Monarch:** Cisco Wheeler and Fritz Springmeier, *The Illuminati Formula Used to Create an Undetectable Total Mind Controlled Slave*, self-published, 1996. Available online at: http://educate-yourself.org/mc/IlluminatiFormulaindex.shtml.

61 **"not impeach a president for unlawful war-making":** Representative Robert Drinan (D-Mass.) Opening Statement, Nixon Impeachment Hearings, U.S. Congress, C-SPAN, July 25, 1974.

64 **On July 18, 1945:** Gerrard-Gough and Christman, *Grand Experiment at Inyokern*, 203.

64 **"you can't shake off":** Al Christman, *Target Hiroshima: Deak Parsons and the Creation of the Atomic Bomb*, Annapolis, MD: Naval Institute Press, 1998.

64 **"sort of crude sense":** Robert Oppenheimer interview about the Trinity explosion, first broadcast as part of the television documentary *The Decision to Drop the Bomb,* produced by Fred Freed, NBC White Paper, New York: NBC News, 1965.

64 **Groves had built:** K. H. Robinson, "Salt Wells Stars in Vital AEC Project for National Defense," *Rocketeer,* November 8, 1958. www.chinalakealumni.org/Downloads/Rocketeer/1958/Rktr11.08.1958.pdf.

64 **"willing to have other people killed and wounded":** Robert S. Norris, *Racing for the Bomb: General Leslie R. Groves, the Manhattan Project's Indispensable Man*, Hanover, NH: Steerforth Press, 2002.

64 **"From the psychological point":** "Minutes of the Second Meeting of the Target Committee Los Alamos, May 10–11, 1945," U.S. National Archives, Record Group 77, Records of the Office of the Chief of Engineers, Manhattan Engineer District, TS Manhattan Project File '42–'46, folder 5D, Selection of Targets, 2 Notes on Target Committee Meetings. Secretary of War Henry L. Stimson struck Kyoto from the list over the objections of General Leslie Groves. According to Professor Edwin O. Reischauer, "The only person deserving credit for saving Kyoto from destruction is Henry L. Stimson, the Secretary of War at the time, who had known and admired Kyoto ever since his honeymoon there several decades earlier." Edwin O. Reischauer, *My Life Between Japan and America*, New York: Harper & Row, 1986, 101. See also Leslie Groves, *Now It Can Be Told: The Story of the Manhattan Project*, New York: Harper & Row, 1962.

69 **sneaking onto the base:** For more information on Charles Manson in the desert, read Bob Murphy, *Desert Shadows: A True Story of the Charles Manson Family in Death Valley*, Morongo Valley, CA: Sagebrush Press, 1993.

69 **another "hippie commune":** "Navy Helicopter Used to Airlift Deadly Chemicals," *Rocketeer,* November 5, 1971. www.chinalakealumni.org/Downloads/Rocketeer/1971/Rktr11.05.1971.pdf.

74 **relied on Dr. Spock:** Benjamin Spock, *Dr. Spock's Baby and Child Care,* 9th ed., New York: Gallery Books, 2012, 438.

77 **"had a prayer breakfast":** This is from a comment by "Bill from Maryland" posted on September 1, 2008, in response to the blog entry "It's a Mountain of Foreclosures in California," in *The Housing Bubble* (blog) by Ben Jones, August 31, 2008. Accessed February 29, 2016. http://the housingbubbleblog.com/?p=4898.

78 **"Although ACE recommends":** Lisa J. L. Kelley, "An Analysis of Accelerated Christian Education and College Preparedness Based on ACT Scores," *Theses, Dissertations and Capstones*, thesis submitted to the Graduate College of Marshall University, paper 95 (2005), 22. http://mds.marshall.edu/etd/95.

80 **"undermined the authority":** Catherine Speck and David Prideaux, "Fundamentalist Education and Creation Science," *Australian Journal of Education* 37 (1993): 279–95.

81 **"father to be head of his family":** Quotes and screen shots from PACEs can be found in Alexis Record's November 2016 post, "Exposing Accelerated Christian Education," in the *Children and Parenting* blog of Karen Garst's website The Faithless Feminist. Accessed December 2016. www.faithlessfeminist.com. Other examples are from memory or from old PACEs I purchased online. It appears the PACEs have not changed much since the 1970s.

81 **near the Paluxy River:** John D. Morris, "The Paluxy River Mystery," *Acts & Facts* 15, no. 1 (1986).

82 **"inconceivable without God":** Wernher von Braun, "Forward," in Harold Hill, *From Goo to You by Way of the Zoo*, Plainfield, NJ: Logos International, 1976.

87 **"Don't spank the child":** Jack Hyles, "Why God Is for War," Sunday evening sermon, March 15, 1970. Accessed March 1, 2005. www.jackhyles.com/godforwar.htm.

104 **we passed "Kennedy's Forest":** "Command Performance: President John F. Kennedy's Visit to Naval Ordnance Test Station, China Lake, California, 7 June 1963," special chapter edition from the *History of the Navy at China Lake California*, vol. 4 (unpublished), NAWCWD TS2013-108, Technical Communication and Library Division, November 2013.

105 **"Idealized missiles"** and **"fair-weather attacks"**: Howard A. Wilcox, "Sidewinder Seminar Notes," China Lake, CA: Naval Weapons Center, 1953. Filed with the National Archives and Records Administration, Riverside, California, under "Naval Weapons Center, Weapons Department, China Lake, California, Project Files 1952–1976."

106 **sixteen percent in Vietnam:** Don Holloway, "Fox Two!" *Aviation History*, March 2013. See also Carlo Kopp, "The Sidewinder Story: The Evolution of the AIM-9 Missile," *Australian Aviation*, April 1994. Kopp writes, "Kill probabilities were in the tens of percent, very sensitive to how the launch craft was positioned."

106 **"trafficking in the black arts":** Quoted in Jason Weindling, "Donald Trump is the Kremlin's Man: A Comprehensive Case for Russian Influence in the GOP Campaign," *Paste*, October 12, 2016. Accessed February 5, 2017. https://www.pastemagazine.com/articles/2016/10/donald-trump-is-the-kremlins-man-a-comprehensive-c.html.

107 **"Like parents bracing":** "Command Performance."

108 **aim a missile at the president's head:** "Command Performance."

108 **defense contractor a cigarette:** Babcock, *Magnificent Mavericks*, 207, 397.

108 **"shot of whiskey":** "Command Performance."

109 **"I cannot think of a prouder occupation":** "Command Performance."

109 **"I am not an atomic playboy":** Gerard J. DeGroot, *The Bomb: A Life*, Cambridge, MA: Harvard University Press, 2004.

109 **"Not a Pax Americana":** John F. Kennedy, "1963 Commencement Speech," American University, Washington, DC, June 10, 1963.

110 **he devised a plan:** James K. Galbraith, "Exit Strategy: In 1963, JFK Ordered a Complete Withdrawal from Vietnam," *Boston Review*, September 1, 2003.

110 **Secretary of Defense Robert McNamara:** James K. Galbraith, "Kennedy, Vietnam, and Iraq," *Salon*, November 22, 2003.

Part Two: A Teenage Weaponeer

135 **"unite in marriage only those who are biblically qualified":** "On The Scandal of Southern Baptist Divorce," Southern Baptist Convention

Resolution, Orlando, Florida, 2010. Available online at: http://www
.sbc.net/resolutions/1205/on-the-scandal-of-southern-baptist-divorce.

135 **"submit herself graciously":** "The Baptist Faith and Message: The
2000 Baptist Faith & Message," Southern Baptist Convention. Available
online at: http://www.sbc.net/bfm2000/bfm2000.asp.

136 **"deadly plague invading our shores":** Quoted in "The LAPD: Chief
Gates," Los Angeles Police Department. Gates used this descriptor fre-
quently throughout his tenure as Chief of Police from 1978 to 1992. Accessed March 1, 2016. https://www.lapdonline.org/history_of_the
_lapd/content_basic_view/1114.

137 **"Red Squad" to infiltrate Communists:** Joe Domanick, *To Protect
and Serve: The LAPD's Century of War in the City of Dreams*, Los Angeles: Figueroa Press, 2003.

138 **"Happy Armageddon Rabbit Masher":** "China Lake Honors Bill
Porter at Farewell Party," *Rocketeer*, January 14, 1993. www.china
lakealumni.org/Downloads/Rocketeer/1993/Rktr01.14.1993.pdf.

142 **"universities teach poverty":** Bill Britt said at the "Free Enterprise Day
Seminar" in Portland, Oregon (1990), "That's why ninety-eight percent
of people are broke in this country; they go to universities that teach them
poverty." See Sidney Schwartz, "The Gospel According to Amway: Religion and Politics According to Dexter Yager, Bill Britt, and other Amway
Luminaries." Accessed April 15, 2012. https://www.cs.cmu.edu/~dst/
Amway/AUS/amwaygospel.htm. These seminars are recorded and can
usually be purchased from Amway, now the "School of Tomorrow."

146 **"When I look at him, I see Jesus":** Quoted in Mike Wallace, *60 Minutes*, "Soap and Hope," CBS, January 9, 1983.

147 **"advance God's Kingdom":** Benjamin Wermund, "Trump's Education Pick Says Reform can 'Advance God's Kingdom,'" *Politico*, December 2, 2016. Accessed February 2, 2017. https://www.politico.com/story
/2016/12/betsy-devos-education-trump-religion-232150.

147 **"Read the story of Moses":** "Yager Network Marketing Institute,"
seminar tape, released 1994. Quoted in Sidney Schwartz, "The Gospel
According to Amway." See also Bill and Peggy Britt, "Free Enterprise
Day Seminar," Boulder, CO, 1990.

151 **"One Kit, Bomb Assembly":** "Secret Weapons of the Secret City," *China Laker* 19, no. 1 (Winter 2013).

151 **not the uranium or plutonium:** Guy C. Throner, "Project Camel and the Pumpkin Bomb," *China Laker* 14, no. 3 (Fall 2008).

151 **"insensitive munitions":** Ian J. Powell, "Insensitive Munitions—Design Principles and Technology Developments," *Propellants, Explosives, Pyrotechnics*, February 24, 2016.

153 **TNT or RDX:** *Proposed Plan for Cleanup Action: Propulsion Laboratory Operable Unit: NAWS China Lake*, U.S. Department of the Navy, Naval Facilities Engineering Command, Southwest, China Lake, CA, September 2008.

158 **"The Aug. 15 flood":** "Answers Sought to Questions Raised by Flood on Aug. 15," *Rocketeer*, September 14, 1984. www.chinalakealumni.org/Downloads/Rocketeer/1984/Rktr09.14.1984.pdf.

Part Four: The Cold War at Home

174 **"OUT OF CONTROL":** Stan McKenzie, "'Out of Control' Party Results in Riot, Arrests," *Register-Guard*, May 6, 1989. See also Brian Denson, "Idealism Fuels Anarchists' Battles," *Oregonian*, August 13, 2000.

175 **Bigeye, full of VX:** Albert J. Mauroni, *Chemical Demilitarization: Public Policy Aspects*, Westport, CT: Praeger, 2003. See also Albert J. Mauroni, *America's Struggle with Chemical-Biological Warfare*, Westport, CT: Praeger, 2000.

178 **"381 Burros Are Slain":** "381 Burros Are Slain by Marksmen to Clear Naval Center on Coast," *New York Times*, March 10, 1981. See also Thomas J. McGill, "Feral Equine Management at the Naval Weapons Center," Proceedings of the Eleventh Vertebrate Pest Conference, March 1, 1984, and "500 Horses, Burros Rounded up on Center's Northern Ranges," *Rocketeer*, July 13, 1984.

179 **paisley fabric–covered button:** Ralph Vartabedian, "Lab Opposes 'Gold Plated' Systems: China Lake Weapons Center Battling with the Navy Brass," *Los Angeles Times*, May 1, 1986.

181 **Fort Irwin:** Alexandra Zavis, "Ft. Irwin Stands in for Iraq," *Los Angeles Times*, August 31, 2009.

185 **Tornado fighter plane:** G. Verner, China Lake Accidents, "Incidents & SOC's, Accident on October 19, 1998," China Lake Alumni Organization, May 15, 2015. Accessed May 30, 2015. www.chinalakealumni.org /accidents.htm.

188 **amused by its "fables":** See Despina Stratigakos, *Hitler at Home*, New Haven and London: Yale University Press, 2015, 151.

188 **survivor Jean Michel:** Gerard J. Degroot, *Dark Side of the Moon: The Magnificent Madness of the American Lunar Quest*, New York: New York University Press, 2006, 21.

188 **According to the *Rocketeer*:** "Thermodynamics Consultant to Leave Pasadena Next Week," *Rocketeer*, August 13, 1954. www.china lakealumni.org/Downloads/Rocketeer/1954/Rktr08.13.1954.pdf.

189 **Noeggerath's file:** Wolfgang C. Noeggerath File, Foreign Scientist Case Files 1945–1958 (Entry A1-1B), boxes 1–186, Records of the Office of the Secretary of Defense (Record Group 330), Joint Intelligence Objectives Agency, National Archives and Records Administration, Washington, DC.

191 **"One Bomb, One Target":** Winslow Wheeler, "The Wastrels of Defense: How Congress Sabotages U.S. Security," Annapolis, MD: Naval Institute Press, 2004. See also Grant T. Hammond, "Myths of the Gulf War: Some 'Lessons' Not to Learn," *Airpower Journal* (Fall 1998).

191 **"this will not be another Vietnam":** "War in the Gulf: The President; Transcript of the Comments by Bush on the Air Strikes Against the Iraqis," *New York Times*, January 17, 1991.

191 **a copy of *What's Happening?*:** "The War at Home," *What's Happening?* (now the *Eugene Weekly*), January 6–13, 1991.

197 **Gulf War syndrome:** Christian Nordqvist, "Proof Gulf War Illness Does Exist," *Medical News Today*, June 15, 2013. See also "Research Advisory Committee on Gulf War Veterans' Illnesses," *Gulf War Illness and the Health of Gulf War Veterans: Scientific Findings and Recommendations*, Washington, DC: U.S. Government Printing Office, November 2008.

199 **"I don't recall"**: Janet Cawley and Linda P. Campbell, "Reagan Hazy on Iran-contra: Knowledge of Diversion Is Denied," *Chicago Tribune*, February 23, 1990.

200 **"I'm not fooling"**: "Reagan's Iran-Contra Deposition, July 24, 1992," *Washington Post*, June 20, 1999.

202 **"My fellow Americans"**: Ronald Reagan letter dated November 5, 1994, to "My Fellow Americans," Ronald Reagan Presidential Foundation and Library, Simi Valley, California.

Part Five: Anything Can Be a Weapon

234 **"We regard the weather as a weapon"**: Quoted in Kathy Johnston, "Weather or Not: A Local Cloud-Seeding Program Aims to Make More Rainfall," *Santa Maria Sun* 12, issue 30 (September 28, 2011).

Part Six: Off Target

254 **On ABC, the World Trade Center:** Peter Jennings, *ABC World News Tonight*, World Trade Center attack, September 11, 2001.

262 **"Beyond the sanity":** Jalal a-Din Rumi, "Let Me be Mad," *The Essential Rumi: New Expanded Edition*, Coleman Barks and John Moyne, trans., New York: HarperOne, 2004.

265 **he was part of Operation Sonnie:** Bob Koch, "The O.S.S. Project," *Gung-Ho* magazine, June 1989.

Part Seven: Life without Weapons

275 **the biggest oil consumer:** Sohbet Karbuz, "How Much Energy Does the U.S. Military Consume?" *Daily Energy Report*, August 5, 2013. Accessed August 10, 2014. http://karbuz.blogspot.com/2013/08/how-much-energy-does-us-military.html.

275 **"poses immediate risks to U.S. national security"**: Jeff Goodall, "The Pentagon and Climate Change: How Deniers Put National Security at Risk," *Rolling Stone*, February 12, 2015.

279 **"sixteen thousand years ago"**: David S. Whitley, *Following the Shaman's Path: A Walking Guide to Little Petroglyph Canyon, Coso Range, California*, Ridgecrest, CA: Maturango Press, 1998.

280 **the shamans were "seeing things"**: Patricia A. Helvenston and Derek Hodgson, "The Neuropsychology of 'Animism': Implications for Understanding Rock Art," *Rock Art Research* 27, no. 1 (2010): 61–94.

288 **"the tropical oceans"**: Howard A. Wilcox, "The Energy-Crunch: Present Trends and Future Prospects for the World and the USA," paper presented to the Marine Technology Society, Washington, DC, June 12, 1973. Filed with the National Archives and Records Administration, Riverside, California, under "Naval Weapons Center, Weapons Department, China Lake, California, Project Files 1952–1976."

288 **"Man is unwittingly conducting"**: "Restoring the Quality of Our Environment: Report of the Environmental Pollution Panel, President's Science Advisory Committee," White House, November 1965. Available online at http://dge.stanford.edu/labs/caldeiralab.

288 **"more garden clubs are getting interested"**: Telephone conversation between President Johnson and Walter Reuther, recorded on February 5, 1965, The LBJ Library, Citation No: 6802. Available at: https://www.youtube.com/watch?v=wUD2ermIErE.

289 **San Clemente Island**: Howard A. Wilcox, "Expected Thermal Effects of a System of Large, Open-Ocean, Mariculture Facilities for Utilizing Solar Energy," paper presented at a meeting of the American Geophysical Union in San Francisco, California, December 12, 1973.

289 **a portable igloo**: Jerry D. Stachiw, "Inflatable Ice Igloo," in *Navy Inventions: Yours for the Asking*, Washington, DC: U.S. Navy, 1973. Filed with the National Archives and Records Administration, Riverside, California, under "Naval Weapons Center, Weapons Department, China Lake, California, Project Files 1952–1976."

289 **"Hidden Knowledge Detector"**: Federick N. Dyer, "Hidden Knowledge Detector," in *Navy Inventions: Yours for the Asking*, Washington,

DC: U.S. Navy, 1973. Filed with the National Archives and Records Administration, Riverside, California, under "Record ID: Naval Weapons Center, Weapons Department, China Lake, California, Project Files 1952–1976."

289 **"quantum mechanics of H$_2$O":** Memo to "Files" from Rudolph J. Marcus regarding "D.S. Villars Objections to NWC IR/IED Evaluation," U.S. Government, February 20, 1969. Filed with the National Archives and Records Administration, Riverside, California, under "Naval Weapons Center, Weapons Department, China Lake, California, Project Files 1952–1976."

290 **"military application of this work":** E. T. Florence, "Technical Review of Naval Weapons Center Independent Research and Exploratory Development Program," Arlington, VA: Office of Naval Research, November 1973. Filed with the National Archives and Records Administration, Riverside, California, under "Naval Weapons Center, Weapons Department, China Lake, California, Project Files 1952–1976."

290 **a book titled *Hothouse Earth*:** "*Hothouse Earth* by Howard A. Wilcox: Kirkus Review," *Kirkus Reviews,* October 1, 1975. Accessed October 15, 2015. https://www.kirkusreviews.com.

292 **I called Burrell Hays:** Karen Piper, personal interview with Burrell Hays, by telephone, June 5, 2008.

302 **"stepping into *The Twilight Zone*":** See "Bringing Together the Laboratory and the Fleet: China Lake Military Leadership," China Lake Museum. Accessed October 15, 2015. www.chinalakemuseum.org.